This Little Piggy GETS EVEN!

A
SUBURBAN
Fairy Tales
C O L L E C T I O N

by Francis Bonnet

Published through CreateSpace. First Edition.

ISBN: 978-1-453-89990-8

Suburban Fairy Tales comic strip is written and drawn by Francis Bonnet. Visit **www.francisbonnet.com** to read the newest comic strips, updated regularly.

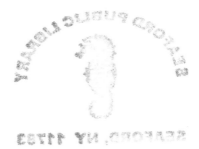

SUBURBAN *Fairy Tales*

MAIN CHARACTERS

Frog Prince
A sweet and somewhat naive boy trapped in the body of a frog. His fondest wish is to become a normal boy again, but that can only happen with a kiss from a girl. He is friendly and outgoing to those around him, but easily becomes nervous when things go unexpectedly. He sometimes feels sadness that he is unpopular and often turns to others for guidance.

Pinocchio
He is quick-tempered and has a low tolerance for stupidity. He has rigid expectations for the way life around him should operate and is frustrated when it doesn't go the way he would like. He is truthful to a fault because of his obvious weakness for lying.

Rapunzel
She is the most popular girl in school. She's preppy, self-absorbed, and also quite vain. She believes she can do no wrong in the eyes of her classmates. To maintain her status, she shuns the likes of Pinocchio or Frog Prince.

Little Pig #3
He is not the brightest bulb in the box. He understands very little about what goes on around him, and yet still manages to annoy his peers to the point where they can't tolerate him. He'll never be well liked, but likely will never know the difference.

Goldilocks
The number 2 most popular girl in school. On the surface she is friends with Rapunzel, but is willing to double-cross her at any time just to become number 1.

Red Riding Hood
Red Riding Hood is the smartest girl in school. She is strong and confident. She and Rapunzel do not get along well, but she is friendly with Pinocchio and Frog Prince.

The Big Bad Wolf
Wolf is the town bully that everyone loves to hate. His greatest amusement is to embarrass, annoy, and beat up on others. Wolf's favorite victim is Little Pig #3, but he ensures everyone gets their fair share of abuse.

Humpty Dumpty
Humpty is a skater punk, which means he lives for performing stunts on his skateboard. He's got a hotheaded attitude and loves to be rebellious.

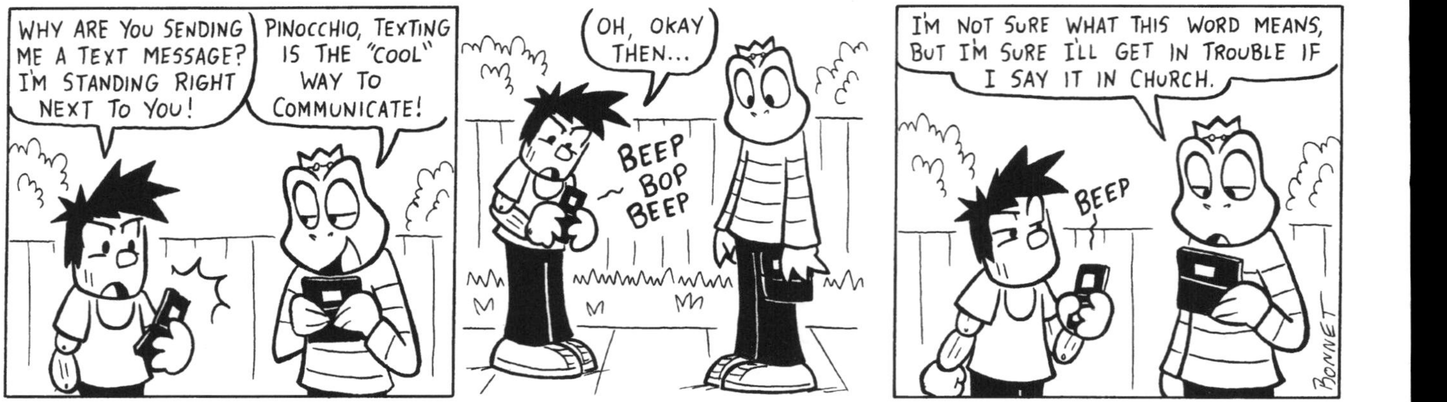
WHY ARE YOU SENDING ME A TEXT MESSAGE? I'M STANDING RIGHT NEXT TO YOU!
PINOCCHIO, TEXTING IS THE "COOL" WAY TO COMMUNICATE!
OH, OKAY THEN...
BEEP BOP BEEP
I'M NOT SURE WHAT THIS WORD MEANS, BUT I'M SURE I'LL GET IN TROUBLE IF I SAY IT IN CHURCH.
BEEP
BONNET

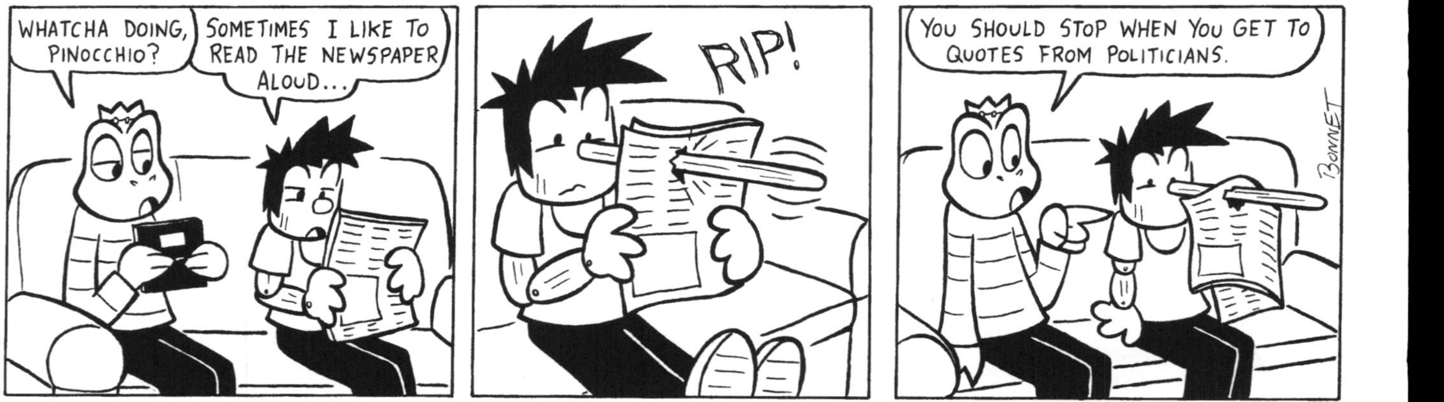
WHATCHA DOING, PINOCCHIO?
SOMETIMES I LIKE TO READ THE NEWSPAPER ALOUD...
RIP!
YOU SHOULD STOP WHEN YOU GET TO QUOTES FROM POLITICIANS.
BONNET

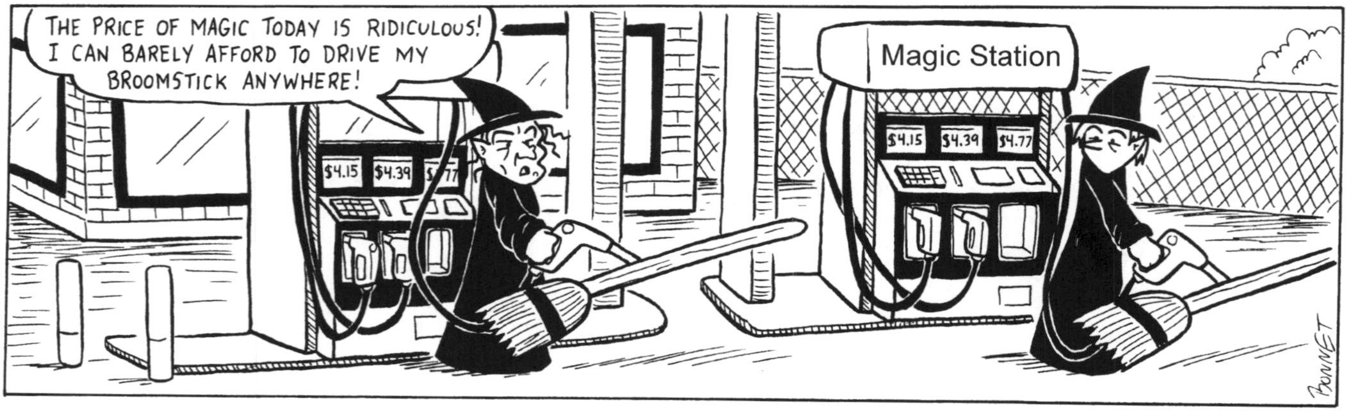
THE PRICE OF MAGIC TODAY IS RIDICULOUS! I CAN BARELY AFFORD TO DRIVE MY BROOMSTICK ANYWHERE!
Magic Station
$4.15
$4.39
$4.77
BONNET

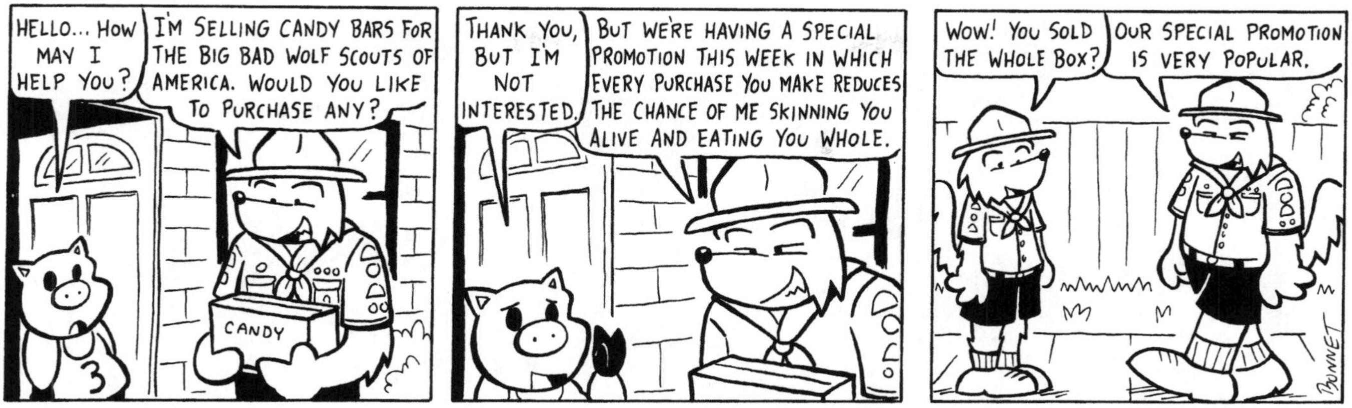
HELLO... HOW MAY I HELP YOU?
I'M SELLING CANDY BARS FOR THE BIG BAD WOLF SCOUTS OF AMERICA. WOULD YOU LIKE TO PURCHASE ANY?
CANDY
THANK YOU, BUT I'M NOT INTERESTED.
BUT WE'RE HAVING A SPECIAL PROMOTION THIS WEEK IN WHICH EVERY PURCHASE YOU MAKE REDUCES THE CHANCE OF ME SKINNING YOU ALIVE AND EATING YOU WHOLE.
WOW! YOU SOLD THE WHOLE BOX?
OUR SPECIAL PROMOTION IS VERY POPULAR.
BONNET

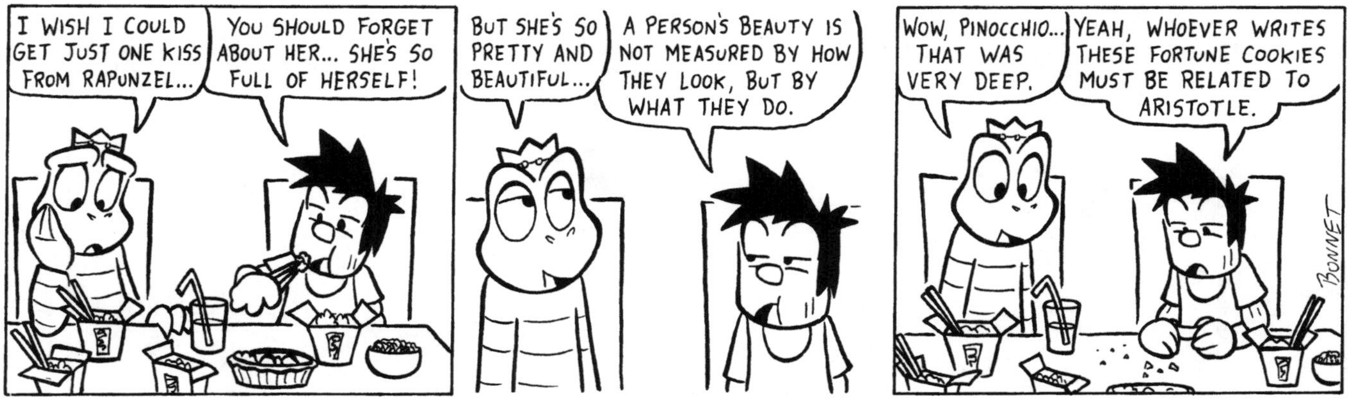
I WISH I COULD GET JUST ONE KISS FROM RAPUNZEL...
YOU SHOULD FORGET ABOUT HER... SHE'S SO FULL OF HERSELF!
BUT SHE'S SO PRETTY AND BEAUTIFUL...
A PERSON'S BEAUTY IS NOT MEASURED BY HOW THEY LOOK, BUT BY WHAT THEY DO.
WOW, PINOCCHIO... THAT WAS VERY DEEP.
YEAH, WHOEVER WRITES THESE FORTUNE COOKIES MUST BE RELATED TO ARISTOTLE.
BONNET

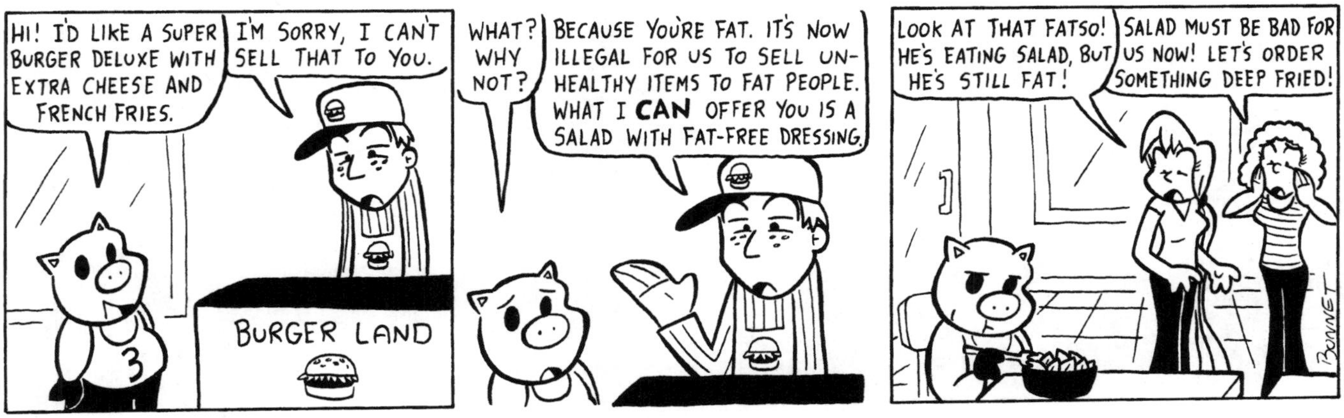
HI! I'D LIKE A SUPER BURGER DELUXE WITH EXTRA CHEESE AND FRENCH FRIES.
I'M SORRY, I CAN'T SELL THAT TO YOU.
BURGER LAND
WHAT? WHY NOT?
BECAUSE YOU'RE FAT. IT'S NOW ILLEGAL FOR US TO SELL UNHEALTHY ITEMS TO FAT PEOPLE. WHAT I **CAN** OFFER YOU IS A SALAD WITH FAT-FREE DRESSING.
LOOK AT THAT FATSO! HE'S EATING SALAD, BUT HE'S STILL FAT!
SALAD MUST BE BAD FOR US NOW! LET'S ORDER SOMETHING DEEP FRIED!
BONNET

Sept. 29, Oct. 1, 3, 2008

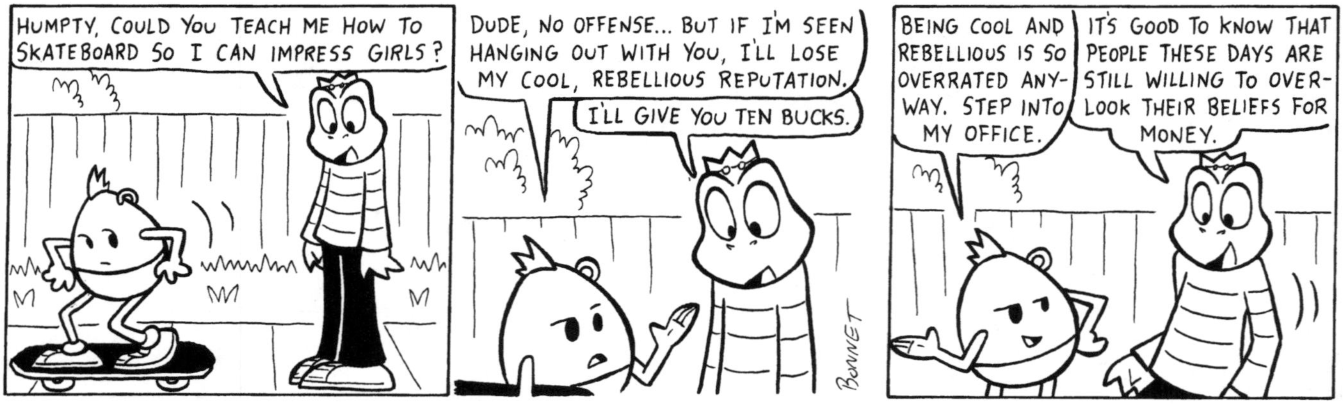
HUMPTY, COULD YOU TEACH ME HOW TO SKATEBOARD SO I CAN IMPRESS GIRLS?
DUDE, NO OFFENSE... BUT IF I'M SEEN HANGING OUT WITH YOU, I'LL LOSE MY COOL, REBELLIOUS REPUTATION.
I'LL GIVE YOU TEN BUCKS.
BONNET
BEING COOL AND REBELLIOUS IS SO OVERRATED ANY-WAY. STEP INTO MY OFFICE.
IT'S GOOD TO KNOW THAT PEOPLE THESE DAYS ARE STILL WILLING TO OVER-LOOK THEIR BELIEFS FOR MONEY.

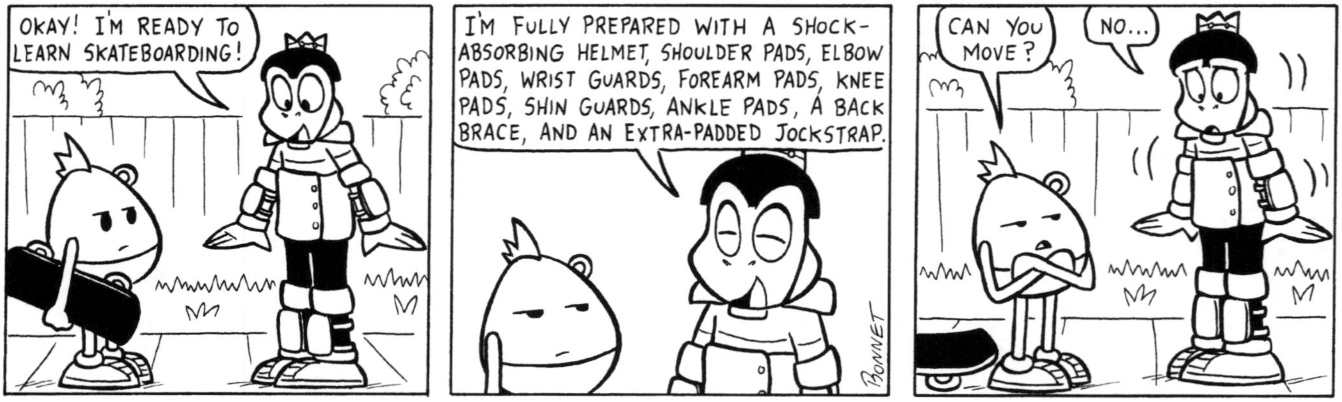
OKAY! I'M READY TO LEARN SKATEBOARDING!
I'M FULLY PREPARED WITH A SHOCK-ABSORBING HELMET, SHOULDER PADS, ELBOW PADS, WRIST GUARDS, FOREARM PADS, KNEE PADS, SHIN GUARDS, ANKLE PADS, A BACK BRACE, AND AN EXTRA-PADDED JOCKSTRAP.
BONNET
CAN YOU MOVE?
NO...

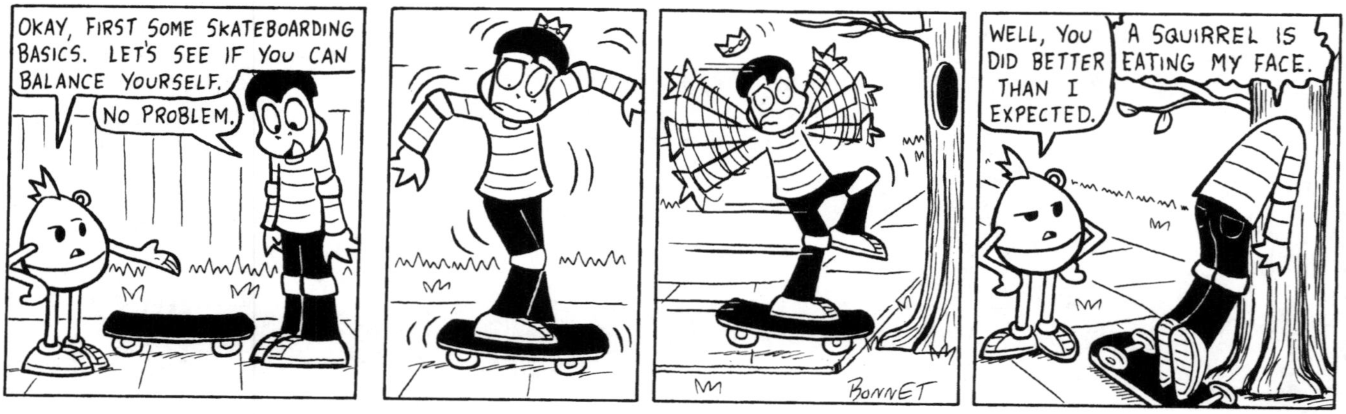
OKAY, FIRST SOME SKATEBOARDING BASICS. LET'S SEE IF YOU CAN BALANCE YOURSELF.
NO PROBLEM.
BONNET
WELL, YOU DID BETTER THAN I EXPECTED.
A SQUIRREL IS EATING MY FACE.

Oct. 6, 8, 10, 2008

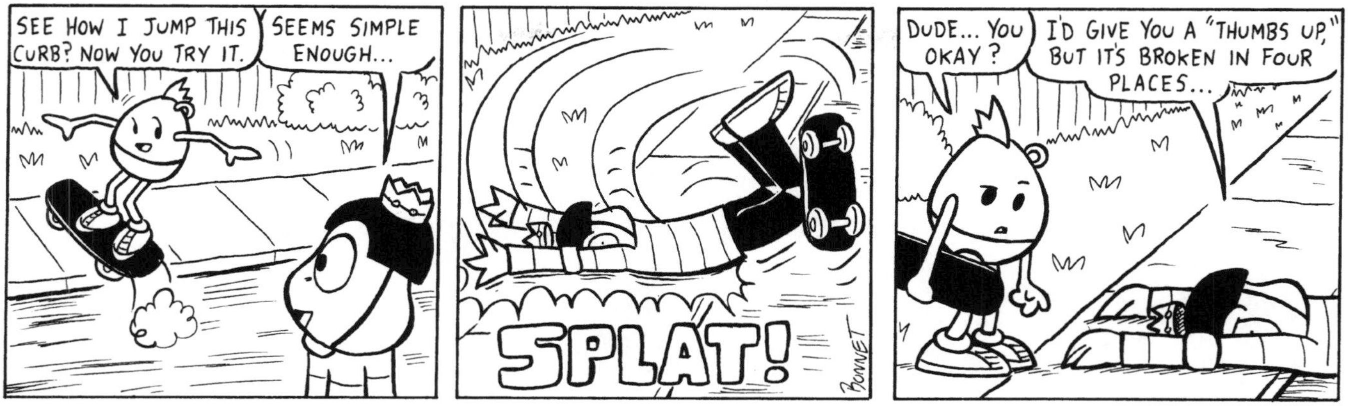
SEE HOW I JUMP THIS CURB? NOW YOU TRY IT.
SEEMS SIMPLE ENOUGH...
SPLAT!
BONNET
DUDE... YOU OKAY?
I'D GIVE YOU A "THUMBS UP," BUT IT'S BROKEN IN FOUR PLACES...

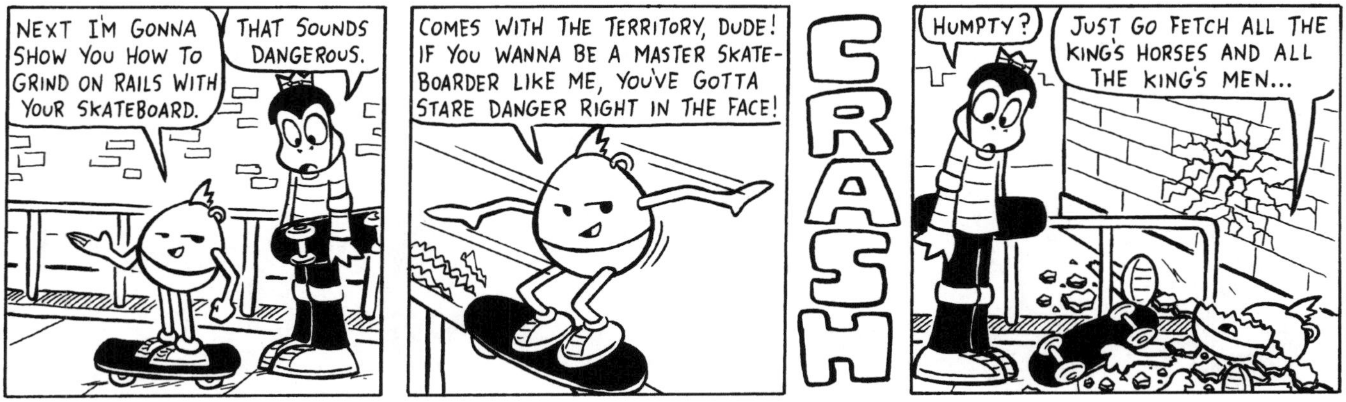
NEXT I'M GONNA SHOW YOU HOW TO GRIND ON RAILS WITH YOUR SKATEBOARD.
THAT SOUNDS DANGEROUS.
COMES WITH THE TERRITORY, DUDE! IF YOU WANNA BE A MASTER SKATE-BOARDER LIKE ME, YOU'VE GOTTA STARE DANGER RIGHT IN THE FACE!
CRASH
HUMPTY?
JUST GO FETCH ALL THE KING'S HORSES AND ALL THE KING'S MEN...

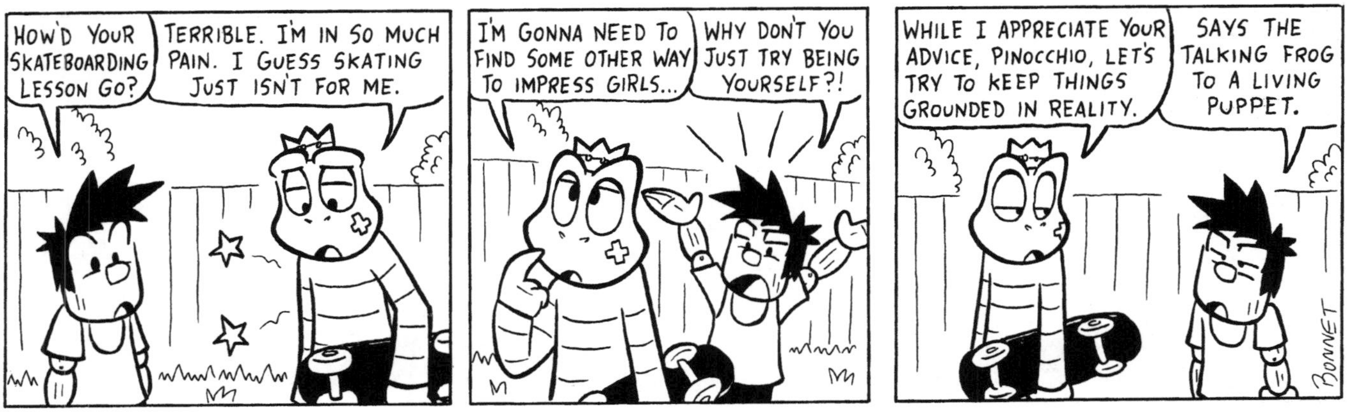
HOW'D YOUR SKATEBOARDING LESSON GO?
TERRIBLE. I'M IN SO MUCH PAIN. I GUESS SKATING JUST ISN'T FOR ME.
I'M GONNA NEED TO FIND SOME OTHER WAY TO IMPRESS GIRLS...
WHY DON'T YOU JUST TRY BEING YOURSELF?!
WHILE I APPRECIATE YOUR ADVICE, PINOCCHIO, LET'S TRY TO KEEP THINGS GROUNDED IN REALITY.
SAYS THE TALKING FROG TO A LIVING PUPPET.
BONNET

Oct. 13, 15, 17, 2008

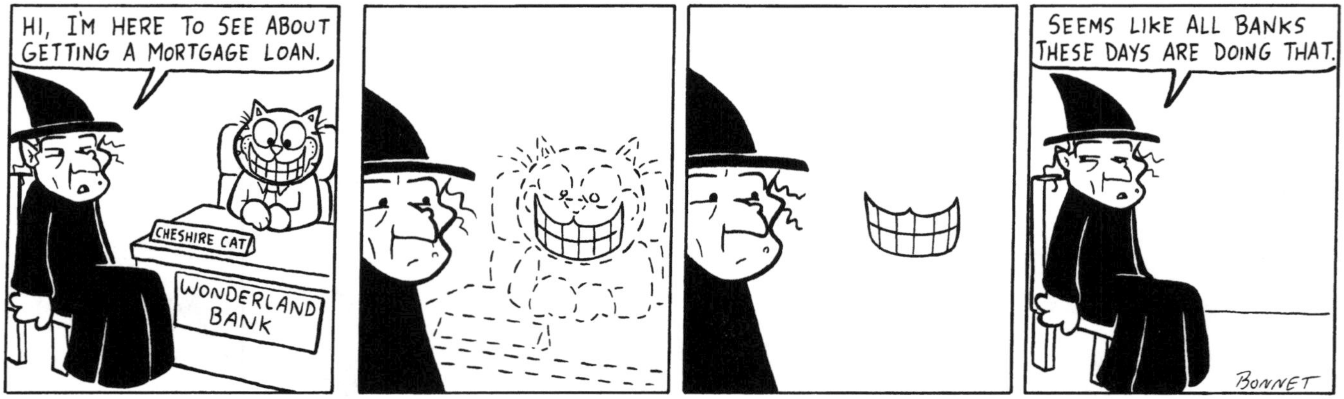
HI, I'M HERE TO SEE ABOUT GETTING A MORTGAGE LOAN.
CHESHIRE CAT
WONDERLAND BANK
SEEMS LIKE ALL BANKS THESE DAYS ARE DOING THAT.
BONNET

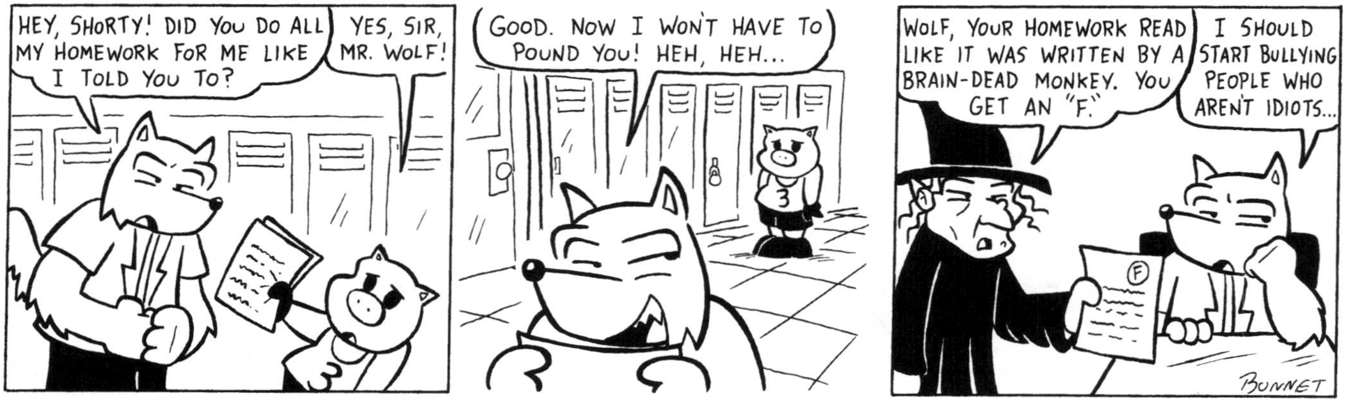
HEY, SHORTY! DID YOU DO ALL MY HOMEWORK FOR ME LIKE I TOLD YOU TO?
YES, SIR, MR. WOLF!
GOOD. NOW I WON'T HAVE TO POUND YOU! HEH, HEH...
WOLF, YOUR HOMEWORK READ LIKE IT WAS WRITTEN BY A BRAIN-DEAD MONKEY. YOU GET AN "F."
I SHOULD START BULLYING PEOPLE WHO AREN'T IDIOTS...
BONNET

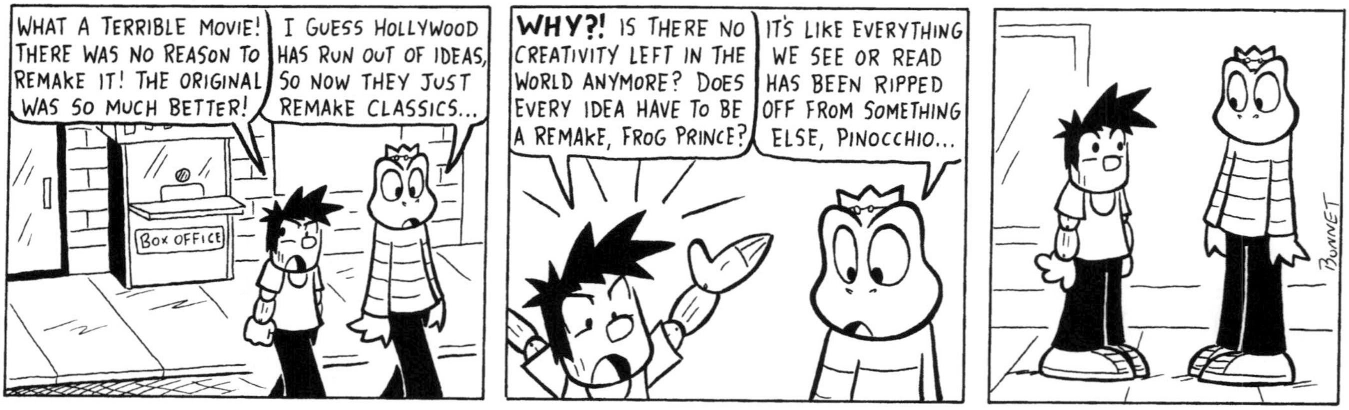
WHAT A TERRIBLE MOVIE! THERE WAS NO REASON TO REMAKE IT! THE ORIGINAL WAS SO MUCH BETTER!
I GUESS HOLLYWOOD HAS RUN OUT OF IDEAS, SO NOW THEY JUST REMAKE CLASSICS...
BOX OFFICE
WHY?! IS THERE NO CREATIVITY LEFT IN THE WORLD ANYMORE? DOES EVERY IDEA HAVE TO BE A REMAKE, FROG PRINCE?
IT'S LIKE EVERYTHING WE SEE OR READ HAS BEEN RIPPED OFF FROM SOMETHING ELSE, PINOCCHIO...
BONNET

Oct. 20, 22, 24, 2008

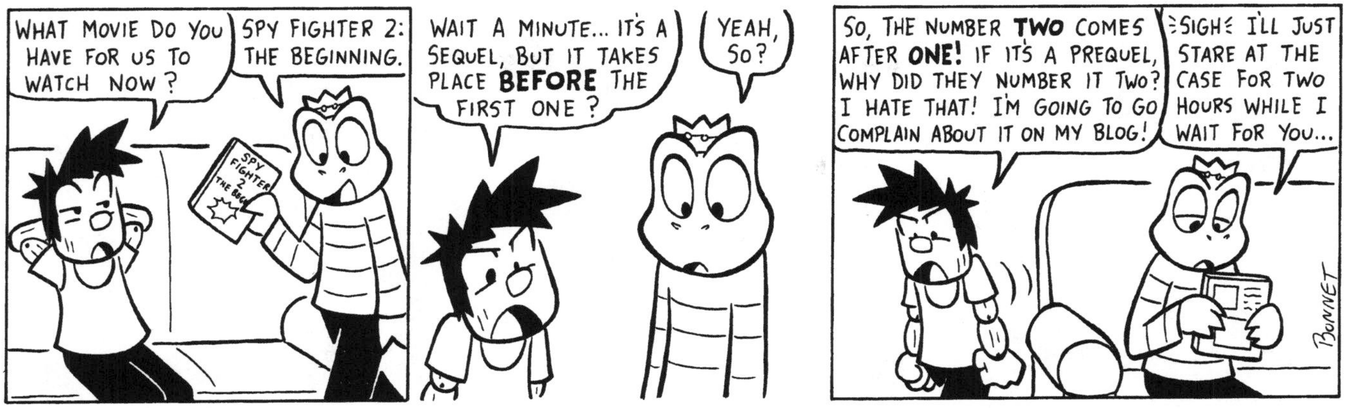
WHAT MOVIE DO YOU HAVE FOR US TO WATCH NOW?
SPY FIGHTER 2: THE BEGINNING.
SPY FIGHTER 2
WAIT A MINUTE... IT'S A SEQUEL, BUT IT TAKES PLACE **BEFORE** THE FIRST ONE?
YEAH, SO?
SO, THE NUMBER **TWO** COMES AFTER **ONE!** IF IT'S A PREQUEL, WHY DID THEY NUMBER IT TWO? I HATE THAT! I'M GOING TO GO COMPLAIN ABOUT IT ON MY BLOG!
SIGH I'LL JUST STARE AT THE CASE FOR TWO HOURS WHILE I WAIT FOR YOU...
BONNET

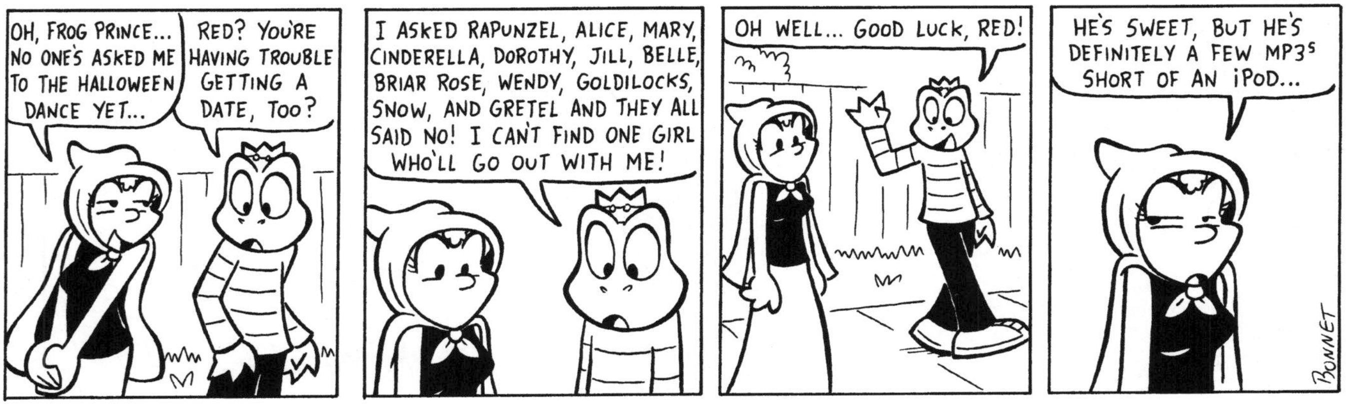
OH, FROG PRINCE... NO ONE'S ASKED ME TO THE HALLOWEEN DANCE YET...
RED? YOU'RE HAVING TROUBLE GETTING A DATE, TOO?
I ASKED RAPUNZEL, ALICE, MARY, CINDERELLA, DOROTHY, JILL, BELLE, BRIAR ROSE, WENDY, GOLDILOCKS, SNOW, AND GRETEL AND THEY ALL SAID NO! I CAN'T FIND ONE GIRL WHO'LL GO OUT WITH ME!
OH WELL... GOOD LUCK, RED!
HE'S SWEET, BUT HE'S DEFINITELY A FEW MP3S SHORT OF AN iPOD...
BONNET

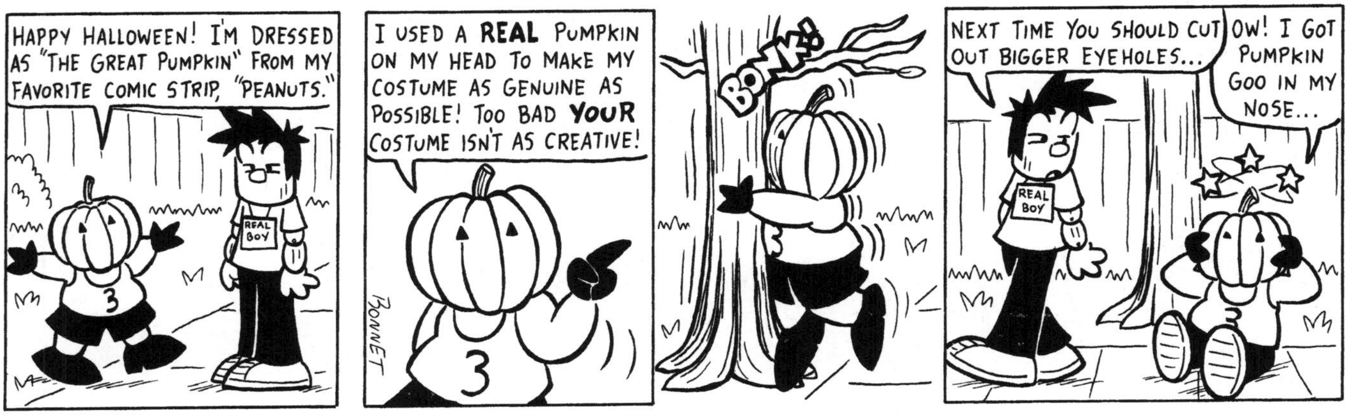
HAPPY HALLOWEEN! I'M DRESSED AS "THE GREAT PUMPKIN" FROM MY FAVORITE COMIC STRIP, "PEANUTS."
REAL BOY
I USED A **REAL** PUMPKIN ON MY HEAD TO MAKE MY COSTUME AS GENUINE AS POSSIBLE! TOO BAD **YOUR** COSTUME ISN'T AS CREATIVE!
BONNET
BONK!
NEXT TIME YOU SHOULD CUT OUT BIGGER EYEHOLES...
OW! I GOT PUMPKIN GOO IN MY NOSE...

Oct. 27, 29, 31, 2008

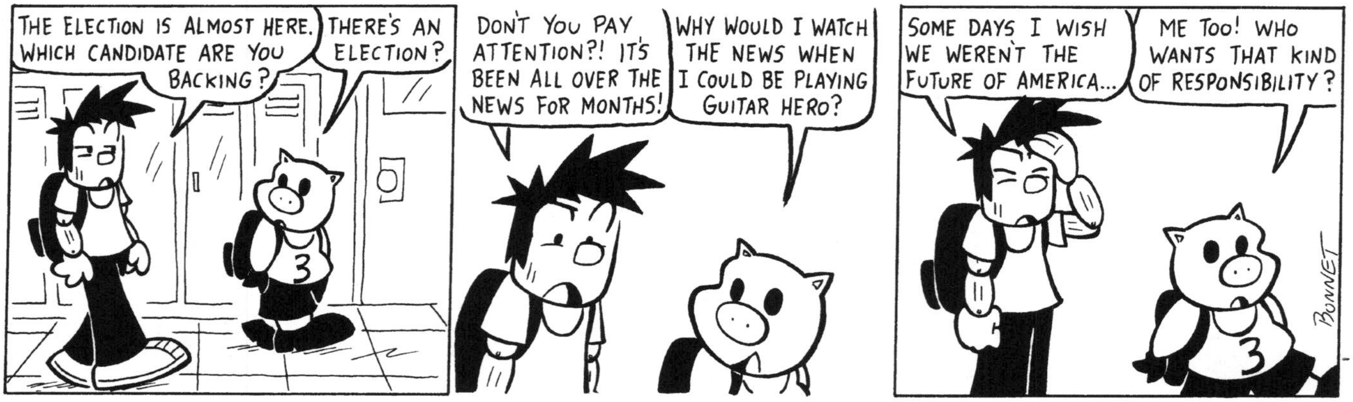
THE ELECTION IS ALMOST HERE. WHICH CANDIDATE ARE YOU BACKING?
THERE'S AN ELECTION?
DON'T YOU PAY ATTENTION?! IT'S BEEN ALL OVER THE NEWS FOR MONTHS!
WHY WOULD I WATCH THE NEWS WHEN I COULD BE PLAYING GUITAR HERO?
SOME DAYS I WISH WE WEREN'T THE FUTURE OF AMERICA...
ME TOO! WHO WANTS THAT KIND OF RESPONSIBILITY?
BONNET

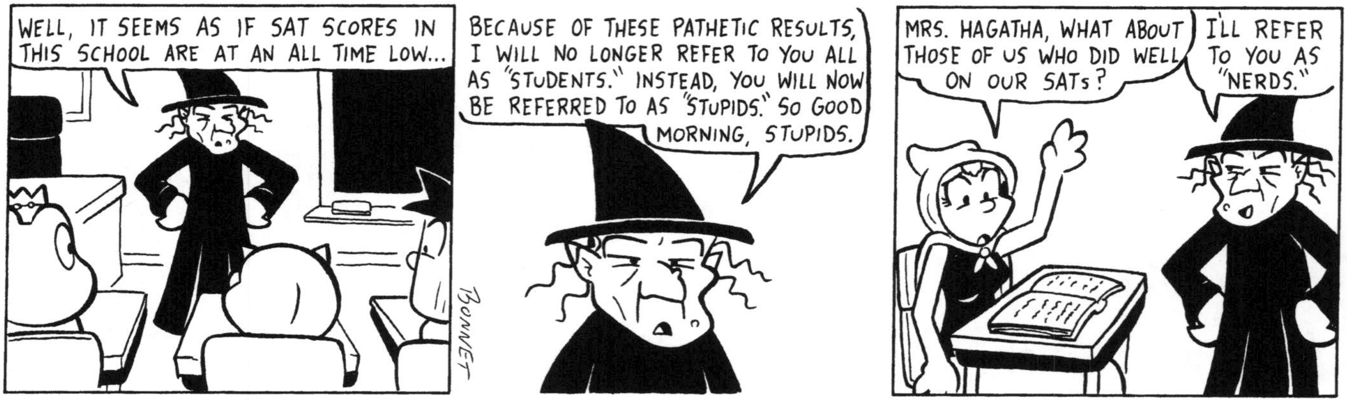
WELL, IT SEEMS AS IF SAT SCORES IN THIS SCHOOL ARE AT AN ALL TIME LOW...
BECAUSE OF THESE PATHETIC RESULTS, I WILL NO LONGER REFER TO YOU ALL AS "STUDENTS." INSTEAD, YOU WILL NOW BE REFERRED TO AS "STUPIDS." SO GOOD MORNING, STUPIDS.
MRS. HAGATHA, WHAT ABOUT THOSE OF US WHO DID WELL ON OUR SATs?
I'LL REFER TO YOU AS "NERDS."
BONNET

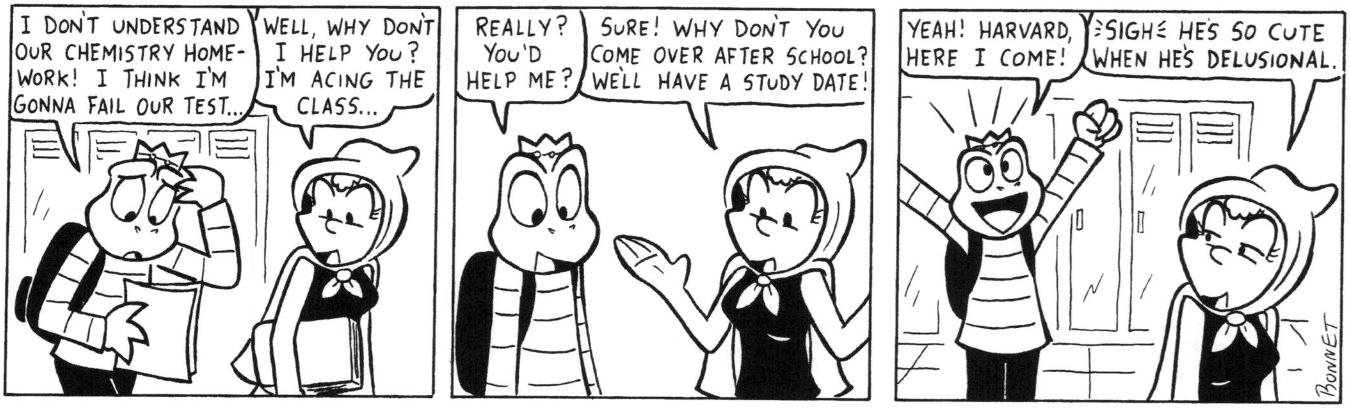
I DON'T UNDERSTAND OUR CHEMISTRY HOME-WORK! I THINK I'M GONNA FAIL OUR TEST...
WELL, WHY DON'T I HELP YOU? I'M ACING THE CLASS...
REALLY? YOU'D HELP ME?
SURE! WHY DON'T YOU COME OVER AFTER SCHOOL? WE'LL HAVE A STUDY DATE!
YEAH! HARVARD, HERE I COME!
⫶SIGH⫶ HE'S SO CUTE WHEN HE'S DELUSIONAL.
BONNET

Nov. 3, 5, 7, 2008

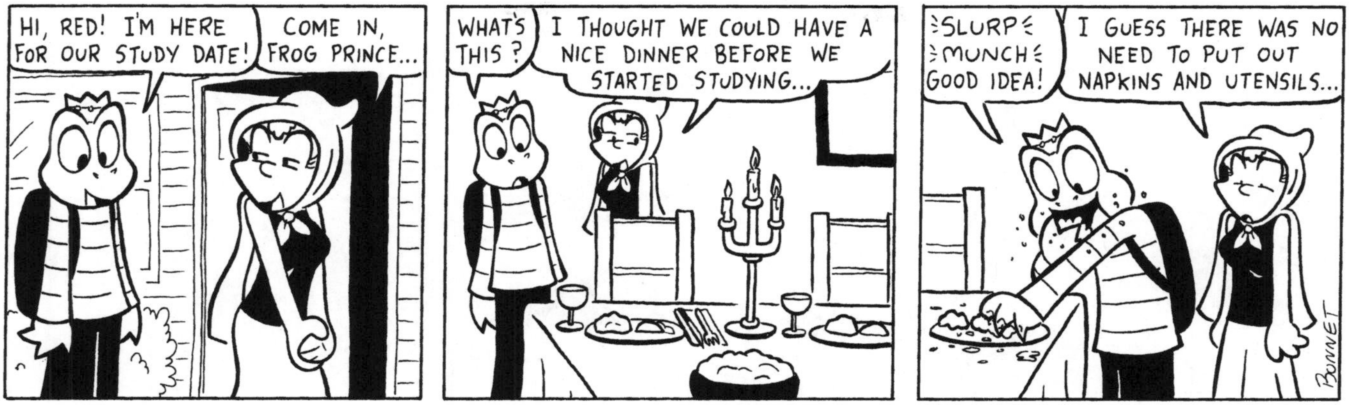
HI, RED! I'M HERE FOR OUR STUDY DATE!
COME IN, FROG PRINCE...
WHAT'S THIS?
I THOUGHT WE COULD HAVE A NICE DINNER BEFORE WE STARTED STUDYING...
SLURP MUNCH GOOD IDEA!
I GUESS THERE WAS NO NEED TO PUT OUT NAPKINS AND UTENSILS...
BONNET

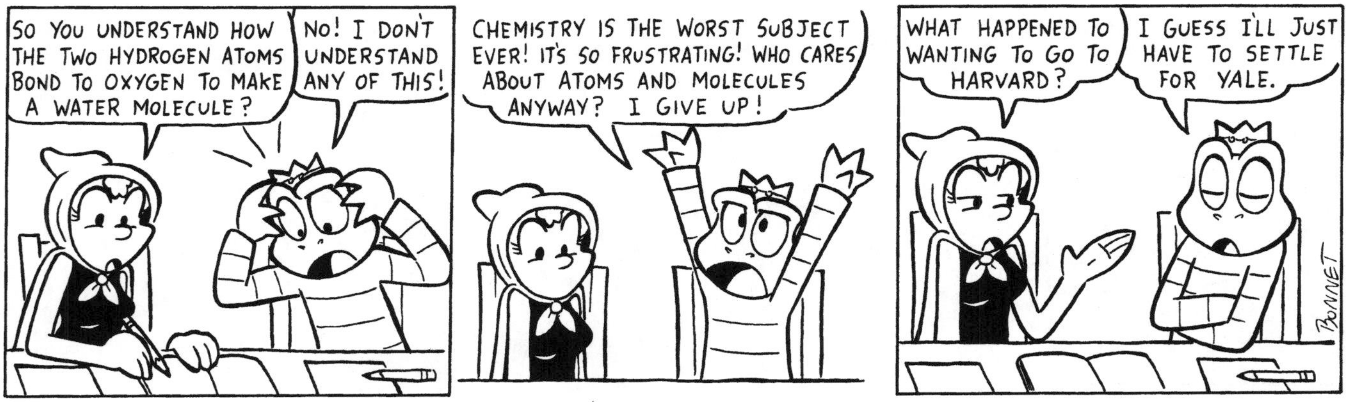
SO YOU UNDERSTAND HOW THE TWO HYDROGEN ATOMS BOND TO OXYGEN TO MAKE A WATER MOLECULE?
NO! I DON'T UNDERSTAND ANY OF THIS!
CHEMISTRY IS THE WORST SUBJECT EVER! IT'S SO FRUSTRATING! WHO CARES ABOUT ATOMS AND MOLECULES ANYWAY? I GIVE UP!
WHAT HAPPENED TO WANTING TO GO TO HARVARD?
I GUESS I'LL JUST HAVE TO SETTLE FOR YALE.
BONNET

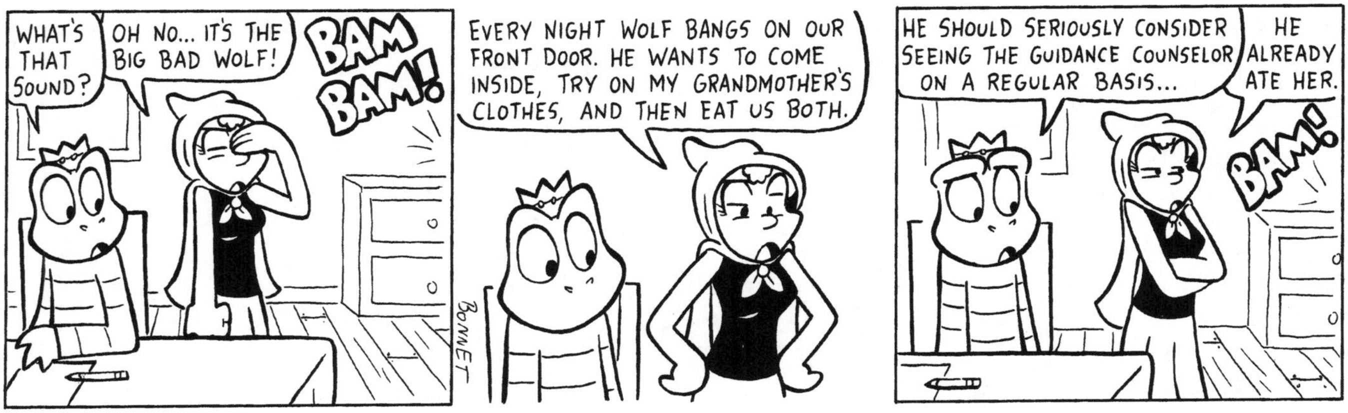
WHAT'S THAT SOUND?
OH NO... IT'S THE BIG BAD WOLF!
BAM BAM!
BONNET
EVERY NIGHT WOLF BANGS ON OUR FRONT DOOR. HE WANTS TO COME INSIDE, TRY ON MY GRANDMOTHER'S CLOTHES, AND THEN EAT US BOTH.
HE SHOULD SERIOUSLY CONSIDER SEEING THE GUIDANCE COUNSELOR ON A REGULAR BASIS...
HE ALREADY ATE HER.
BAM!

Nov. 10, 12, 14, 2008

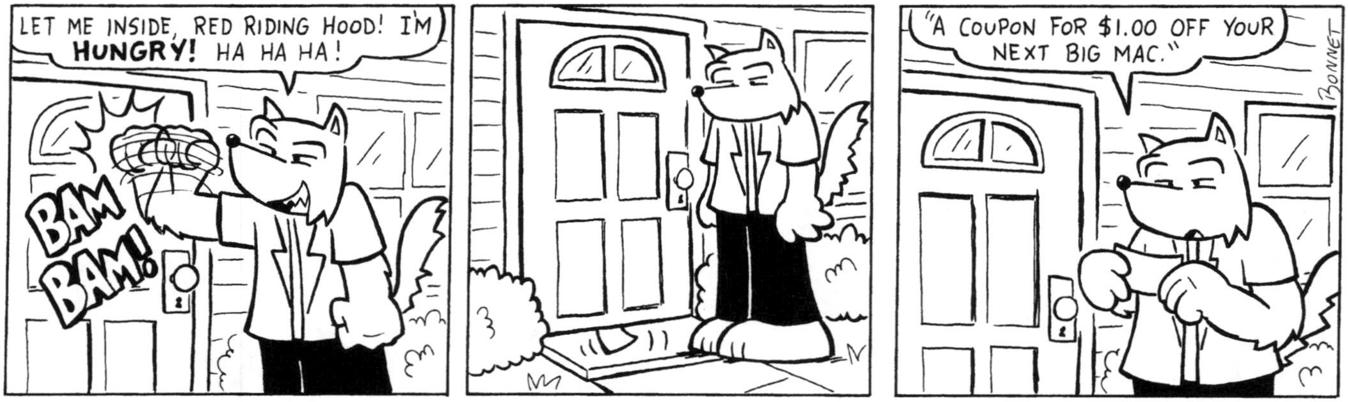
LET ME INSIDE, RED RIDING HOOD! I'M **HUNGRY!** HA HA HA!
BAM BAM!
"A COUPON FOR $1.00 OFF YOUR NEXT BIG MAC."
BONNET

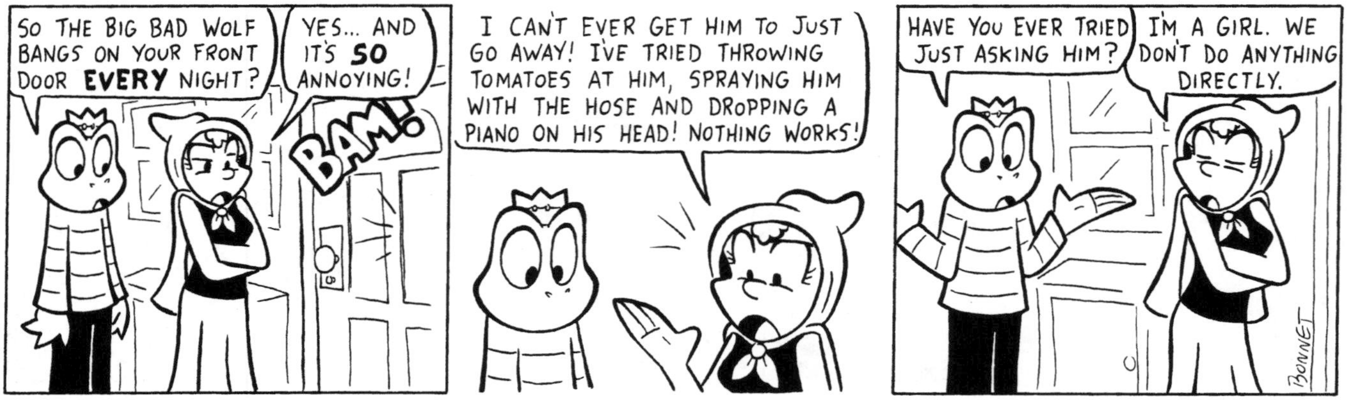
SO THE BIG BAD WOLF BANGS ON YOUR FRONT DOOR **EVERY** NIGHT?
YES... AND IT'S **SO** ANNOYING!
BAM!
I CAN'T EVER GET HIM TO JUST GO AWAY! I'VE TRIED THROWING TOMATOES AT HIM, SPRAYING HIM WITH THE HOSE AND DROPPING A PIANO ON HIS HEAD! NOTHING WORKS!
HAVE YOU EVER TRIED JUST ASKING HIM?
I'M A GIRL. WE DON'T DO ANYTHING DIRECTLY.
BONNET

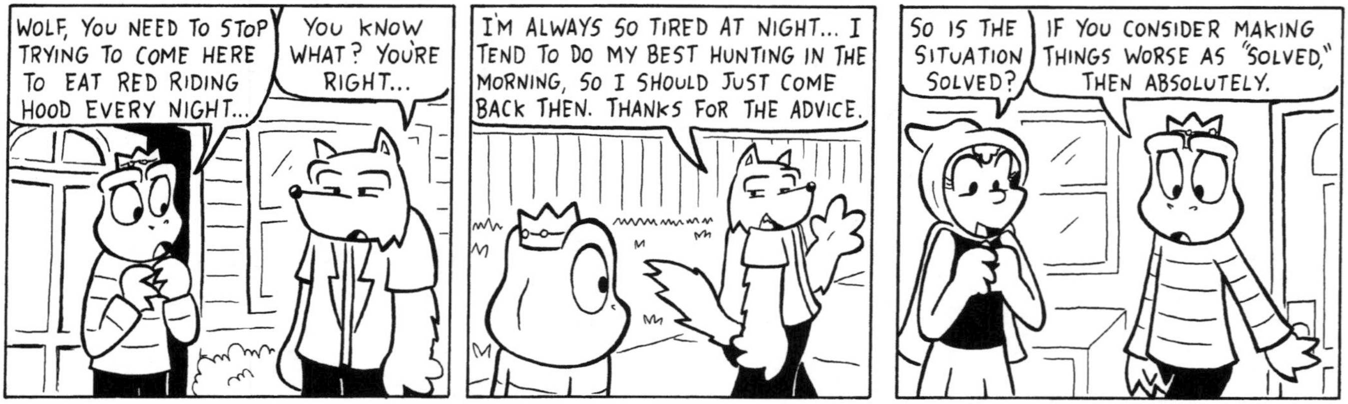
WOLF, YOU NEED TO STOP TRYING TO COME HERE TO EAT RED RIDING HOOD EVERY NIGHT...
YOU KNOW WHAT? YOU'RE RIGHT...
I'M ALWAYS SO TIRED AT NIGHT... I TEND TO DO MY BEST HUNTING IN THE MORNING, SO I SHOULD JUST COME BACK THEN. THANKS FOR THE ADVICE.
SO IS THE SITUATION SOLVED?
IF YOU CONSIDER MAKING THINGS WORSE AS "SOLVED," THEN ABSOLUTELY.

Nov. 17, 19, 21, 2008

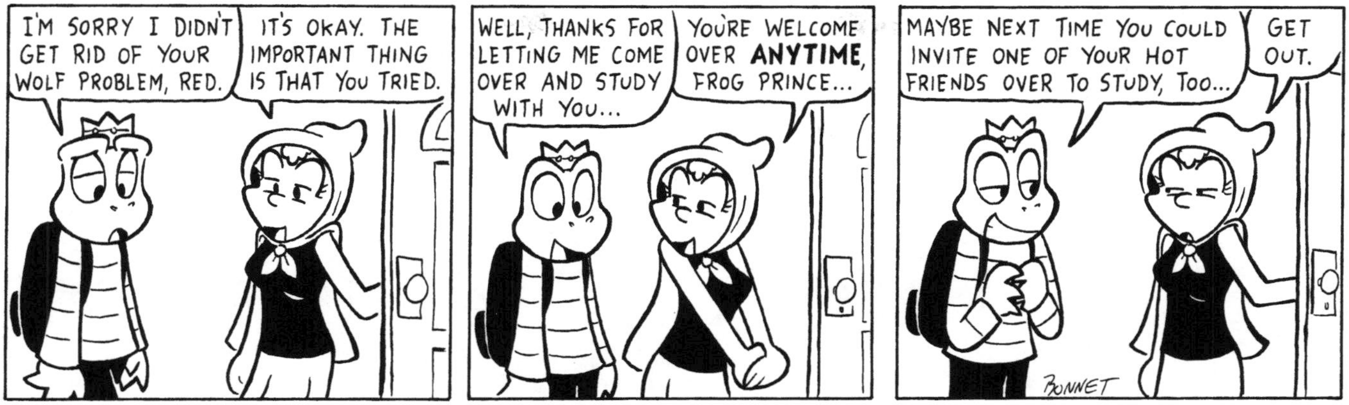
I'M SORRY I DIDN'T GET RID OF YOUR WOLF PROBLEM, RED.
IT'S OKAY. THE IMPORTANT THING IS THAT YOU TRIED.
WELL, THANKS FOR LETTING ME COME OVER AND STUDY WITH YOU...
YOU'RE WELCOME OVER **ANYTIME**, FROG PRINCE...
MAYBE NEXT TIME YOU COULD INVITE ONE OF YOUR HOT FRIENDS OVER TO STUDY, TOO...
GET OUT.
BONNET

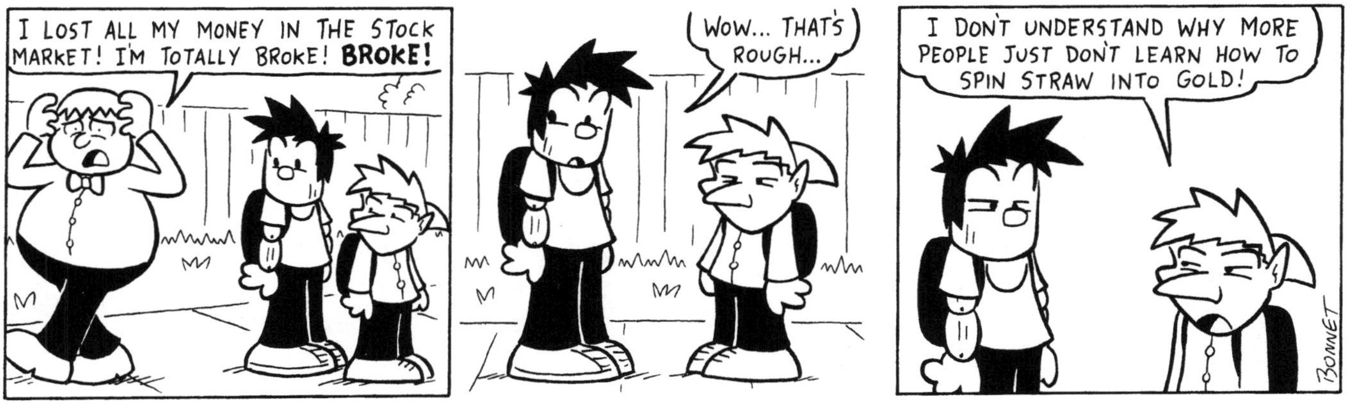
I LOST ALL MY MONEY IN THE STOCK MARKET! I'M TOTALLY BROKE! **BROKE!**
WOW... THAT'S ROUGH...
I DON'T UNDERSTAND WHY MORE PEOPLE JUST DON'T LEARN HOW TO SPIN STRAW INTO GOLD!
BONNET

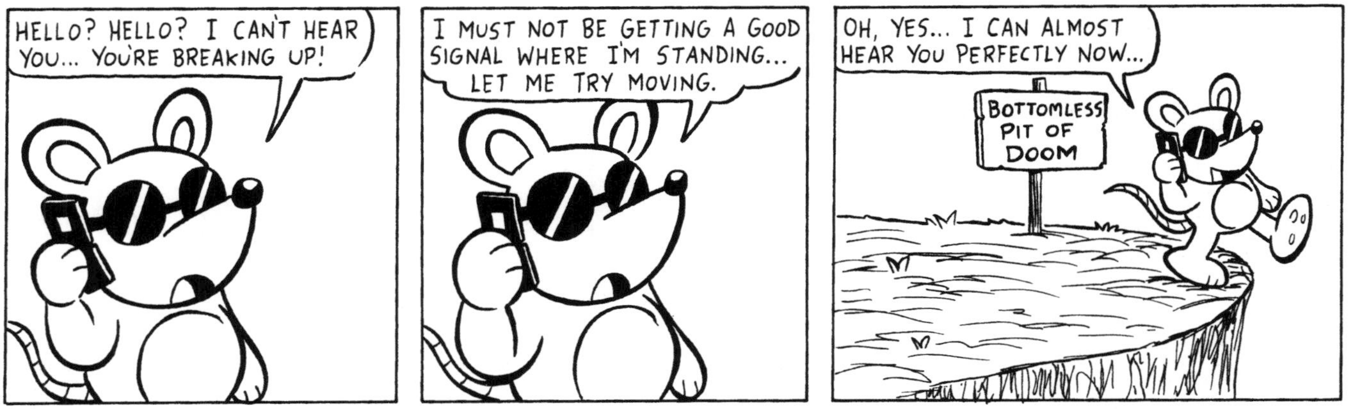
HELLO? HELLO? I CAN'T HEAR YOU... YOU'RE BREAKING UP!
I MUST NOT BE GETTING A GOOD SIGNAL WHERE I'M STANDING... LET ME TRY MOVING.
OH, YES... I CAN ALMOST HEAR YOU PERFECTLY NOW...
BOTTOMLESS PIT OF DOOM

Nov. 24, 26, 28, 2008

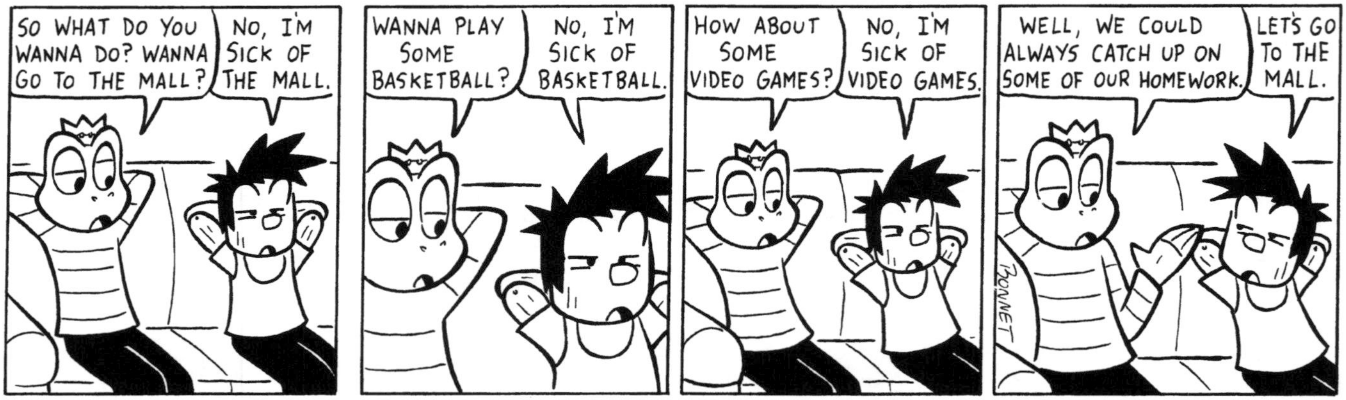
SO WHAT DO YOU WANNA DO? WANNA GO TO THE MALL?
NO, I'M SICK OF THE MALL.
WANNA PLAY SOME BASKETBALL?
NO, I'M SICK OF BASKETBALL.
HOW ABOUT SOME VIDEO GAMES?
NO, I'M SICK OF VIDEO GAMES.
BONNET
WELL, WE COULD ALWAYS CATCH UP ON SOME OF OUR HOMEWORK.
LET'S GO TO THE MALL.

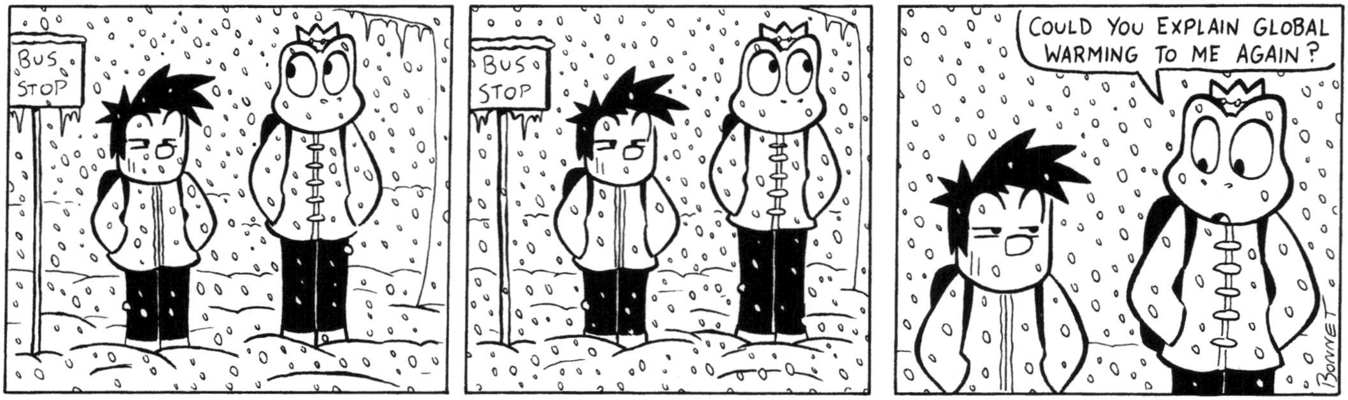
BUS STOP
BUS STOP
COULD YOU EXPLAIN GLOBAL WARMING TO ME AGAIN?
BONNET

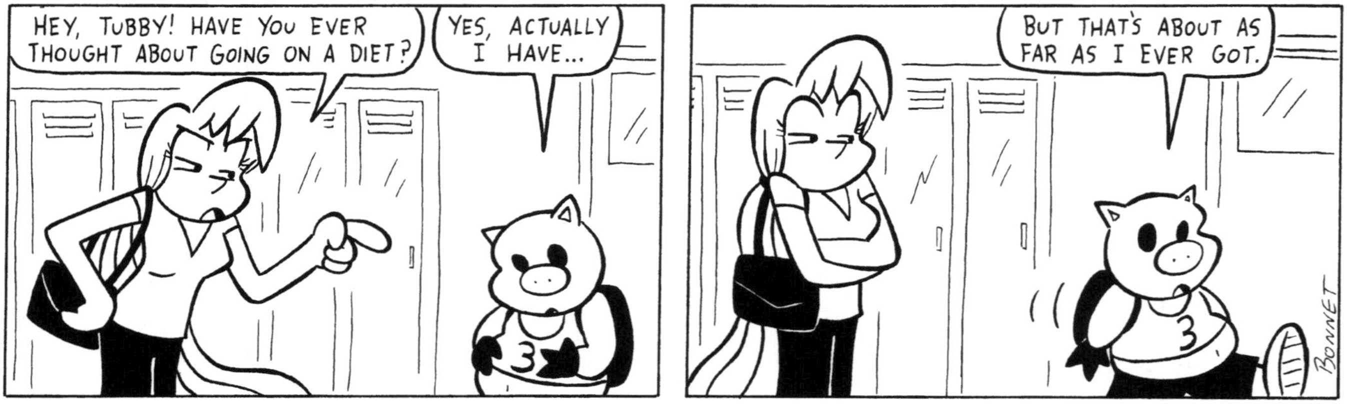
HEY, TUBBY! HAVE YOU EVER THOUGHT ABOUT GOING ON A DIET?
YES, ACTUALLY I HAVE...
BUT THAT'S ABOUT AS FAR AS I EVER GOT.
BONNET

Dec. 1, 3, 5, 2008

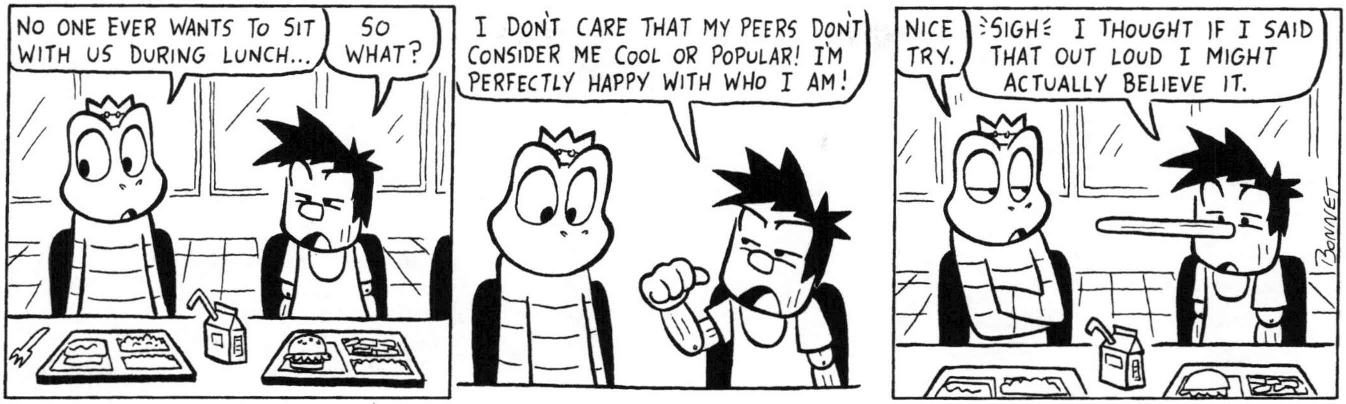
NO ONE EVER WANTS TO SIT WITH US DURING LUNCH...
SO WHAT?
I DON'T CARE THAT MY PEERS DON'T CONSIDER ME COOL OR POPULAR! I'M PERFECTLY HAPPY WITH WHO I AM!
NICE TRY.
SIGH I THOUGHT IF I SAID THAT OUT LOUD I MIGHT ACTUALLY BELIEVE IT.
BONNET

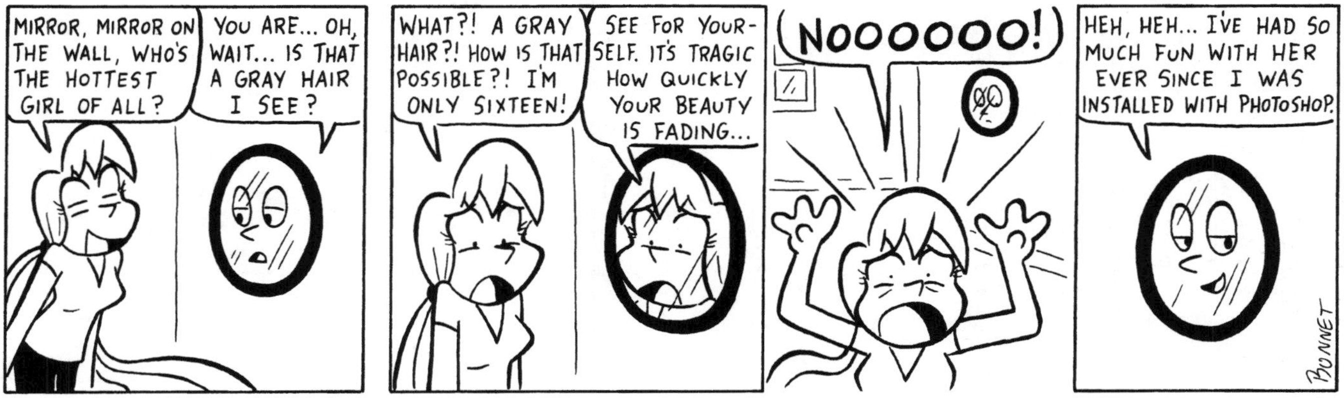
MIRROR, MIRROR ON THE WALL, WHO'S THE HOTTEST GIRL OF ALL?
YOU ARE... OH, WAIT... IS THAT A GRAY HAIR I SEE?
WHAT?! A GRAY HAIR?! HOW IS THAT POSSIBLE?! I'M ONLY SIXTEEN!
SEE FOR YOURSELF. IT'S TRAGIC HOW QUICKLY YOUR BEAUTY IS FADING...
NOOOOOO!
HEH, HEH... I'VE HAD SO MUCH FUN WITH HER EVER SINCE I WAS INSTALLED WITH PHOTOSHOP.
BONNET

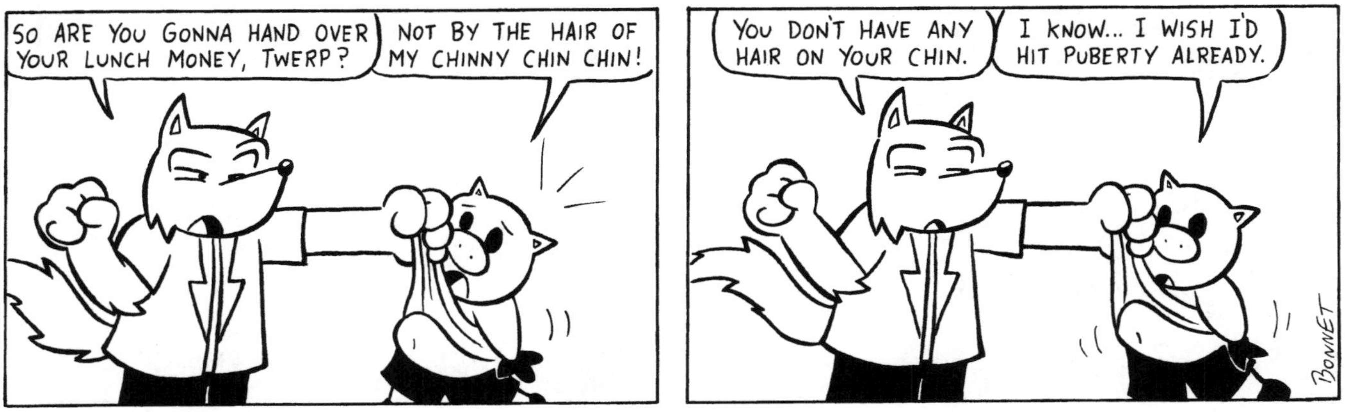
SO ARE YOU GONNA HAND OVER YOUR LUNCH MONEY, TWERP?
NOT BY THE HAIR OF MY CHINNY CHIN CHIN!
YOU DON'T HAVE ANY HAIR ON YOUR CHIN.
I KNOW... I WISH I'D HIT PUBERTY ALREADY.
BONNET

Dec. 8, 10, 12, 2008

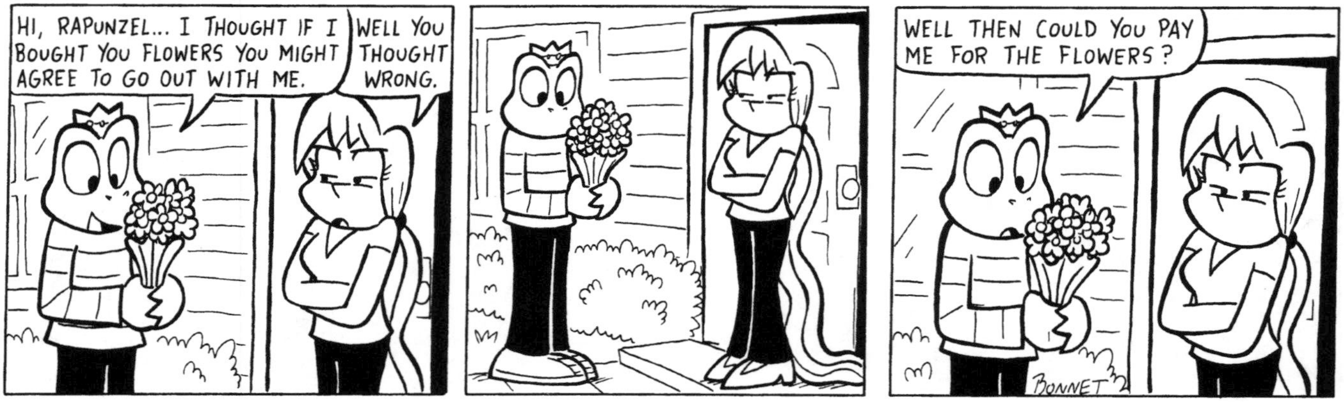
HI, RAPUNZEL... I THOUGHT IF I BOUGHT YOU FLOWERS YOU MIGHT AGREE TO GO OUT WITH ME.
WELL YOU THOUGHT WRONG.
WELL THEN COULD YOU PAY ME FOR THE FLOWERS?
BONNET

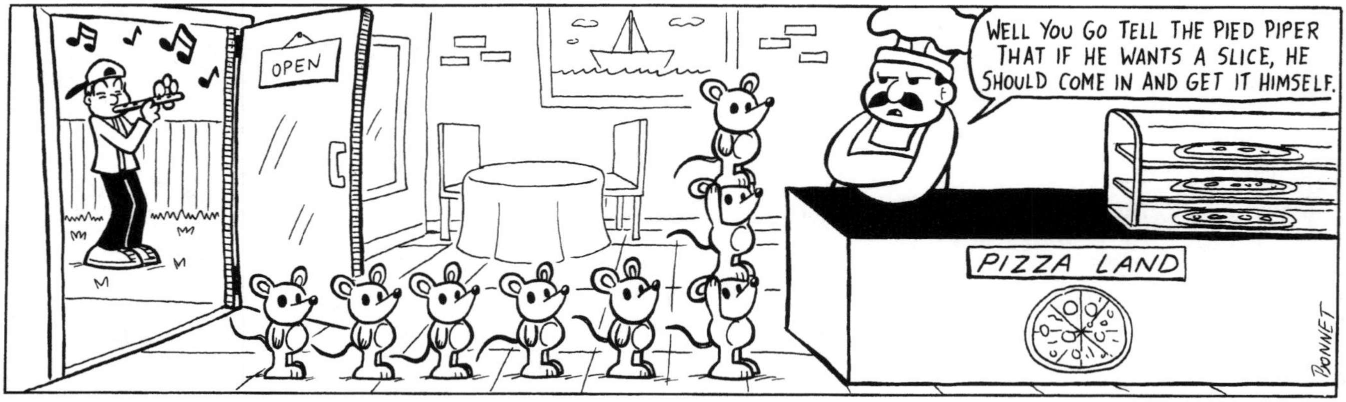
OPEN
WELL YOU GO TELL THE PIED PIPER THAT IF HE WANTS A SLICE, HE SHOULD COME IN AND GET IT HIMSELF.
PIZZA LAND
BONNET

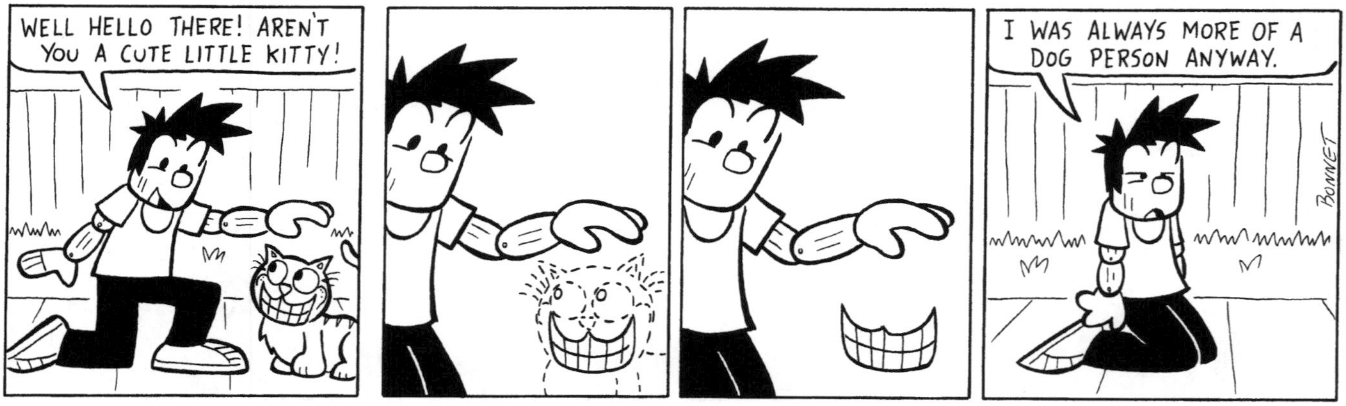
WELL HELLO THERE! AREN'T YOU A CUTE LITTLE KITTY!
I WAS ALWAYS MORE OF A DOG PERSON ANYWAY.
BONNET

Dec. 15, 17, 19, 2008

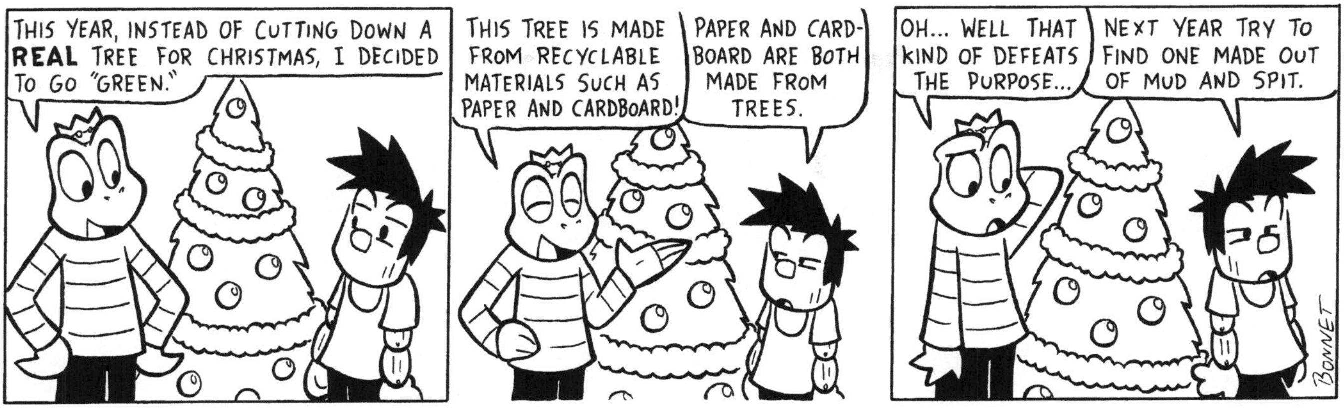
THIS YEAR, INSTEAD OF CUTTING DOWN A **REAL** TREE FOR CHRISTMAS, I DECIDED TO GO "GREEN."
THIS TREE IS MADE FROM RECYCLABLE MATERIALS SUCH AS PAPER AND CARDBOARD!
PAPER AND CARD-BOARD ARE BOTH MADE FROM TREES.
OH... WELL THAT KIND OF DEFEATS THE PURPOSE...
NEXT YEAR TRY TO FIND ONE MADE OUT OF MUD AND SPIT.
BONNET

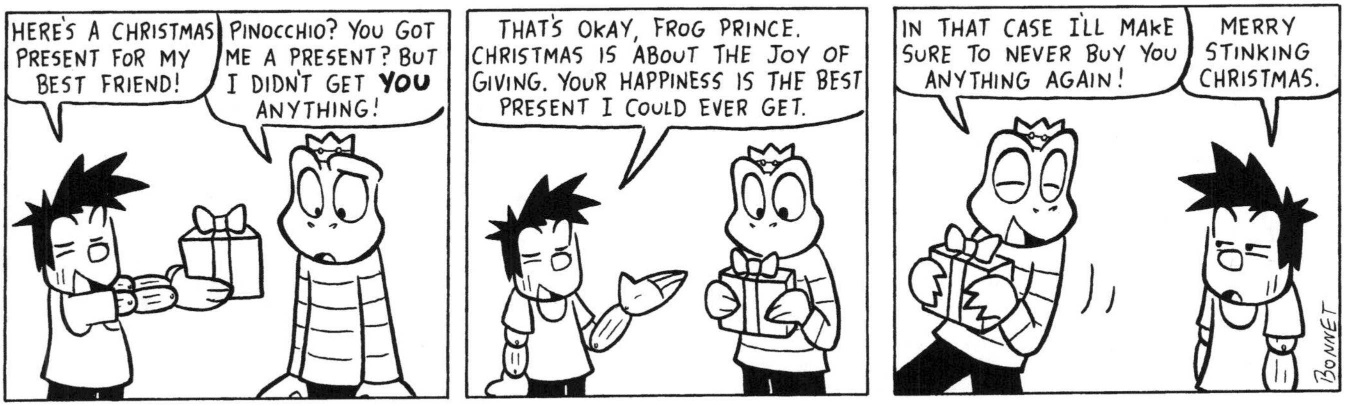
HERE'S A CHRISTMAS PRESENT FOR MY BEST FRIEND!
PINOCCHIO? YOU GOT ME A PRESENT? BUT I DIDN'T GET **YOU** ANYTHING!
THAT'S OKAY, FROG PRINCE. CHRISTMAS IS ABOUT THE JOY OF GIVING. YOUR HAPPINESS IS THE BEST PRESENT I COULD EVER GET.
IN THAT CASE I'LL MAKE SURE TO NEVER BUY YOU ANYTHING AGAIN!
MERRY STINKING CHRISTMAS.
BONNET

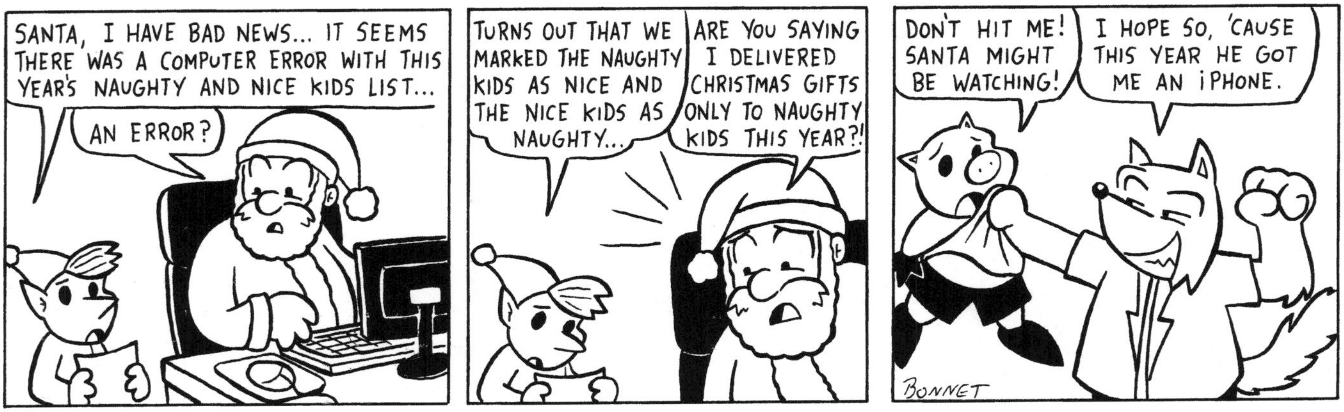
SANTA, I HAVE BAD NEWS... IT SEEMS THERE WAS A COMPUTER ERROR WITH THIS YEAR'S NAUGHTY AND NICE KIDS LIST...
AN ERROR?
TURNS OUT THAT WE MARKED THE NAUGHTY KIDS AS NICE AND THE NICE KIDS AS NAUGHTY...
ARE YOU SAYING I DELIVERED CHRISTMAS GIFTS ONLY TO NAUGHTY KIDS THIS YEAR?!
DON'T HIT ME! SANTA MIGHT BE WATCHING!
I HOPE SO, 'CAUSE THIS YEAR HE GOT ME AN iPHONE.
BONNET

Dec. 22, 24, 26, 2008

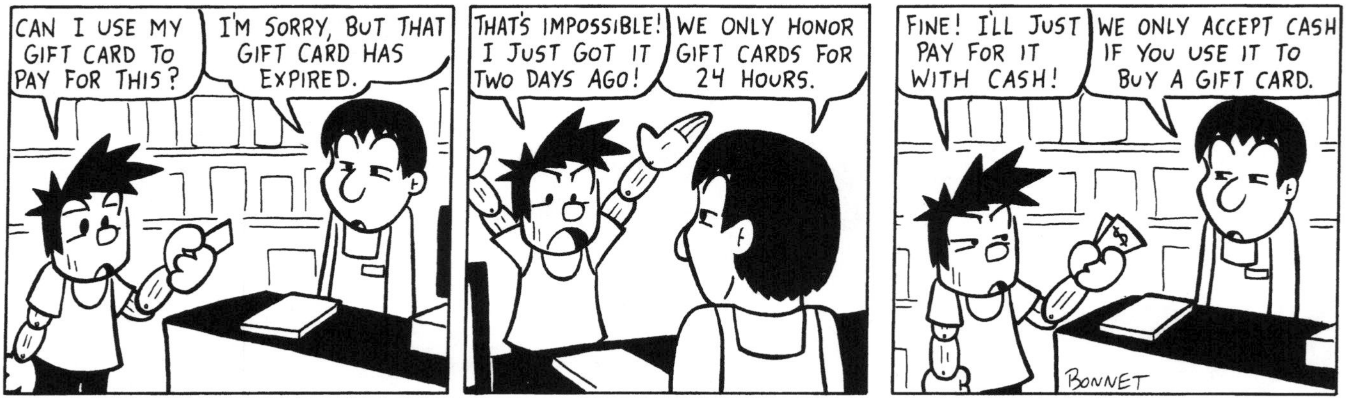
CAN I USE MY GIFT CARD TO PAY FOR THIS?
I'M SORRY, BUT THAT GIFT CARD HAS EXPIRED.
THAT'S IMPOSSIBLE! I JUST GOT IT TWO DAYS AGO!
WE ONLY HONOR GIFT CARDS FOR 24 HOURS.
FINE! I'LL JUST PAY FOR IT WITH CASH!
WE ONLY ACCEPT CASH IF YOU USE IT TO BUY A GIFT CARD.
BONNET

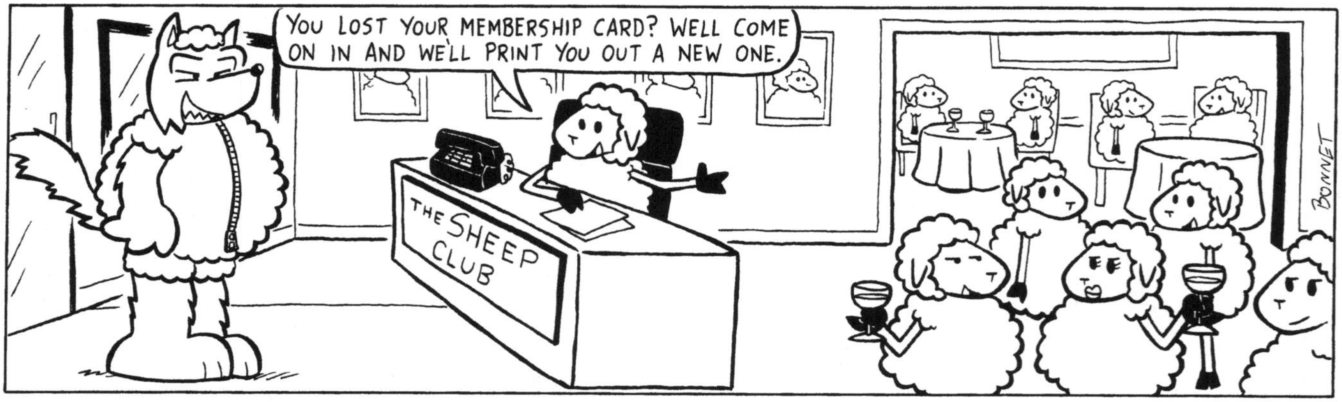
YOU LOST YOUR MEMBERSHIP CARD? WELL COME ON IN AND WE'LL PRINT YOU OUT A NEW ONE.
THE SHEEP CLUB
BONNET

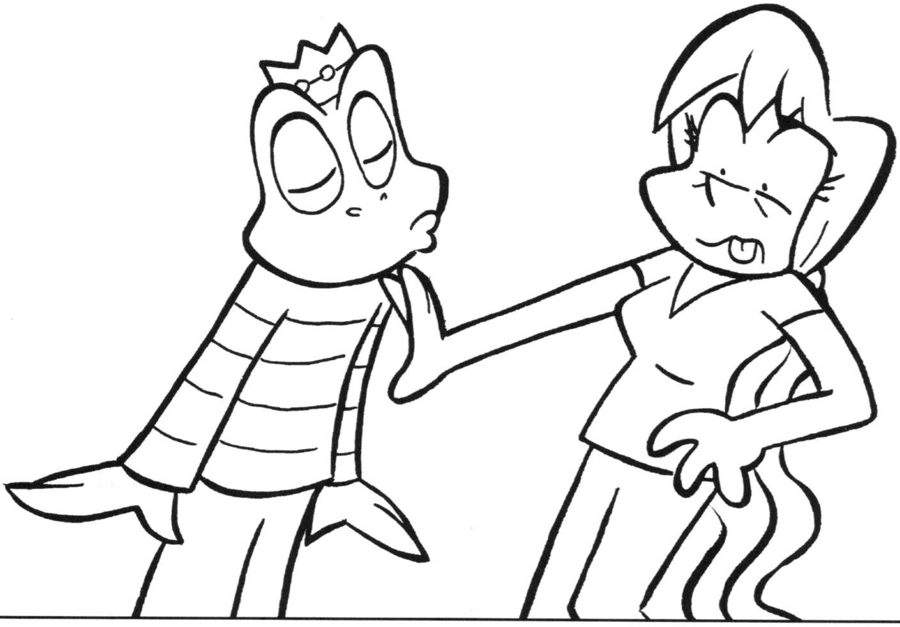

Dec, 29, 31, 2008

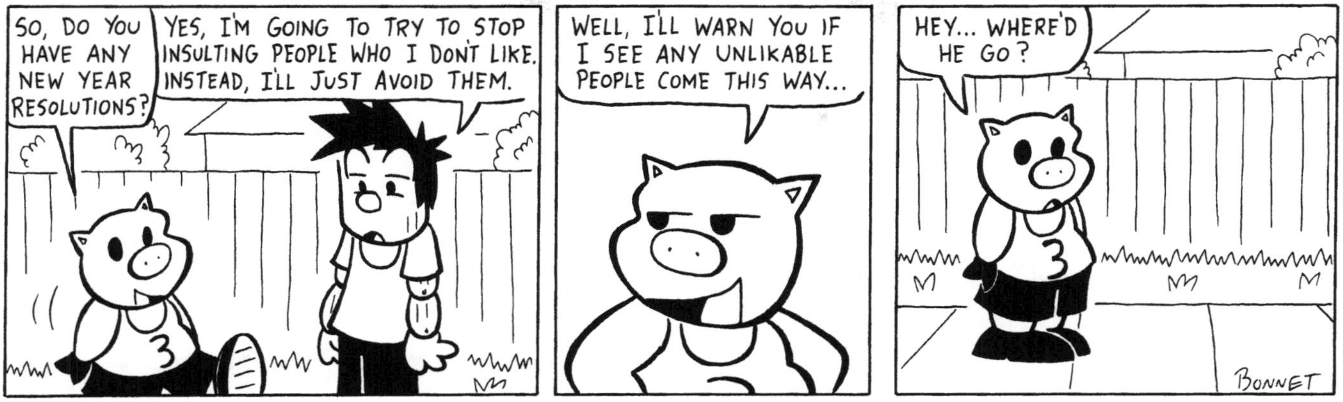
SO, DO YOU HAVE ANY NEW YEAR RESOLUTIONS?
YES, I'M GOING TO TRY TO STOP INSULTING PEOPLE WHO I DON'T LIKE. INSTEAD, I'LL JUST AVOID THEM.
WELL, I'LL WARN YOU IF I SEE ANY UNLIKABLE PEOPLE COME THIS WAY...
HEY... WHERE'D HE GO?
BONNET

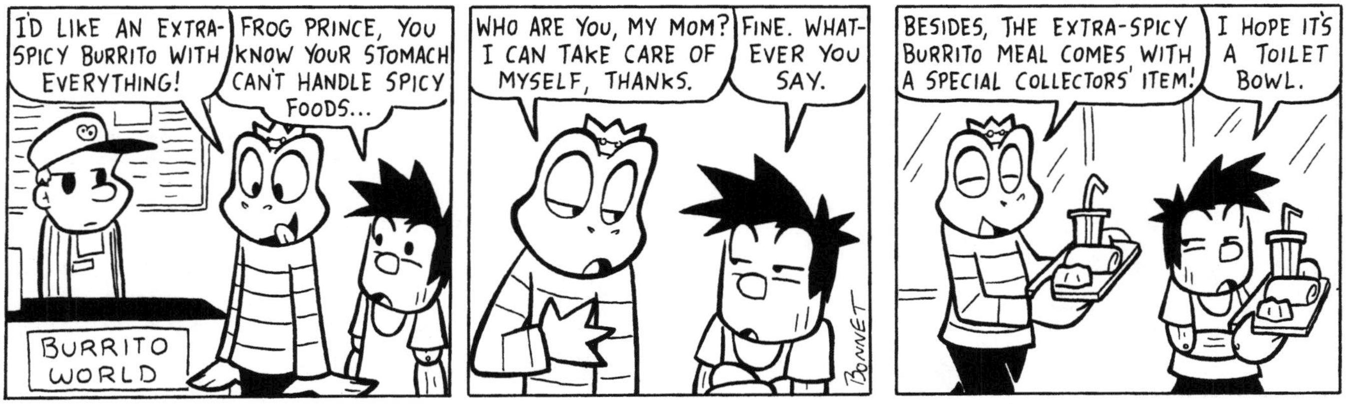
I'D LIKE AN EXTRA-SPICY BURRITO WITH EVERYTHING!
FROG PRINCE, YOU KNOW YOUR STOMACH CAN'T HANDLE SPICY FOODS...
BURRITO WORLD
WHO ARE YOU, MY MOM? I CAN TAKE CARE OF MYSELF, THANKS.
FINE. WHATEVER YOU SAY.
BONNET
BESIDES, THE EXTRA-SPICY BURRITO MEAL COMES WITH A SPECIAL COLLECTORS' ITEM!
I HOPE IT'S A TOILET BOWL.

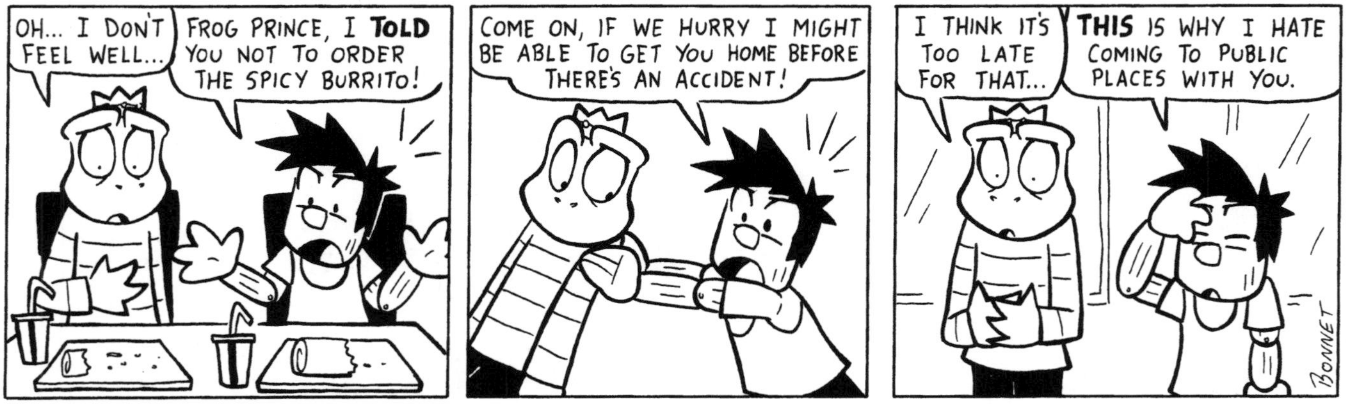
OH... I DON'T FEEL WELL...
FROG PRINCE, I **TOLD** YOU NOT TO ORDER THE SPICY BURRITO!
COME ON, IF WE HURRY I MIGHT BE ABLE TO GET YOU HOME BEFORE THERE'S AN ACCIDENT!
I THINK IT'S TOO LATE FOR THAT...
THIS IS WHY I HATE COMING TO PUBLIC PLACES WITH YOU.
BONNET

Jan. 2, 5, 7, 2009

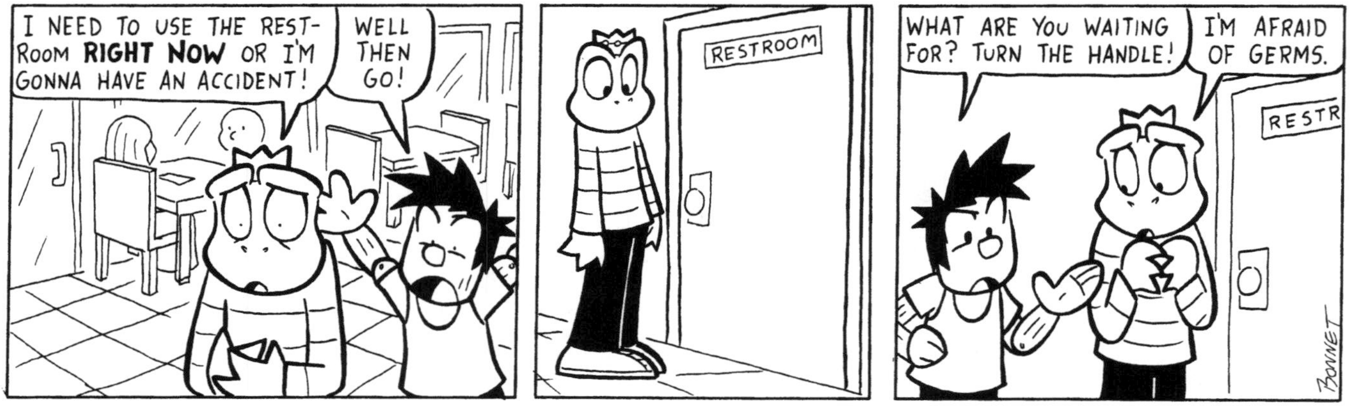
I NEED TO USE THE REST-ROOM **RIGHT NOW** OR I'M GONNA HAVE AN ACCIDENT!
WELL THEN GO!
RESTROOM
WHAT ARE YOU WAITING FOR? TURN THE HANDLE!
I'M AFRAID OF GERMS.
RESTR
BONNET

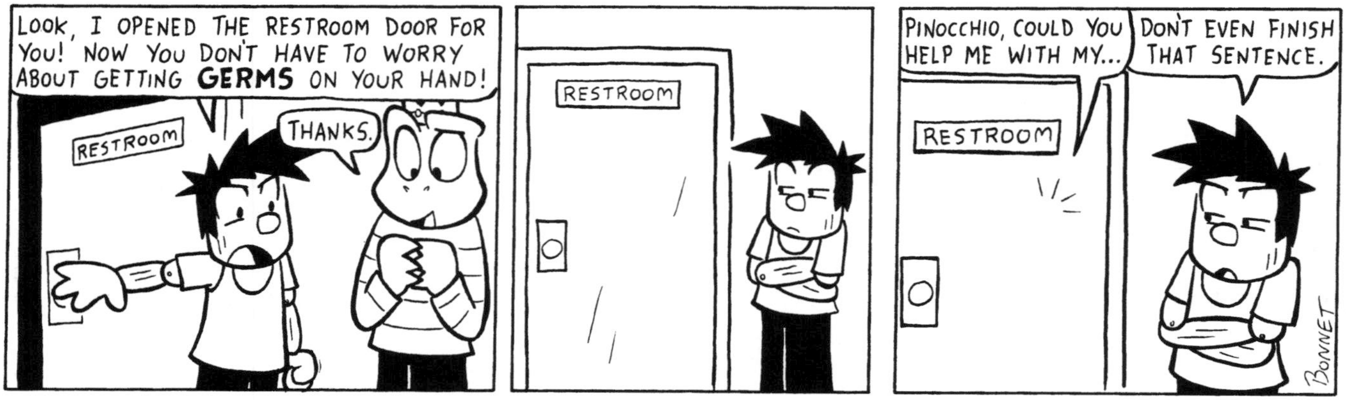
LOOK, I OPENED THE RESTROOM DOOR FOR YOU! NOW YOU DON'T HAVE TO WORRY ABOUT GETTING **GERMS** ON YOUR HAND!
RESTROOM
THANKS.
RESTROOM
PINOCCHIO, COULD YOU HELP ME WITH MY...
DON'T EVEN FINISH THAT SENTENCE.
RESTROOM
BONNET

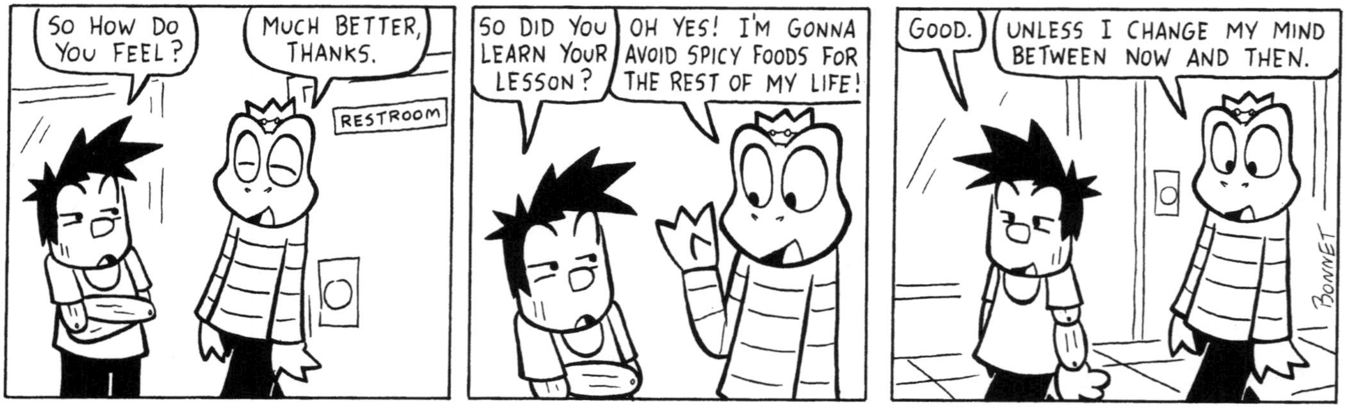
SO HOW DO YOU FEEL?
MUCH BETTER, THANKS.
RESTROOM
SO DID YOU LEARN YOUR LESSON?
OH YES! I'M GONNA AVOID SPICY FOODS FOR THE REST OF MY LIFE!
GOOD.
UNLESS I CHANGE MY MIND BETWEEN NOW AND THEN.
BONNET

Jan. 9, 12, 14, 2009

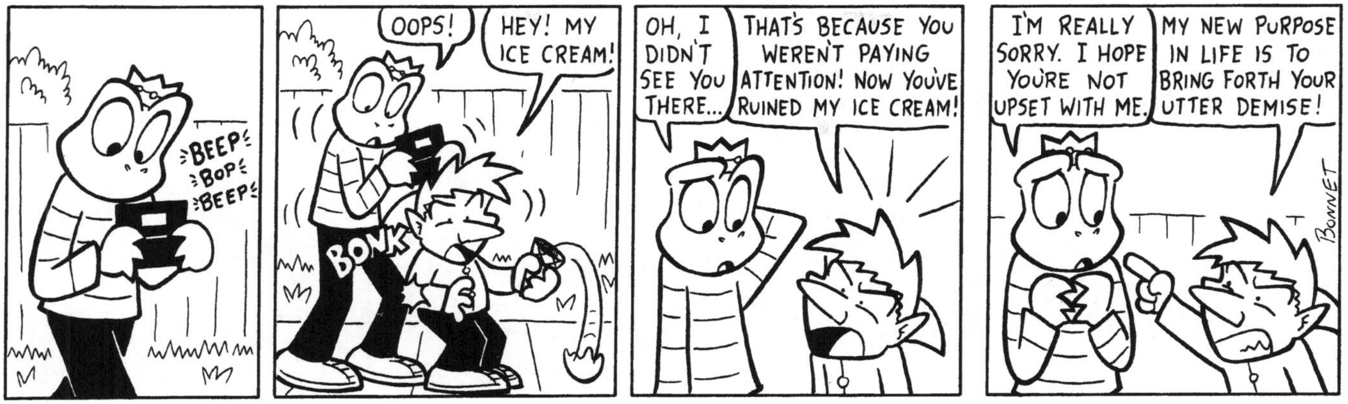
BEEP BOP BEEP
OOPS!
HEY! MY ICE CREAM!
BONK
OH, I DIDN'T SEE YOU THERE...
THAT'S BECAUSE YOU WEREN'T PAYING ATTENTION! NOW YOU'VE RUINED MY ICE CREAM!
I'M REALLY SORRY. I HOPE YOU'RE NOT UPSET WITH ME.
MY NEW PURPOSE IN LIFE IS TO BRING FORTH YOUR UTTER DEMISE!
BONNET

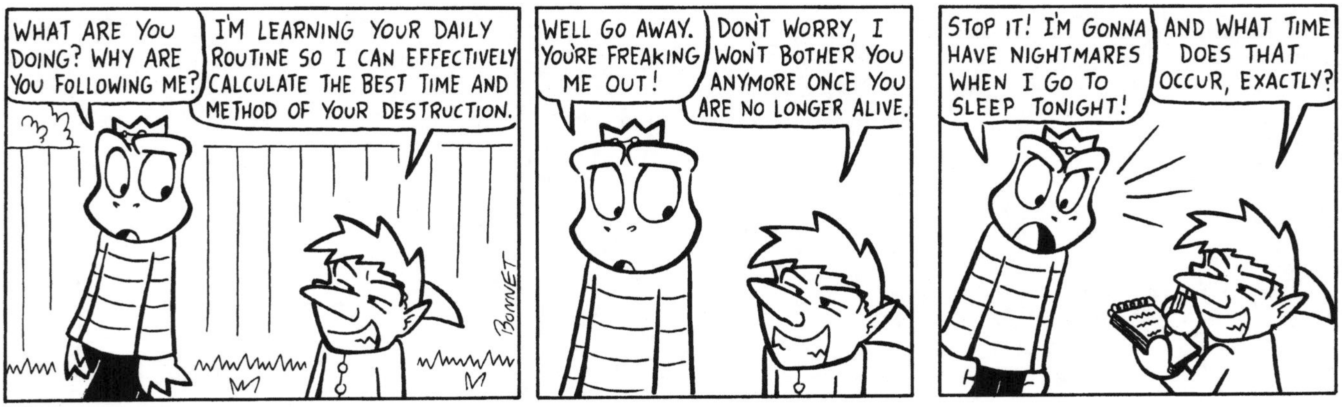
WHAT ARE YOU DOING? WHY ARE YOU FOLLOWING ME?
I'M LEARNING YOUR DAILY ROUTINE SO I CAN EFFECTIVELY CALCULATE THE BEST TIME AND METHOD OF YOUR DESTRUCTION.
BONNET
WELL GO AWAY. YOU'RE FREAKING ME OUT!
DON'T WORRY, I WON'T BOTHER YOU ANYMORE ONCE YOU ARE NO LONGER ALIVE.
STOP IT! I'M GONNA HAVE NIGHTMARES WHEN I GO TO SLEEP TONIGHT!
AND WHAT TIME DOES THAT OCCUR, EXACTLY?

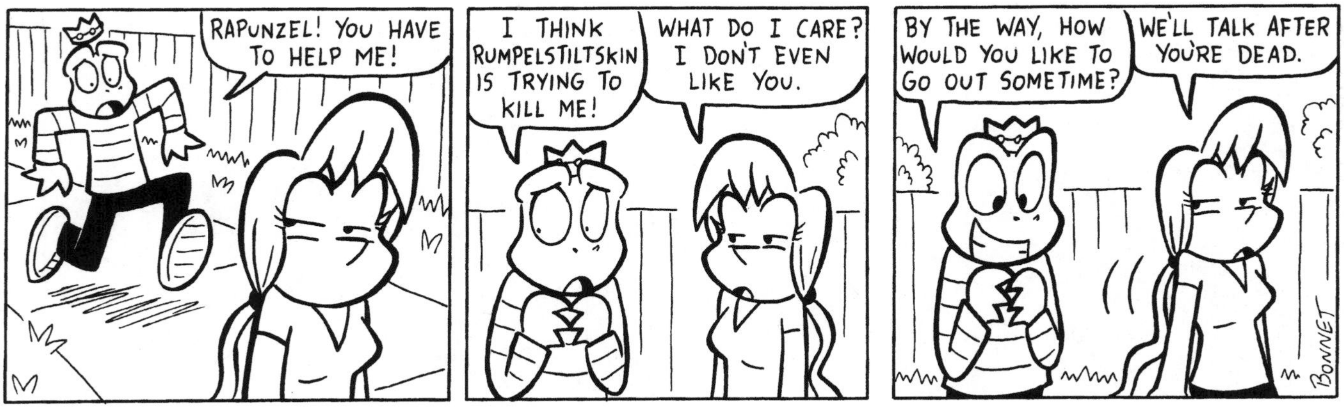
RAPUNZEL! YOU HAVE TO HELP ME!
I THINK RUMPELSTILTSKIN IS TRYING TO KILL ME!
WHAT DO I CARE? I DON'T EVEN LIKE YOU.
BY THE WAY, HOW WOULD YOU LIKE TO GO OUT SOMETIME?
WE'LL TALK AFTER YOU'RE DEAD.
BONNET

Jan. 16, 19, 21, 2009

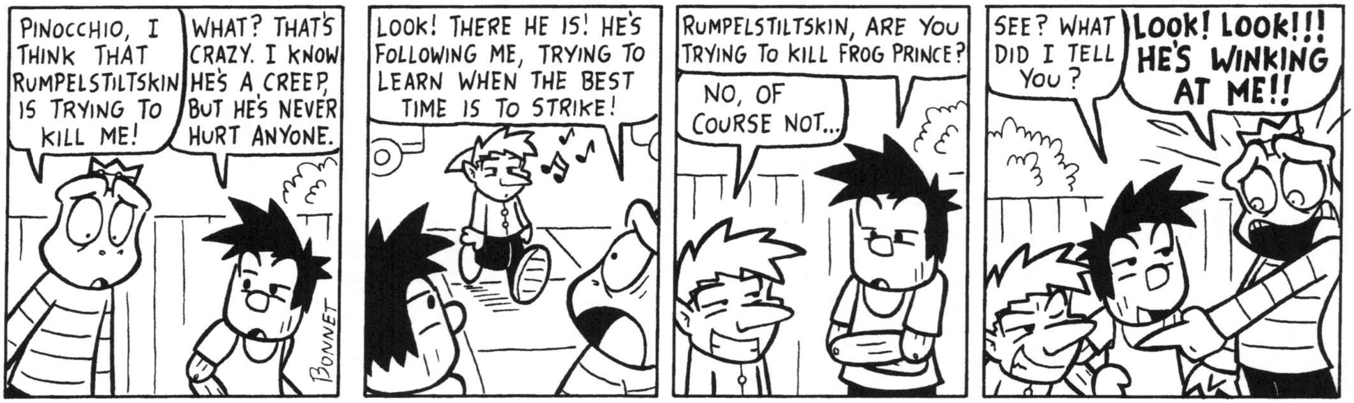
PINOCCHIO, I THINK THAT RUMPELSTILTSKIN IS TRYING TO KILL ME!
WHAT? THAT'S CRAZY. I KNOW HE'S A CREEP, BUT HE'S NEVER HURT ANYONE.
BONNET
LOOK! THERE HE IS! HE'S FOLLOWING ME, TRYING TO LEARN WHEN THE BEST TIME IS TO STRIKE!
RUMPELSTILTSKIN, ARE YOU TRYING TO KILL FROG PRINCE?
NO, OF COURSE NOT...
SEE? WHAT DID I TELL YOU?
LOOK! LOOK!!! HE'S WINKING AT ME!!

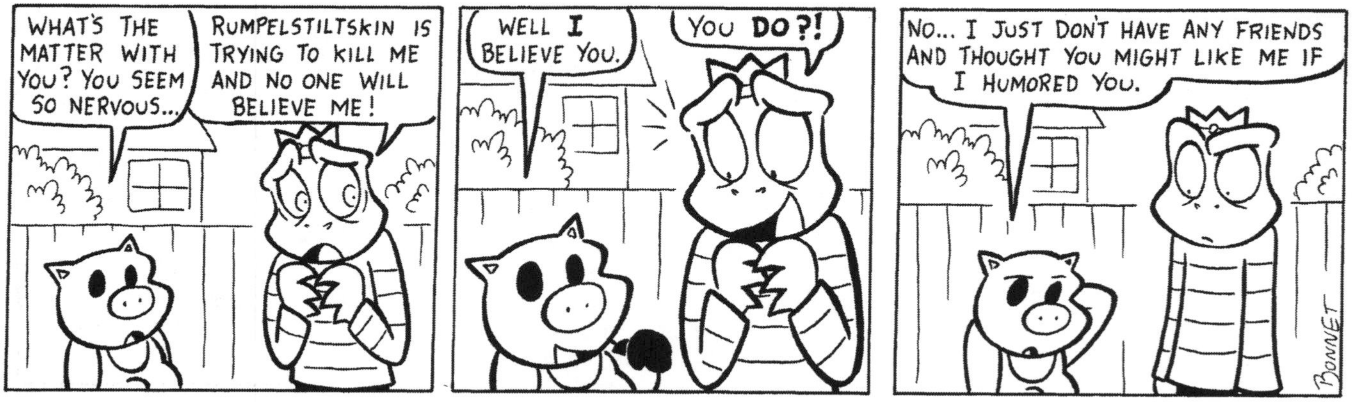
WHAT'S THE MATTER WITH YOU? YOU SEEM SO NERVOUS...
RUMPELSTILTSKIN IS TRYING TO KILL ME AND NO ONE WILL BELIEVE ME!
WELL I BELIEVE YOU.
YOU DO?!
NO... I JUST DON'T HAVE ANY FRIENDS AND THOUGHT YOU MIGHT LIKE ME IF I HUMORED YOU.
BONNET

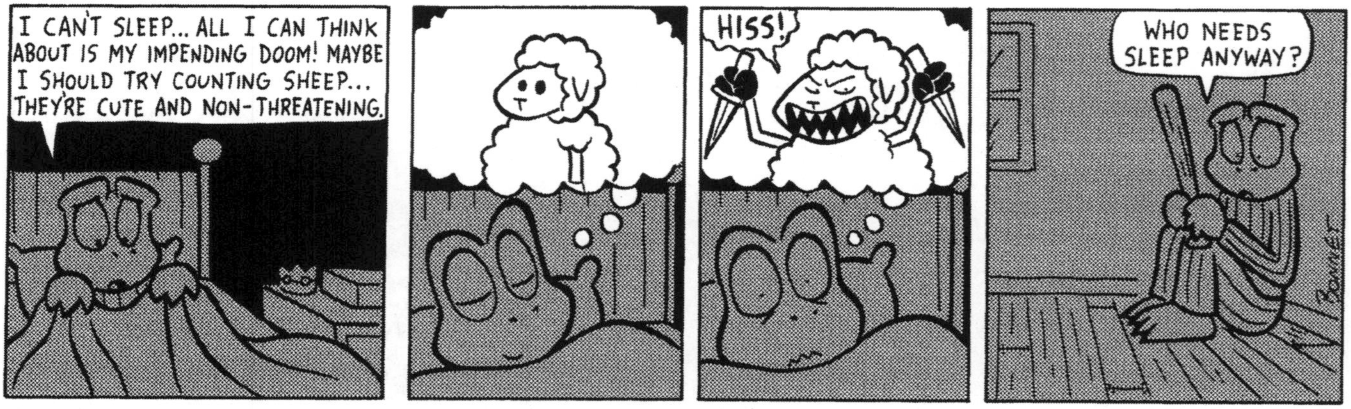
I CAN'T SLEEP... ALL I CAN THINK ABOUT IS MY IMPENDING DOOM! MAYBE I SHOULD TRY COUNTING SHEEP... THEY'RE CUTE AND NON-THREATENING.
HISS!
WHO NEEDS SLEEP ANYWAY?
BONNET

Jan. 23, 26, 28, 2009

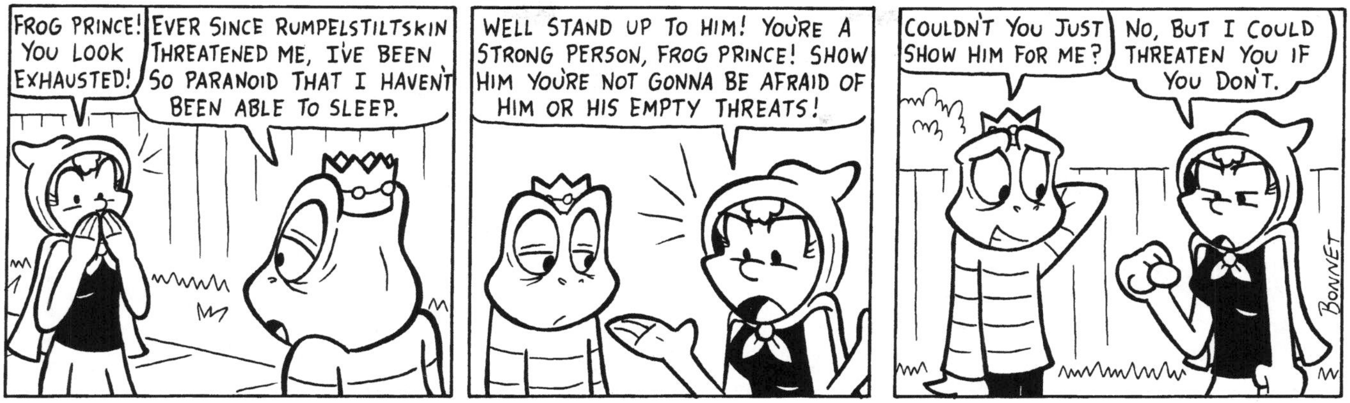
FROG PRINCE! YOU LOOK EXHAUSTED!
EVER SINCE RUMPELSTILTSKIN THREATENED ME, I'VE BEEN SO PARANOID THAT I HAVEN'T BEEN ABLE TO SLEEP.
WELL STAND UP TO HIM! YOU'RE A STRONG PERSON, FROG PRINCE! SHOW HIM YOU'RE NOT GONNA BE AFRAID OF HIM OR HIS EMPTY THREATS!
COULDN'T YOU JUST SHOW HIM FOR ME?
NO, BUT I COULD THREATEN YOU IF YOU DON'T.
BONNET

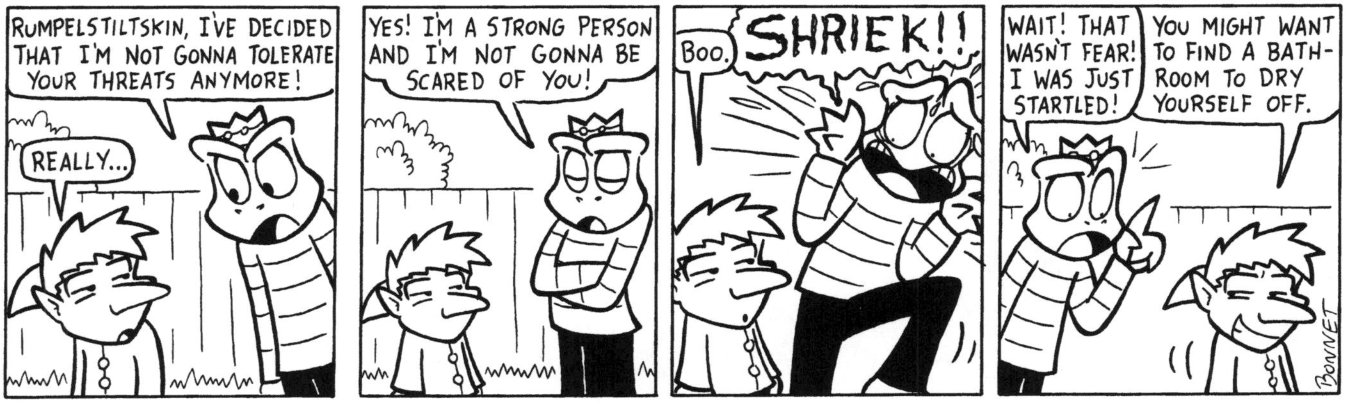
RUMPELSTILTSKIN, I'VE DECIDED THAT I'M NOT GONNA TOLERATE YOUR THREATS ANYMORE!
REALLY...
YES! I'M A STRONG PERSON AND I'M NOT GONNA BE SCARED OF YOU!
BOO.
SHRIEK!!
WAIT! THAT WASN'T FEAR! I WAS JUST STARTLED!
YOU MIGHT WANT TO FIND A BATH-ROOM TO DRY YOURSELF OFF.
BONNET

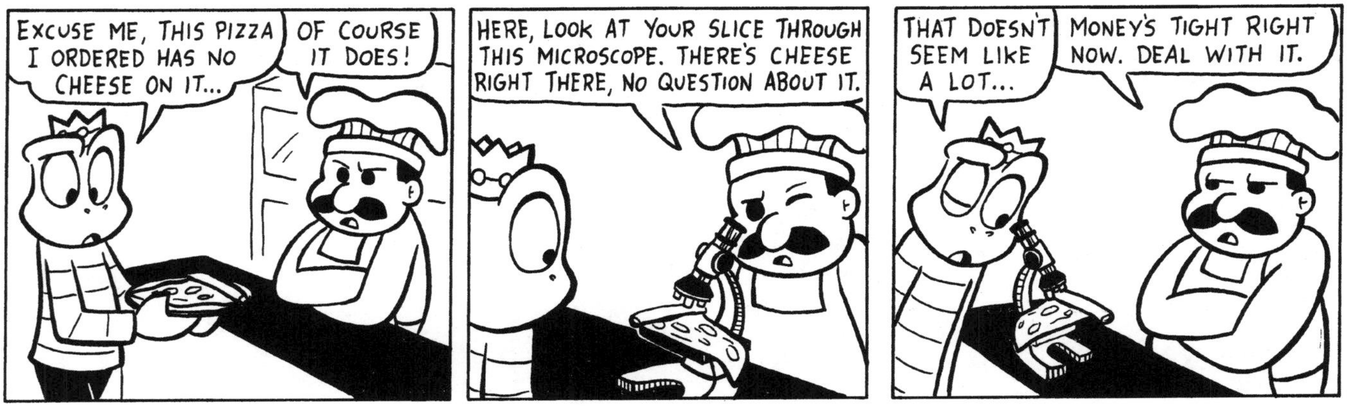
EXCUSE ME, THIS PIZZA I ORDERED HAS NO CHEESE ON IT...
OF COURSE IT DOES!
HERE, LOOK AT YOUR SLICE THROUGH THIS MICROSCOPE. THERE'S CHEESE RIGHT THERE, NO QUESTION ABOUT IT.
THAT DOESN'T SEEM LIKE A LOT...
MONEY'S TIGHT RIGHT NOW. DEAL WITH IT.

Jan. 30, Feb. 2, 4, 2009

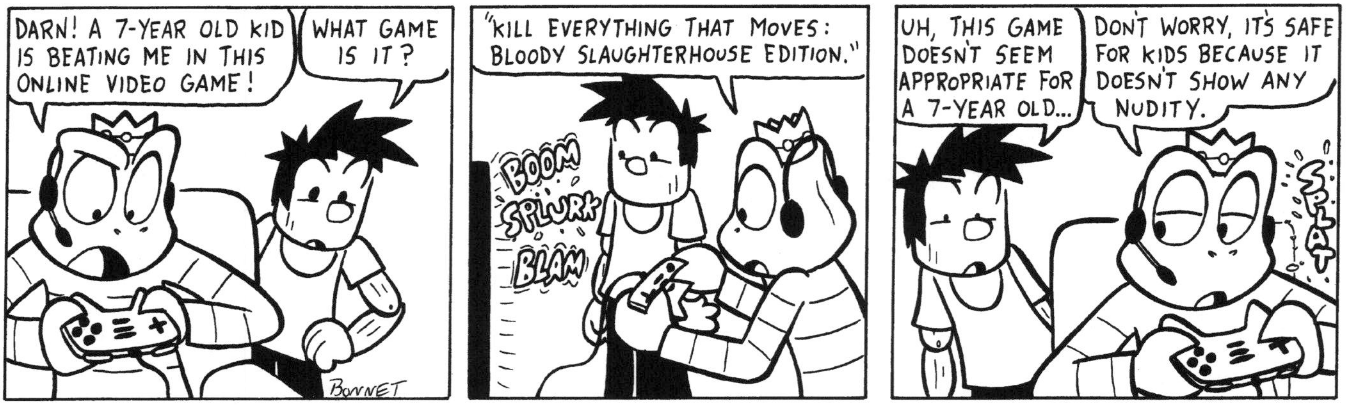
DARN! A 7-YEAR OLD KID IS BEATING ME IN THIS ONLINE VIDEO GAME!
WHAT GAME IS IT?
BONNET
"KILL EVERYTHING THAT MOVES: BLOODY SLAUGHTERHOUSE EDITION."
BOOM
SPLURK
BLAM
UH, THIS GAME DOESN'T SEEM APPROPRIATE FOR A 7-YEAR OLD...
DON'T WORRY, IT'S SAFE FOR KIDS BECAUSE IT DOESN'T SHOW ANY NUDITY.
SPLAT

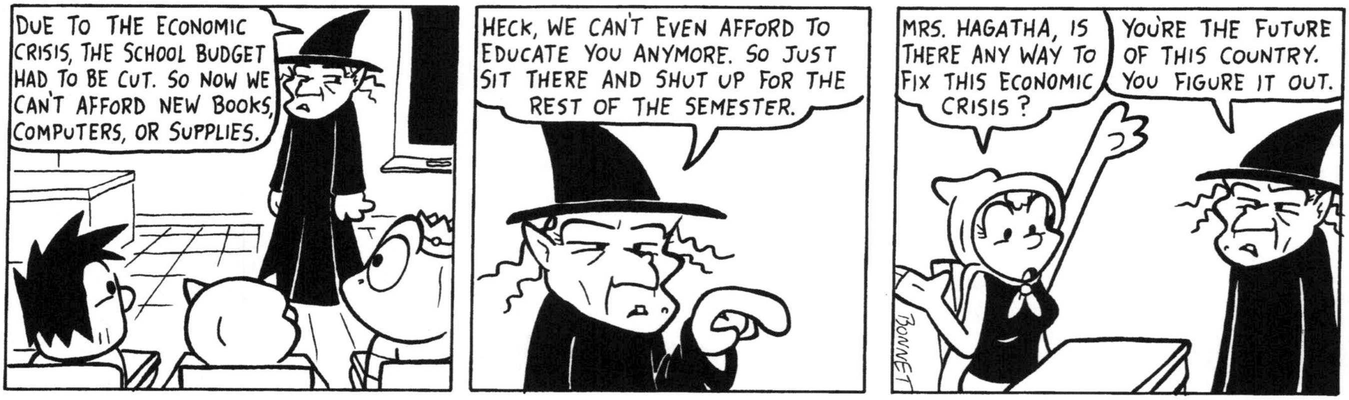
DUE TO THE ECONOMIC CRISIS, THE SCHOOL BUDGET HAD TO BE CUT. SO NOW WE CAN'T AFFORD NEW BOOKS, COMPUTERS, OR SUPPLIES.
HECK, WE CAN'T EVEN AFFORD TO EDUCATE YOU ANYMORE. SO JUST SIT THERE AND SHUT UP FOR THE REST OF THE SEMESTER.
MRS. HAGATHA, IS THERE ANY WAY TO FIX THIS ECONOMIC CRISIS?
YOU'RE THE FUTURE OF THIS COUNTRY. YOU FIGURE IT OUT.
BONNET

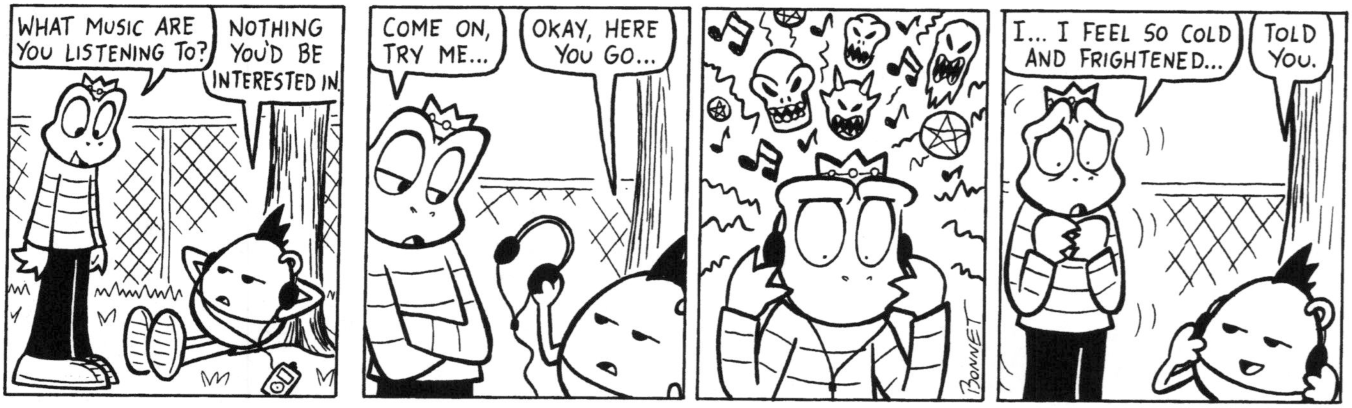
WHAT MUSIC ARE YOU LISTENING TO?
NOTHING YOU'D BE INTERESTED IN.
COME ON, TRY ME...
OKAY, HERE YOU GO...
BONNET
I... I FEEL SO COLD AND FRIGHTENED...
TOLD YOU.

Feb. 6, 9, 11, 2009

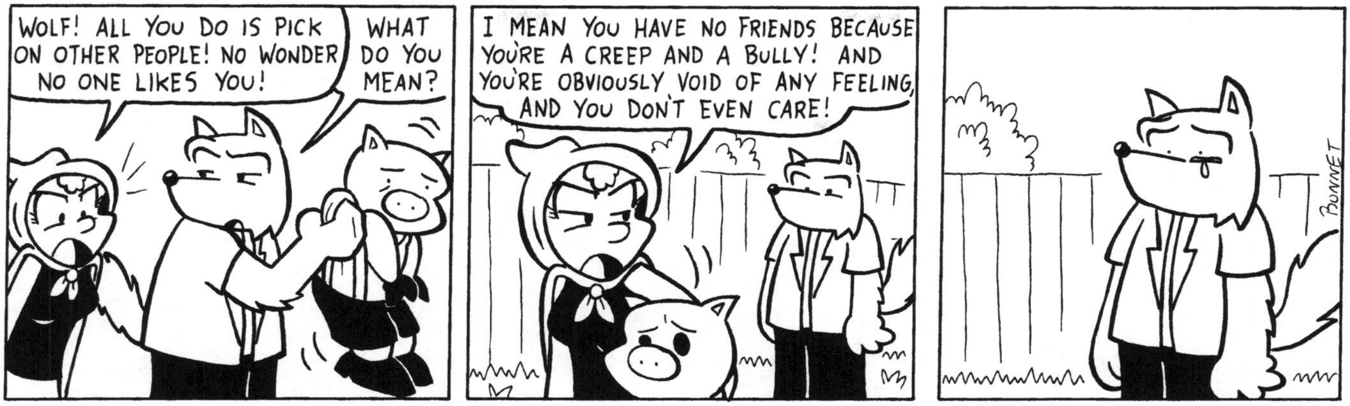
WOLF! ALL YOU DO IS PICK ON OTHER PEOPLE! NO WONDER NO ONE LIKES YOU!
WHAT DO YOU MEAN?
I MEAN YOU HAVE NO FRIENDS BECAUSE YOU'RE A CREEP AND A BULLY! AND YOU'RE OBVIOUSLY VOID OF ANY FEELING, AND YOU DON'T EVEN CARE!
BONNET

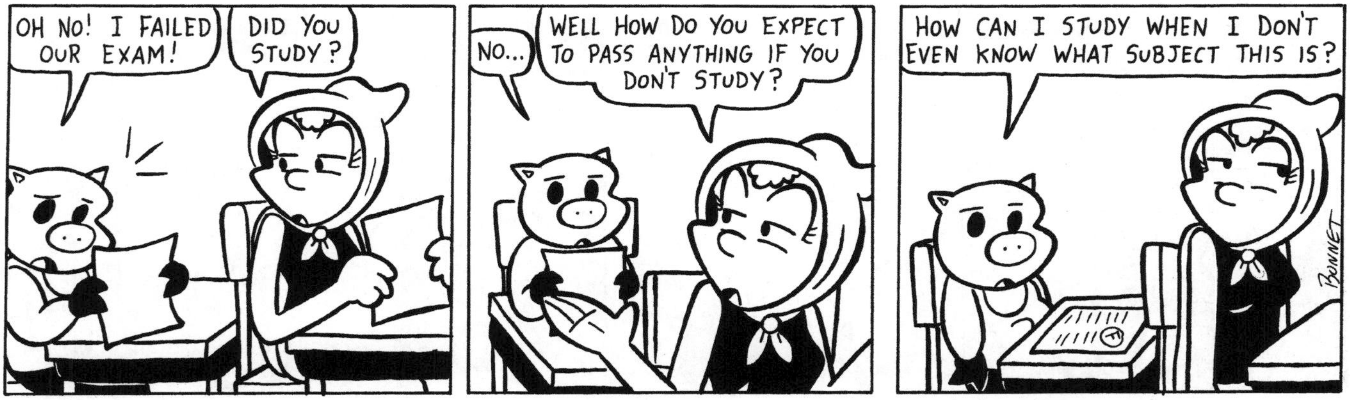
OH NO! I FAILED OUR EXAM!
DID YOU STUDY?
NO...
WELL HOW DO YOU EXPECT TO PASS ANYTHING IF YOU DON'T STUDY?
HOW CAN I STUDY WHEN I DON'T EVEN KNOW WHAT SUBJECT THIS IS?
BONNET

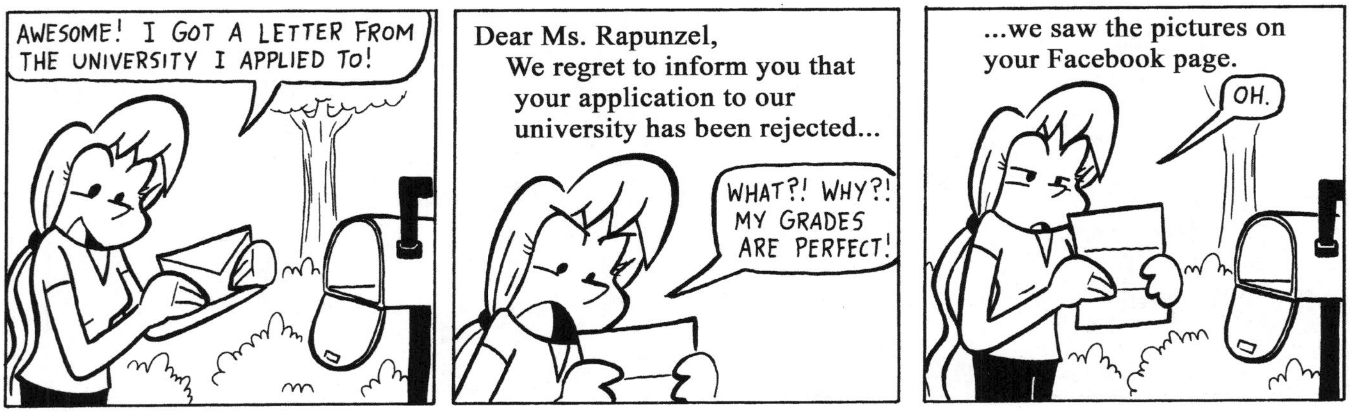
AWESOME! I GOT A LETTER FROM THE UNIVERSITY I APPLIED TO!
Dear Ms. Rapunzel,
We regret to inform you that your application to our university has been rejected...
WHAT?! WHY?! MY GRADES ARE PERFECT!
...we saw the pictures on your Facebook page.
OH.

Feb. 13, 16, 18, 2009

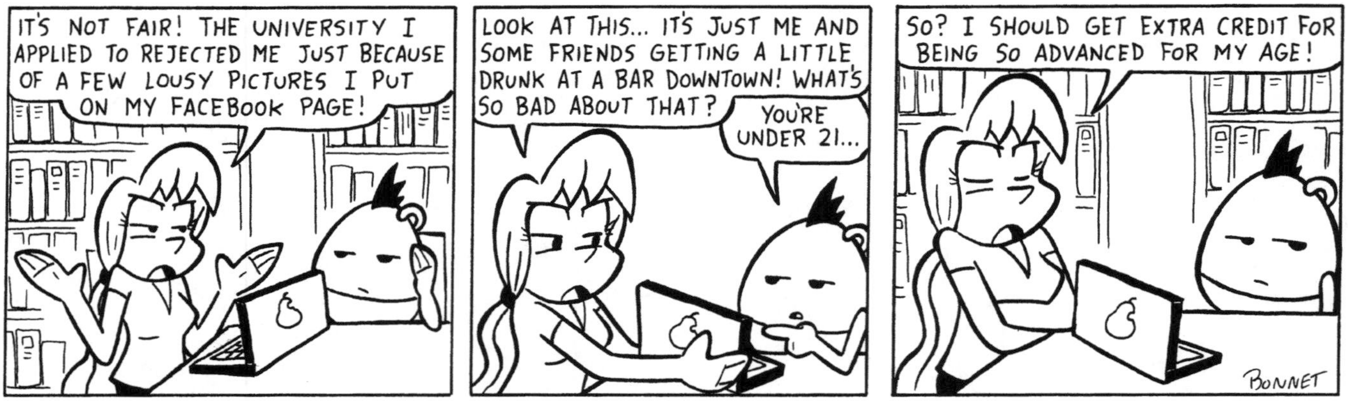
IT'S NOT FAIR! THE UNIVERSITY I APPLIED TO REJECTED ME JUST BECAUSE OF A FEW LOUSY PICTURES I PUT ON MY FACEBOOK PAGE!
LOOK AT THIS... IT'S JUST ME AND SOME FRIENDS GETTING A LITTLE DRUNK AT A BAR DOWNTOWN! WHAT'S SO BAD ABOUT THAT?
YOU'RE UNDER 21...
SO? I SHOULD GET EXTRA CREDIT FOR BEING SO ADVANCED FOR MY AGE!
BONNET

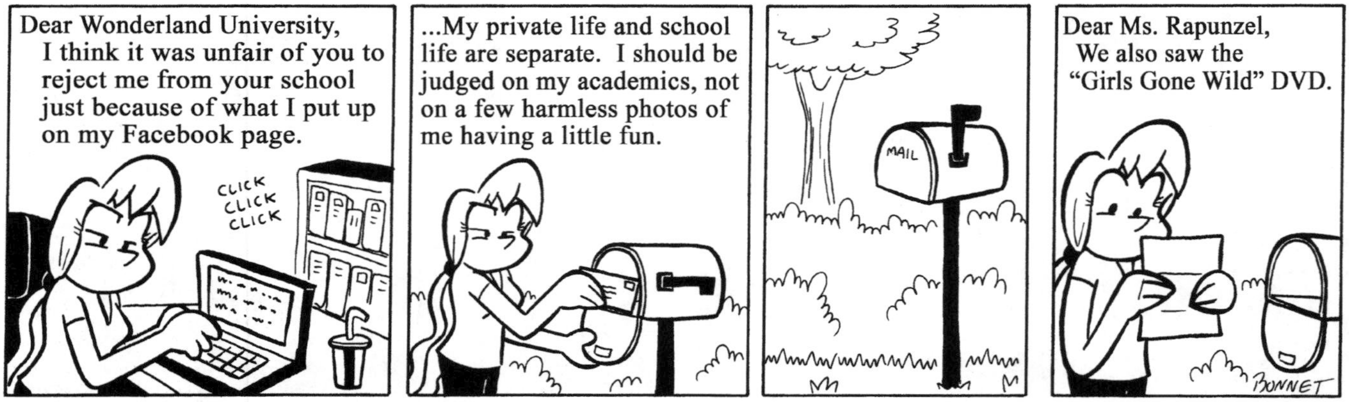
Dear Wonderland University,
I think it was unfair of you to reject me from your school just because of what I put up on my Facebook page.
CLICK CLICK CLICK
...My private life and school life are separate. I should be judged on my academics, not on a few harmless photos of me having a little fun.
MAIL
Dear Ms. Rapunzel,
We also saw the "Girls Gone Wild" DVD.
BONNET

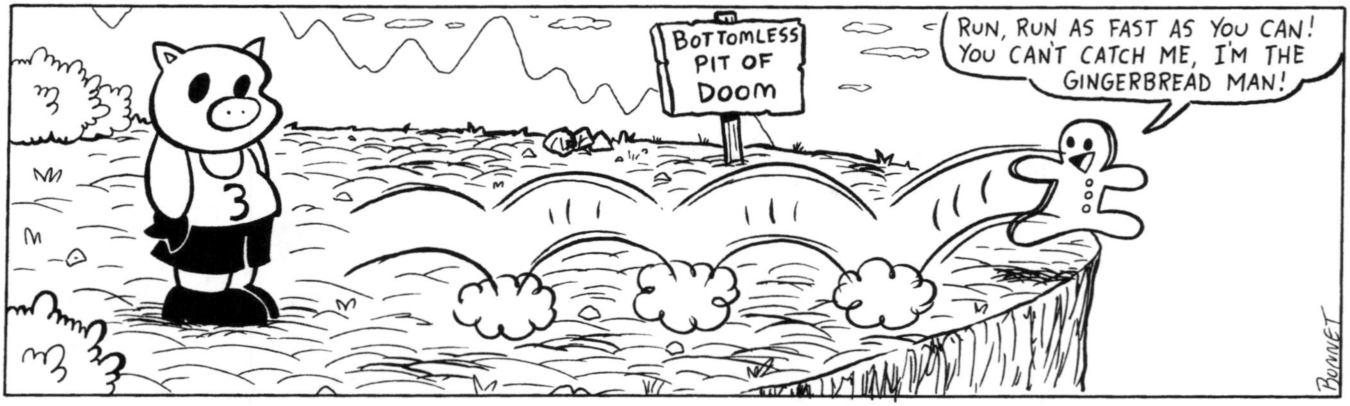
BOTTOMLESS PIT OF DOOM
RUN, RUN AS FAST AS YOU CAN! YOU CAN'T CATCH ME, I'M THE GINGERBREAD MAN!
3
BONNET

Feb. 20, 23, 25, 2009

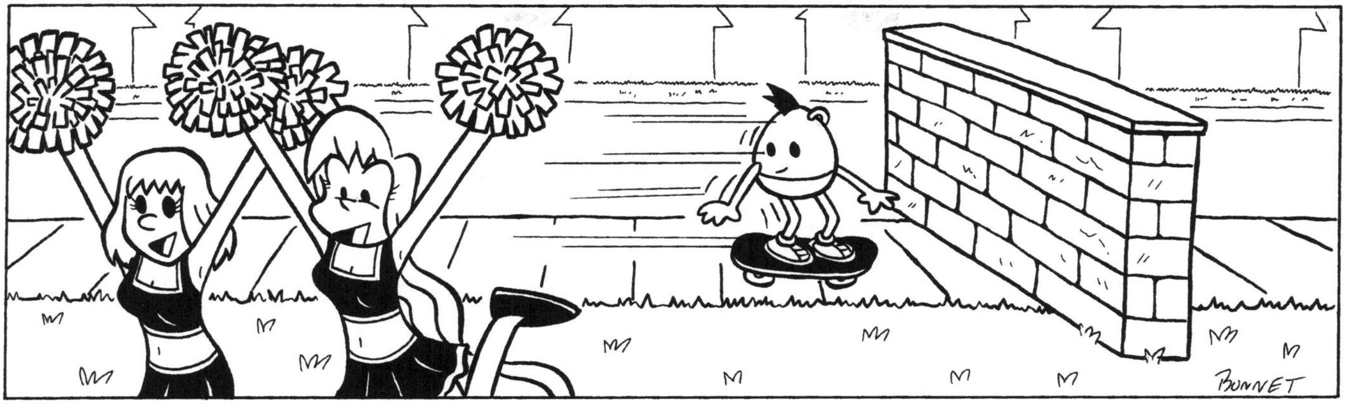
BONNET

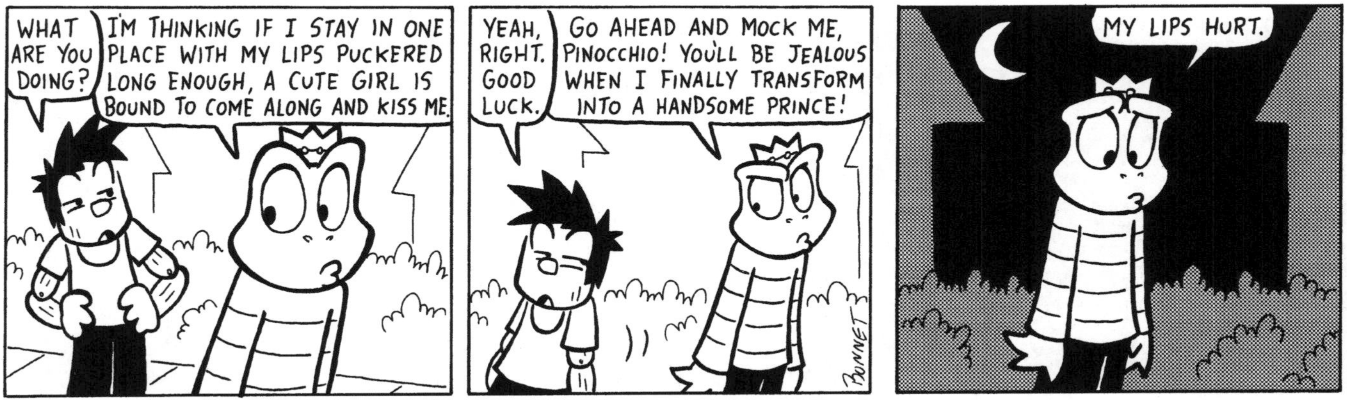
WHAT ARE YOU DOING?
I'M THINKING IF I STAY IN ONE PLACE WITH MY LIPS PUCKERED LONG ENOUGH, A CUTE GIRL IS BOUND TO COME ALONG AND KISS ME.
YEAH, RIGHT. GOOD LUCK.
GO AHEAD AND MOCK ME, PINOCCHIO! YOU'LL BE JEALOUS WHEN I FINALLY TRANSFORM INTO A HANDSOME PRINCE!
BONNET
MY LIPS HURT.

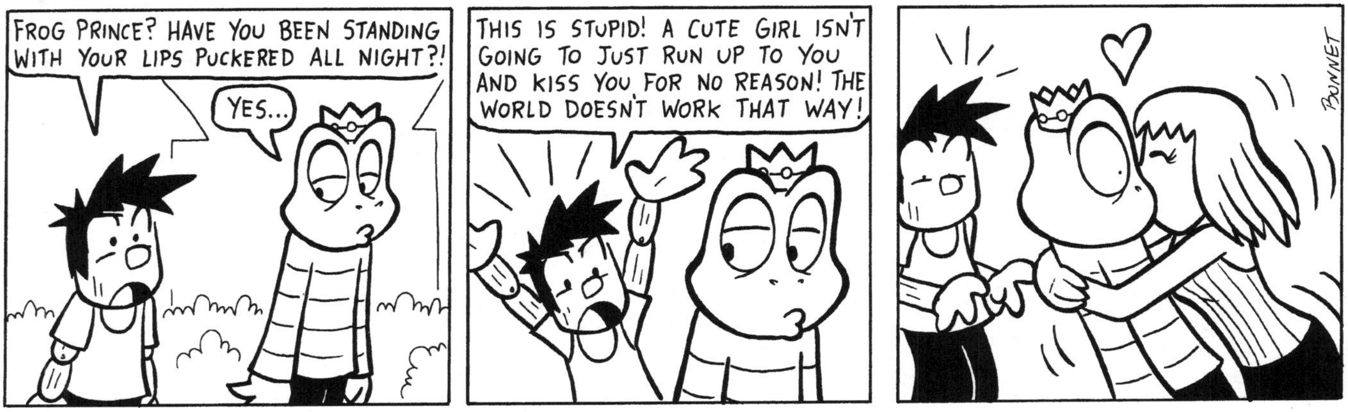
FROG PRINCE? HAVE YOU BEEN STANDING WITH YOUR LIPS PUCKERED ALL NIGHT?!
YES...
THIS IS STUPID! A CUTE GIRL ISN'T GOING TO JUST RUN UP TO YOU AND KISS YOU FOR NO REASON! THE WORLD DOESN'T WORK THAT WAY!
BONNET

Feb. 27, March 2, 4, 2009

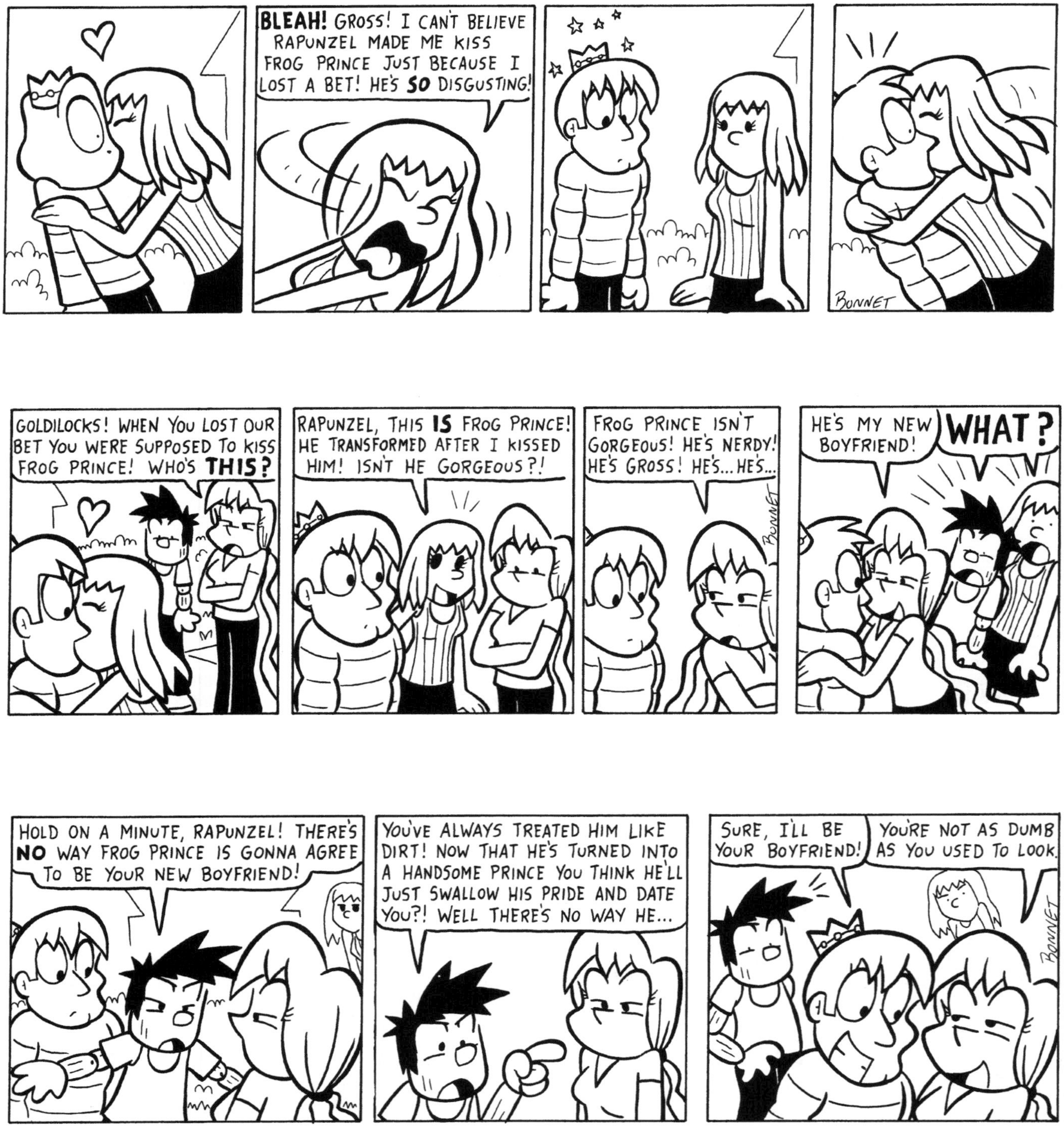
BLEAH! GROSS! I CAN'T BELIEVE RAPUNZEL MADE ME KISS FROG PRINCE JUST BECAUSE I LOST A BET! HE'S SO DISGUSTING!
BONNET
GOLDILOCKS! WHEN YOU LOST OUR BET YOU WERE SUPPOSED TO KISS FROG PRINCE! WHO'S THIS?
RAPUNZEL, THIS IS FROG PRINCE! HE TRANSFORMED AFTER I KISSED HIM! ISN'T HE GORGEOUS?!
FROG PRINCE ISN'T GORGEOUS! HE'S NERDY! HE'S GROSS! HE'S... HE'S...
BONNET
HE'S MY NEW BOYFRIEND!
WHAT?
HOLD ON A MINUTE, RAPUNZEL! THERE'S NO WAY FROG PRINCE IS GONNA AGREE TO BE YOUR NEW BOYFRIEND!
YOU'VE ALWAYS TREATED HIM LIKE DIRT! NOW THAT HE'S TURNED INTO A HANDSOME PRINCE YOU THINK HE'LL JUST SWALLOW HIS PRIDE AND DATE YOU?! WELL THERE'S NO WAY HE...
SURE, I'LL BE YOUR BOYFRIEND!
YOU'RE NOT AS DUMB AS YOU USED TO LOOK.
BONNET

March 6, 9, 11, 2009

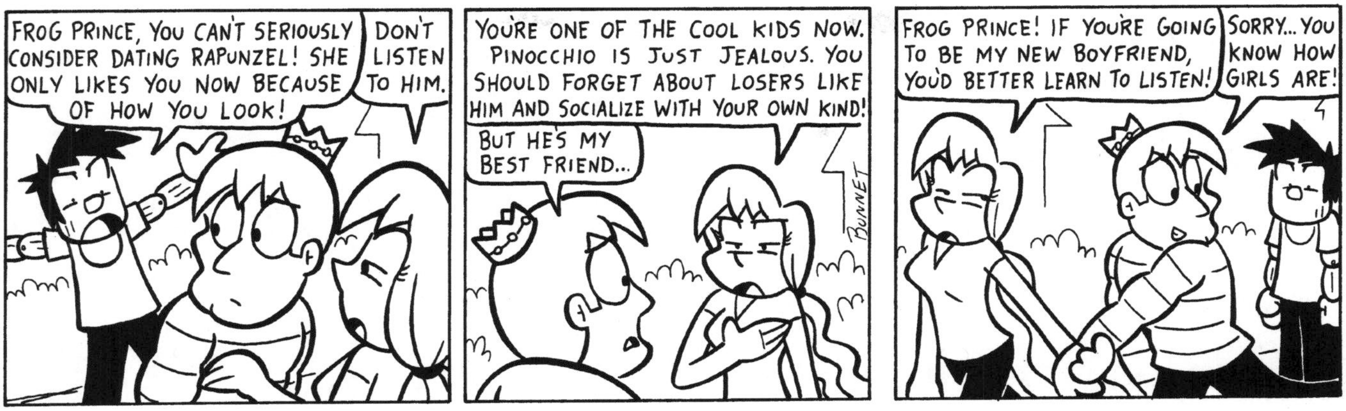
FROG PRINCE, YOU CAN'T SERIOUSLY CONSIDER DATING RAPUNZEL! SHE ONLY LIKES YOU NOW BECAUSE OF HOW YOU LOOK!
DON'T LISTEN TO HIM.
YOU'RE ONE OF THE COOL KIDS NOW. PINOCCHIO IS JUST JEALOUS. YOU SHOULD FORGET ABOUT LOSERS LIKE HIM AND SOCIALIZE WITH YOUR OWN KIND!
BUT HE'S MY BEST FRIEND...
FROG PRINCE! IF YOU'RE GOING TO BE MY NEW BOYFRIEND, YOU'D BETTER LEARN TO LISTEN!
SORRY... YOU KNOW HOW GIRLS ARE!

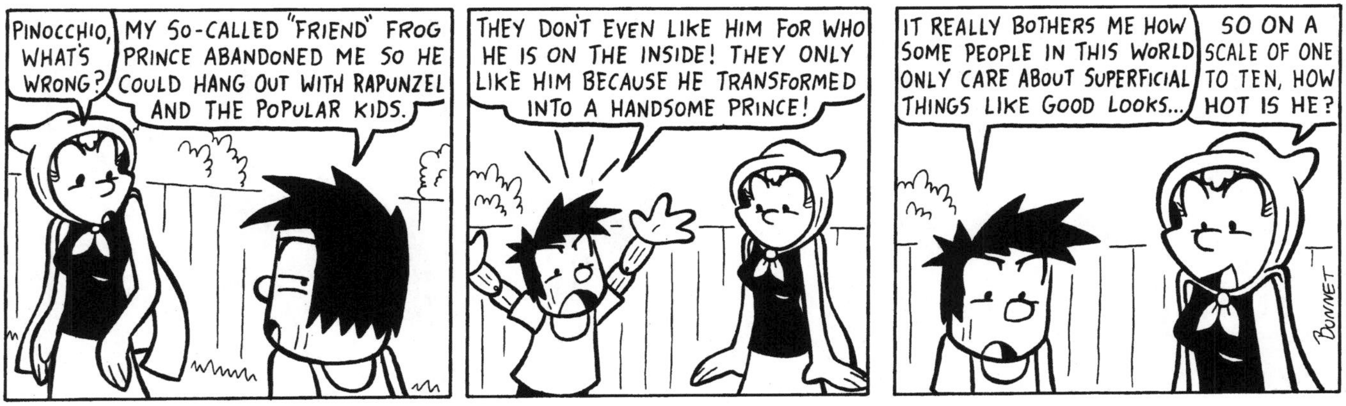
PINOCCHIO, WHAT'S WRONG?
MY SO-CALLED "FRIEND" FROG PRINCE ABANDONED ME SO HE COULD HANG OUT WITH RAPUNZEL AND THE POPULAR KIDS.
THEY DON'T EVEN LIKE HIM FOR WHO HE IS ON THE INSIDE! THEY ONLY LIKE HIM BECAUSE HE TRANSFORMED INTO A HANDSOME PRINCE!
IT REALLY BOTHERS ME HOW SOME PEOPLE IN THIS WORLD ONLY CARE ABOUT SUPERFICIAL THINGS LIKE GOOD LOOKS...
SO ON A SCALE OF ONE TO TEN, HOW HOT IS HE?

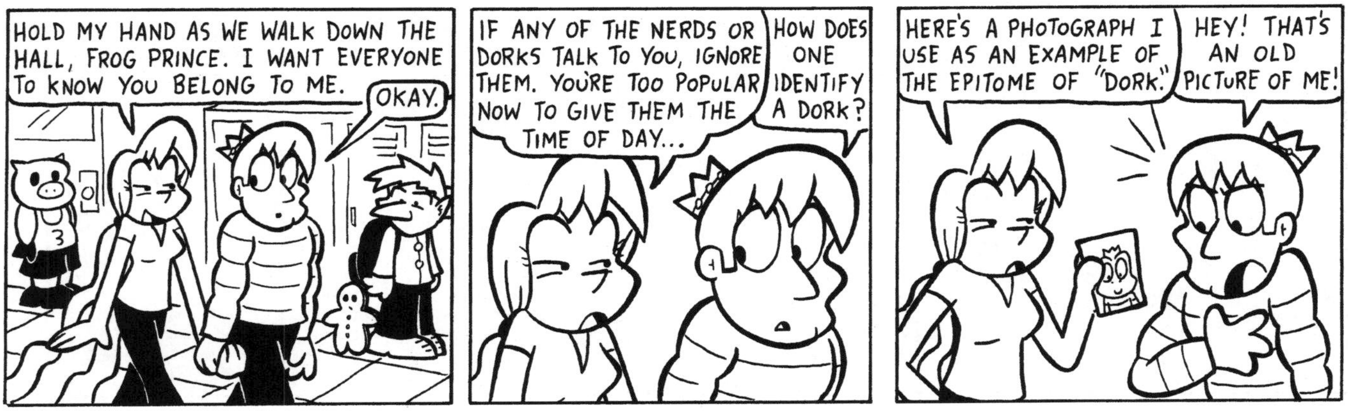
HOLD MY HAND AS WE WALK DOWN THE HALL, FROG PRINCE. I WANT EVERYONE TO KNOW YOU BELONG TO ME.
OKAY.
IF ANY OF THE NERDS OR DORKS TALK TO YOU, IGNORE THEM. YOU'RE TOO POPULAR NOW TO GIVE THEM THE TIME OF DAY...
HOW DOES ONE IDENTIFY A DORK?
HERE'S A PHOTOGRAPH I USE AS AN EXAMPLE OF THE EPITOME OF "DORK."
HEY! THAT'S AN OLD PICTURE OF ME!

March 13, 16, 18, 2009

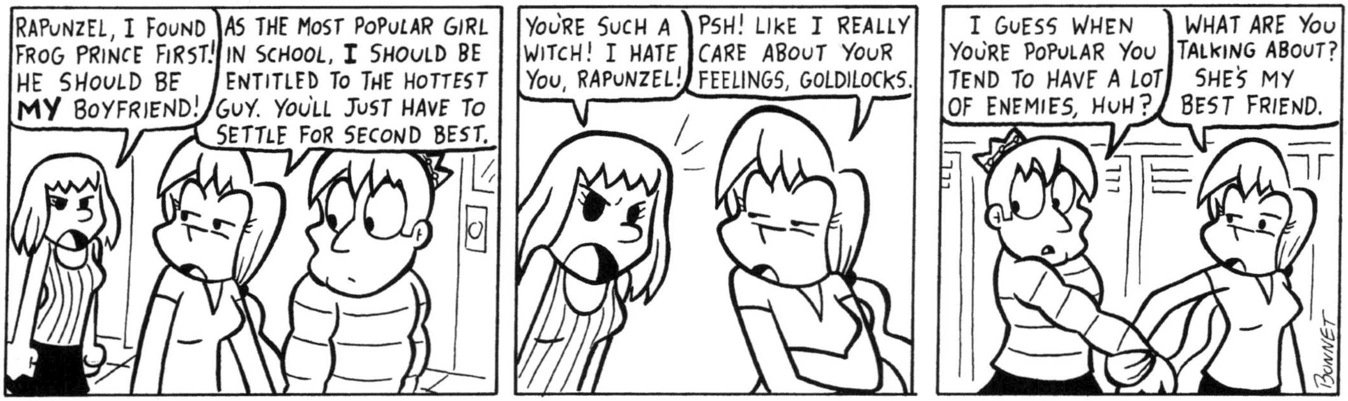
RAPUNZEL, I FOUND FROG PRINCE FIRST! HE SHOULD BE MY BOYFRIEND!
AS THE MOST POPULAR GIRL IN SCHOOL, I SHOULD BE ENTITLED TO THE HOTTEST GUY. YOU'LL JUST HAVE TO SETTLE FOR SECOND BEST.
YOU'RE SUCH A WITCH! I HATE YOU, RAPUNZEL!
PSH! LIKE I REALLY CARE ABOUT YOUR FEELINGS, GOLDILOCKS.
I GUESS WHEN YOU'RE POPULAR YOU TEND TO HAVE A LOT OF ENEMIES, HUH?
WHAT ARE YOU TALKING ABOUT? SHE'S MY BEST FRIEND.
BONNET

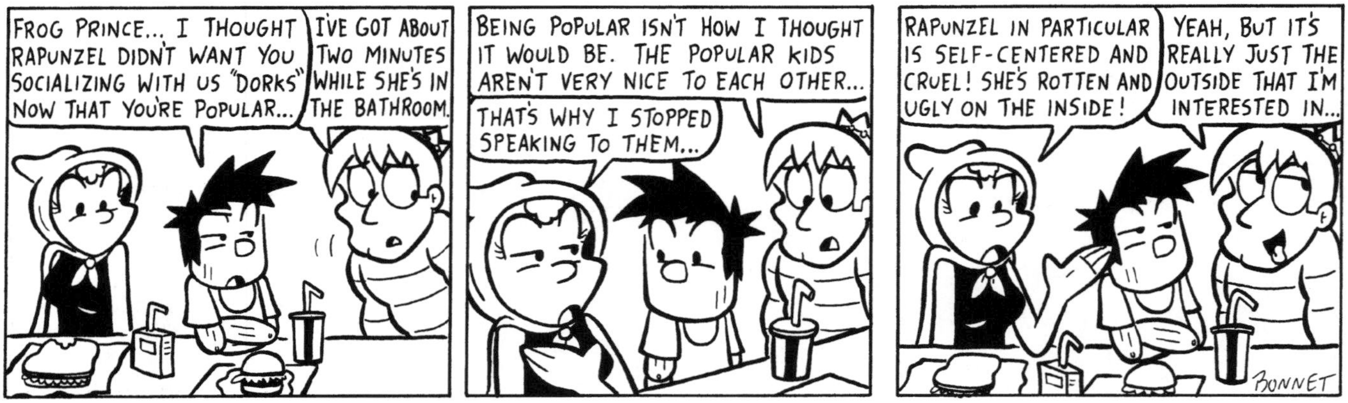
FROG PRINCE... I THOUGHT RAPUNZEL DIDN'T WANT YOU SOCIALIZING WITH US "DORKS" NOW THAT YOU'RE POPULAR...
I'VE GOT ABOUT TWO MINUTES WHILE SHE'S IN THE BATHROOM.
BEING POPULAR ISN'T HOW I THOUGHT IT WOULD BE. THE POPULAR KIDS AREN'T VERY NICE TO EACH OTHER...
THAT'S WHY I STOPPED SPEAKING TO THEM...
RAPUNZEL IN PARTICULAR IS SELF-CENTERED AND CRUEL! SHE'S ROTTEN AND UGLY ON THE INSIDE!
YEAH, BUT IT'S REALLY JUST THE OUTSIDE THAT I'M INTERESTED IN...
BONNET

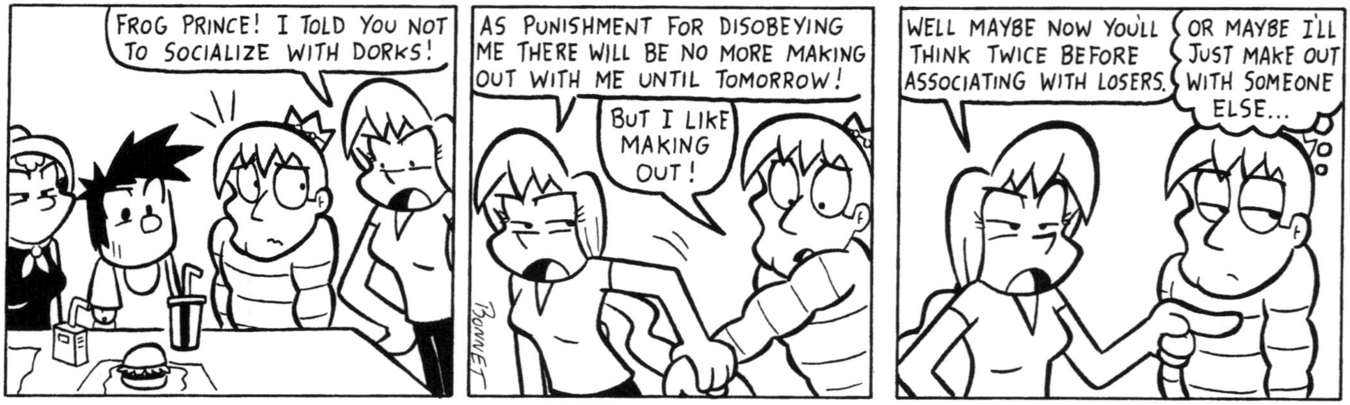
FROG PRINCE! I TOLD YOU NOT TO SOCIALIZE WITH DORKS!
BONNET
AS PUNISHMENT FOR DISOBEYING ME THERE WILL BE NO MORE MAKING OUT WITH ME UNTIL TOMORROW!
BUT I LIKE MAKING OUT!
WELL MAYBE NOW YOU'LL THINK TWICE BEFORE ASSOCIATING WITH LOSERS.
OR MAYBE I'LL JUST MAKE OUT WITH SOMEONE ELSE...

March 20, 23, 25, 2009

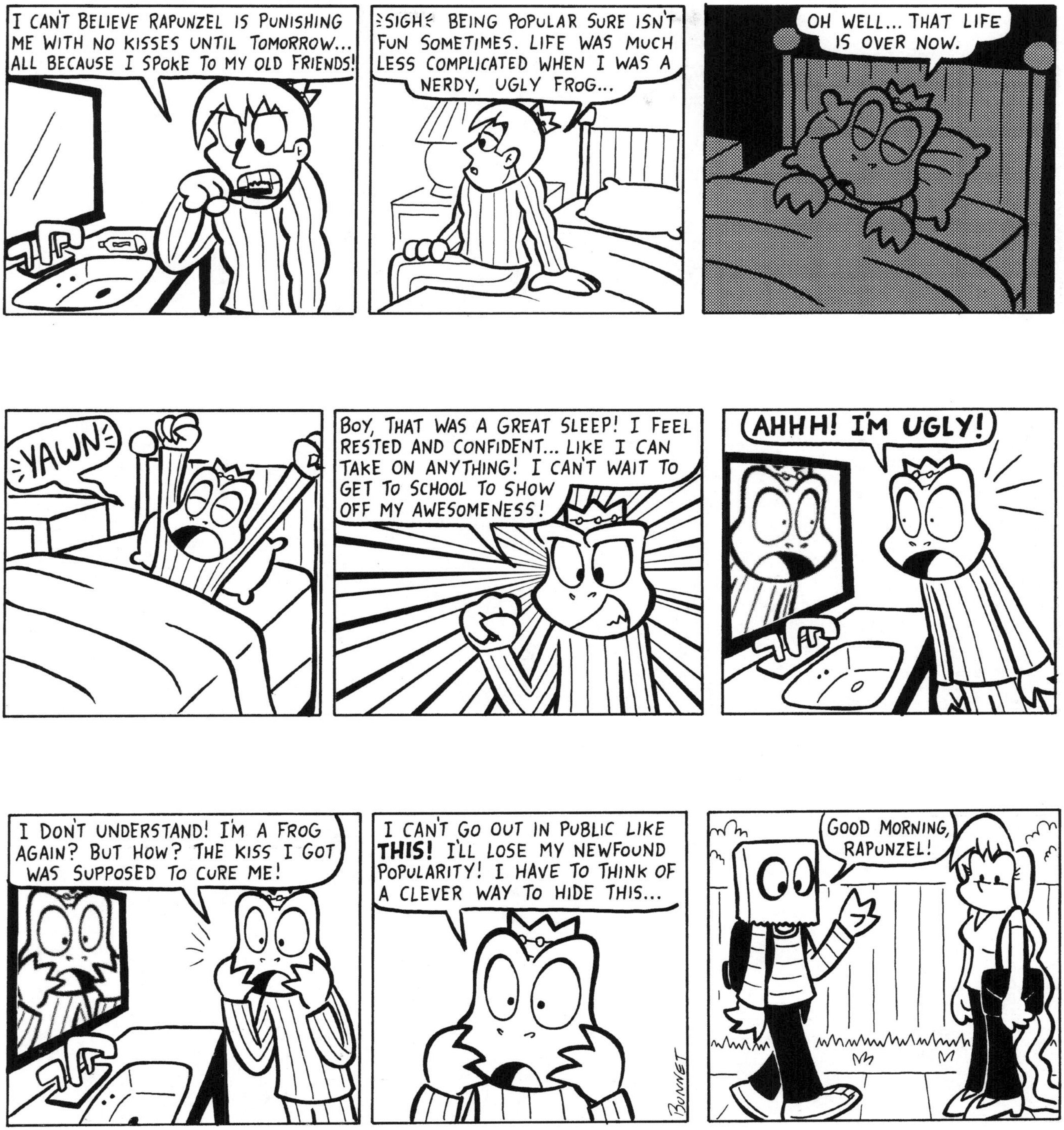
I CAN'T BELIEVE RAPUNZEL IS PUNISHING ME WITH NO KISSES UNTIL TOMORROW... ALL BECAUSE I SPOKE TO MY OLD FRIENDS!
SIGH BEING POPULAR SURE ISN'T FUN SOMETIMES. LIFE WAS MUCH LESS COMPLICATED WHEN I WAS A NERDY, UGLY FROG...
OH WELL... THAT LIFE IS OVER NOW.
YAWN
BOY, THAT WAS A GREAT SLEEP! I FEEL RESTED AND CONFIDENT... LIKE I CAN TAKE ON ANYTHING! I CAN'T WAIT TO GET TO SCHOOL TO SHOW OFF MY AWESOMENESS!
AHHH! I'M UGLY!
I DON'T UNDERSTAND! I'M A FROG AGAIN? BUT HOW? THE KISS I GOT WAS SUPPOSED TO CURE ME!
I CAN'T GO OUT IN PUBLIC LIKE THIS! I'LL LOSE MY NEWFOUND POPULARITY! I HAVE TO THINK OF A CLEVER WAY TO HIDE THIS...
BONNET
GOOD MORNING, RAPUNZEL!

March 27, 30, April 1, 2009

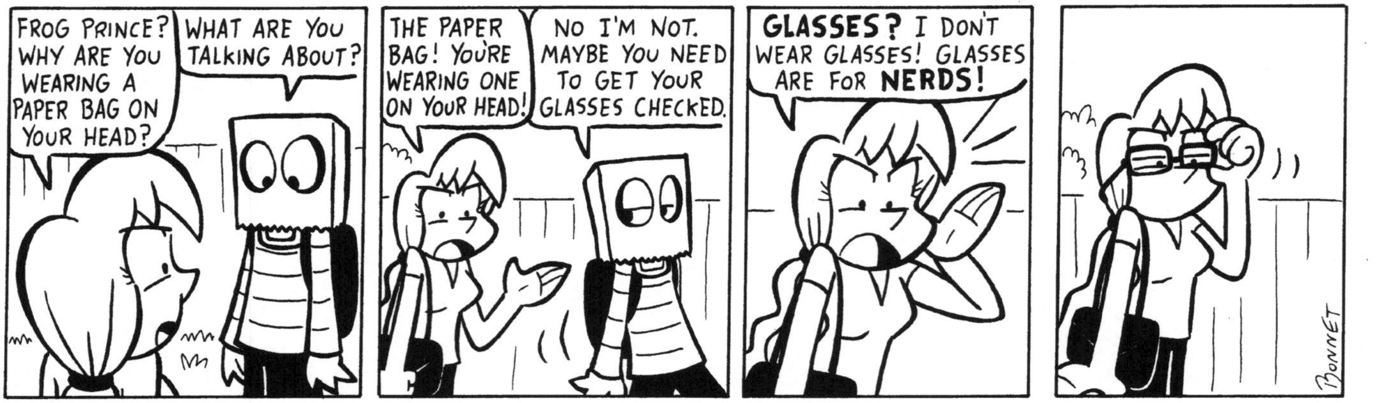
FROG PRINCE? WHY ARE YOU WEARING A PAPER BAG ON YOUR HEAD?
WHAT ARE YOU TALKING ABOUT?
THE PAPER BAG! YOU'RE WEARING ONE ON YOUR HEAD!
NO I'M NOT. MAYBE YOU NEED TO GET YOUR GLASSES CHECKED.
GLASSES? I DON'T WEAR GLASSES! GLASSES ARE FOR **NERDS!**
BONNET

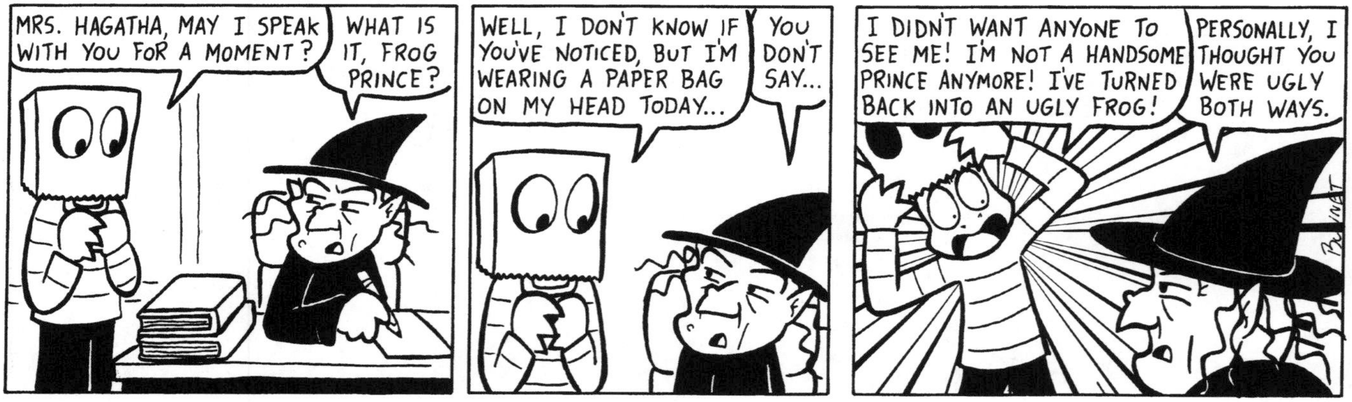
MRS. HAGATHA, MAY I SPEAK WITH YOU FOR A MOMENT?
WHAT IS IT, FROG PRINCE?
WELL, I DON'T KNOW IF YOU'VE NOTICED, BUT I'M WEARING A PAPER BAG ON MY HEAD TODAY...
YOU DON'T SAY...
I DIDN'T WANT ANYONE TO SEE ME! I'M NOT A HANDSOME PRINCE ANYMORE! I'VE TURNED BACK INTO AN UGLY FROG!
PERSONALLY, I THOUGHT YOU WERE UGLY BOTH WAYS.
BONNET

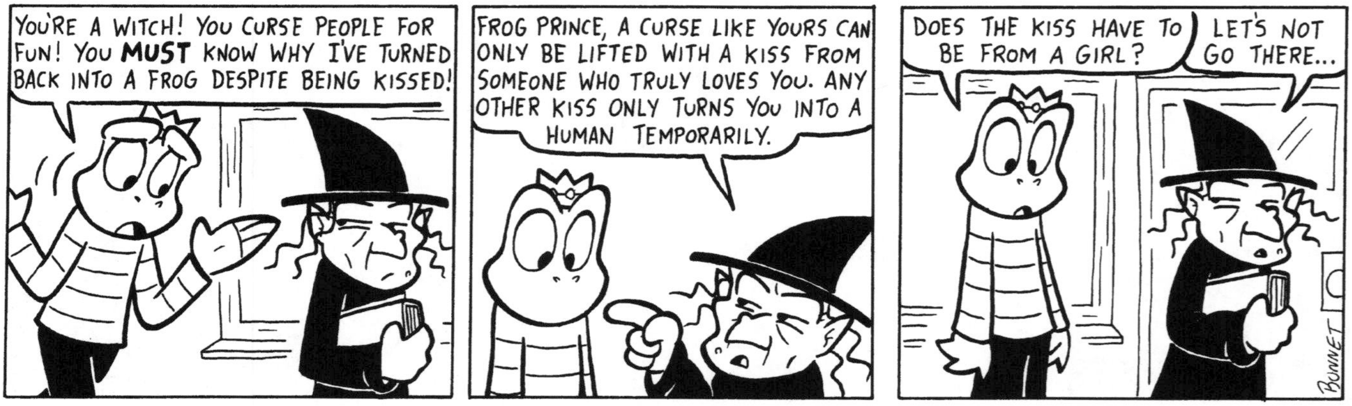
YOU'RE A WITCH! YOU CURSE PEOPLE FOR FUN! YOU **MUST** KNOW WHY I'VE TURNED BACK INTO A FROG DESPITE BEING KISSED!
FROG PRINCE, A CURSE LIKE YOURS CAN ONLY BE LIFTED WITH A KISS FROM SOMEONE WHO TRULY LOVES YOU. ANY OTHER KISS ONLY TURNS YOU INTO A HUMAN TEMPORARILY.
DOES THE KISS HAVE TO BE FROM A GIRL?
LET'S NOT GO THERE...
BONNET

April 3, 6, 8, 2009

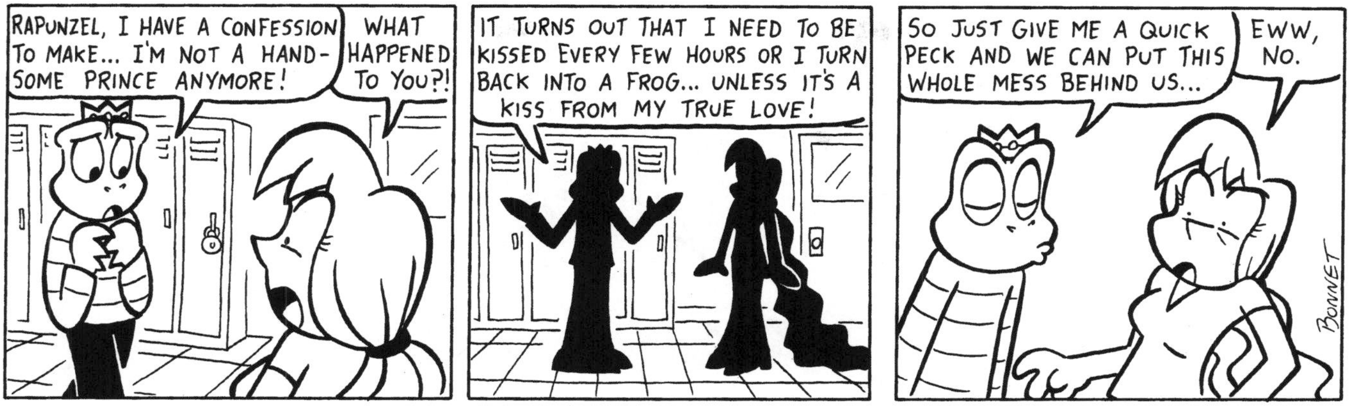
RAPUNZEL, I HAVE A CONFESSION TO MAKE... I'M NOT A HAND-SOME PRINCE ANYMORE!
WHAT HAPPENED TO YOU?!
IT TURNS OUT THAT I NEED TO BE KISSED EVERY FEW HOURS OR I TURN BACK INTO A FROG... UNLESS IT'S A KISS FROM MY TRUE LOVE!
SO JUST GIVE ME A QUICK PECK AND WE CAN PUT THIS WHOLE MESS BEHIND US...
EWW, NO.
BONNET

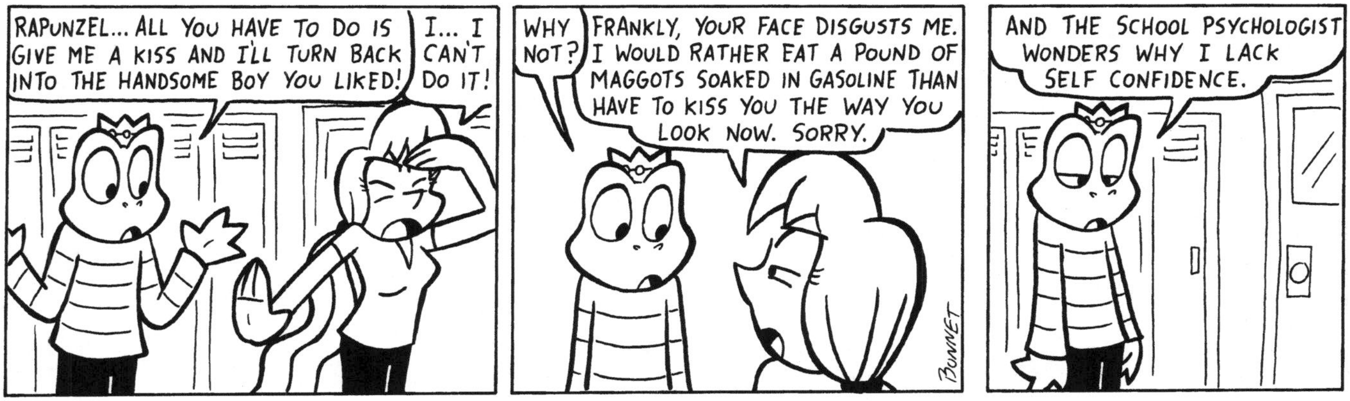
RAPUNZEL... ALL YOU HAVE TO DO IS GIVE ME A KISS AND I'LL TURN BACK INTO THE HANDSOME BOY YOU LIKED!
I... I CAN'T DO IT!
WHY NOT?
FRANKLY, YOUR FACE DISGUSTS ME. I WOULD RATHER EAT A POUND OF MAGGOTS SOAKED IN GASOLINE THAN HAVE TO KISS YOU THE WAY YOU LOOK NOW. SORRY.
BONNET
AND THE SCHOOL PSYCHOLOGIST WONDERS WHY I LACK SELF CONFIDENCE.

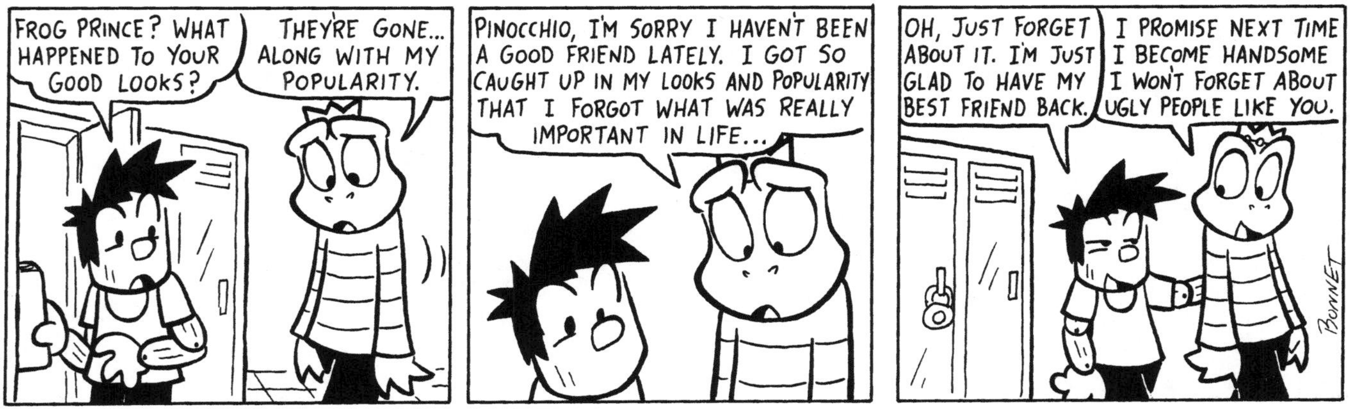
FROG PRINCE? WHAT HAPPENED TO YOUR GOOD LOOKS?
THEY'RE GONE... ALONG WITH MY POPULARITY.
PINOCCHIO, I'M SORRY I HAVEN'T BEEN A GOOD FRIEND LATELY. I GOT SO CAUGHT UP IN MY LOOKS AND POPULARITY THAT I FORGOT WHAT WAS REALLY IMPORTANT IN LIFE...
OH, JUST FORGET ABOUT IT. I'M JUST GLAD TO HAVE MY BEST FRIEND BACK.
I PROMISE NEXT TIME I BECOME HANDSOME I WON'T FORGET ABOUT UGLY PEOPLE LIKE YOU.
BONNET

April 10, 13, 15, 2009

April 17, 20, 22, 2009

34   Suburban Fairy Tales: This Little Piggy Gets Even

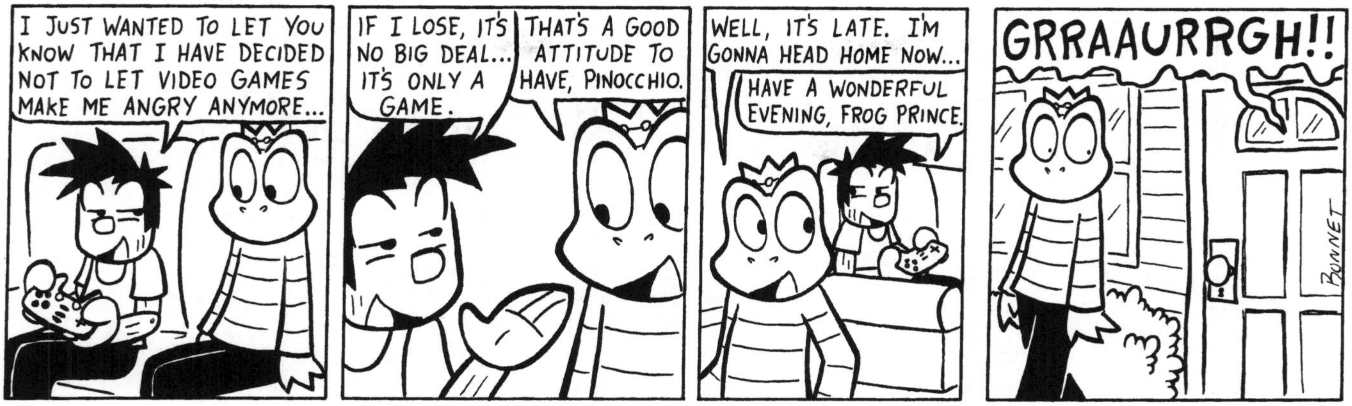
I JUST WANTED TO LET YOU KNOW THAT I HAVE DECIDED NOT TO LET VIDEO GAMES MAKE ME ANGRY ANYMORE...
IF I LOSE, IT'S NO BIG DEAL... IT'S ONLY A GAME.
THAT'S A GOOD ATTITUDE TO HAVE, PINOCCHIO.
WELL, IT'S LATE. I'M GONNA HEAD HOME NOW...
HAVE A WONDERFUL EVENING, FROG PRINCE.
GRRAAURRGH!!
BONNET

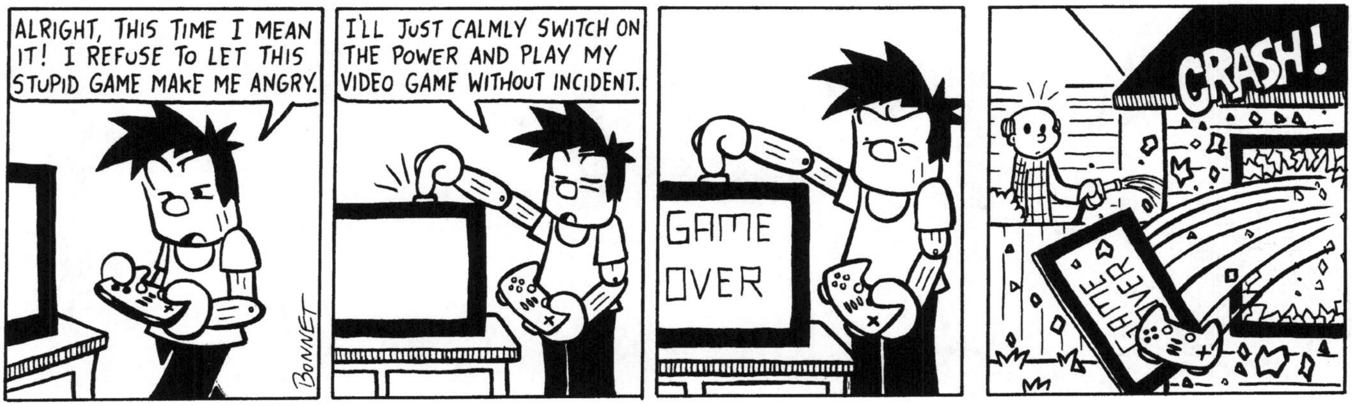
ALRIGHT, THIS TIME I MEAN IT! I REFUSE TO LET THIS STUPID GAME MAKE ME ANGRY.
BONNET
I'LL JUST CALMLY SWITCH ON THE POWER AND PLAY MY VIDEO GAME WITHOUT INCIDENT.
GAME OVER
CRASH!
GAME OVER

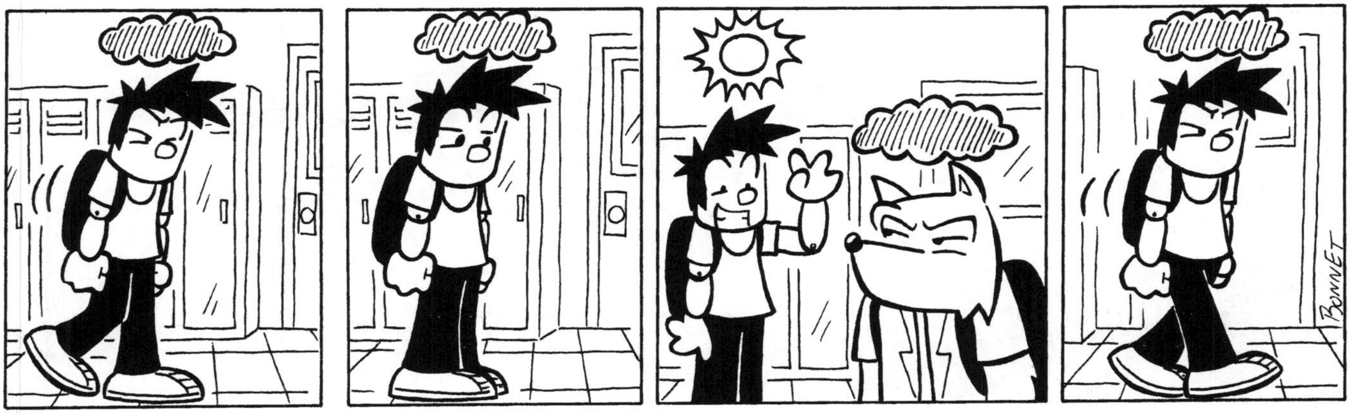
BONNET

April 24, 27, 29, 2009

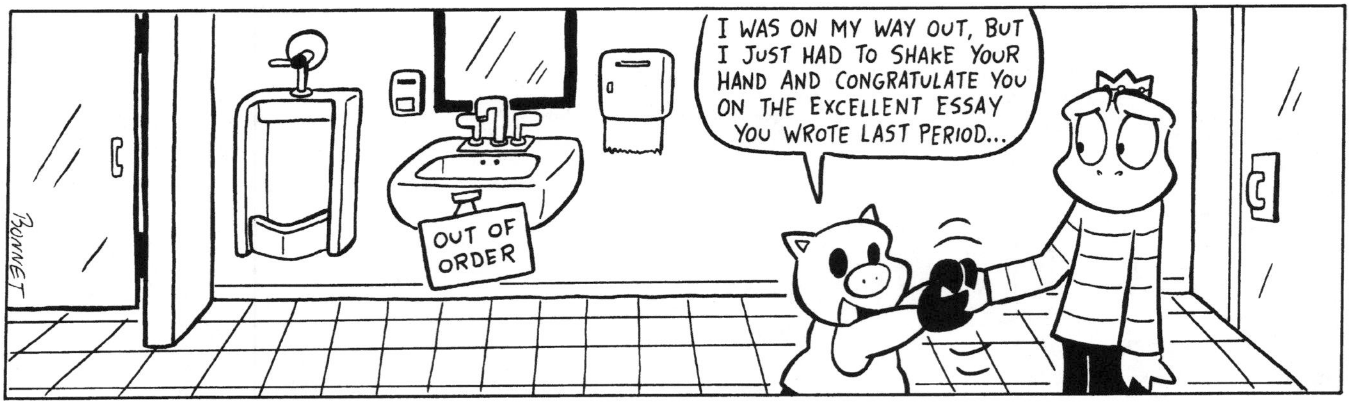
I WAS ON MY WAY OUT, BUT I JUST HAD TO SHAKE YOUR HAND AND CONGRATULATE YOU ON THE EXCELLENT ESSAY YOU WROTE LAST PERIOD...
OUT OF ORDER
BONNET

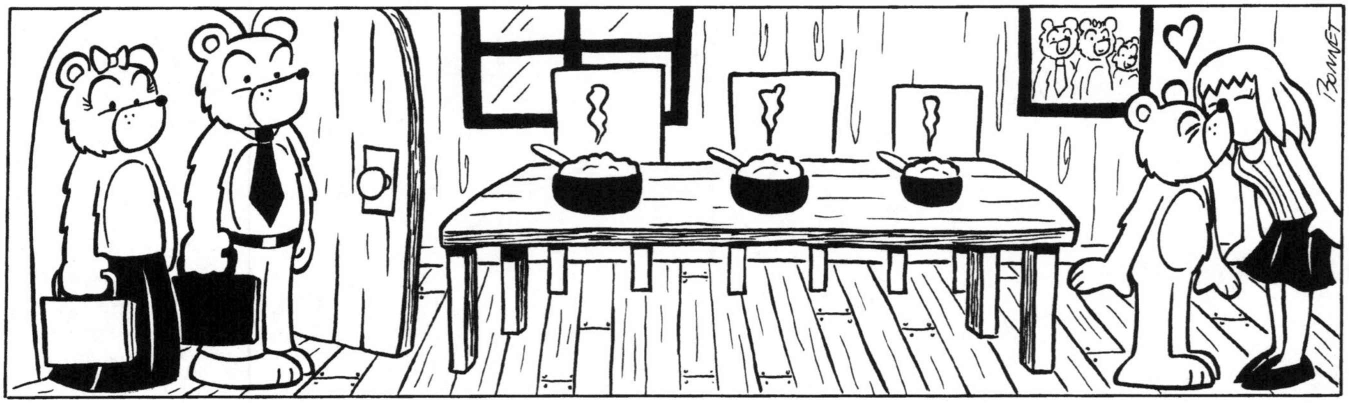
BONNET

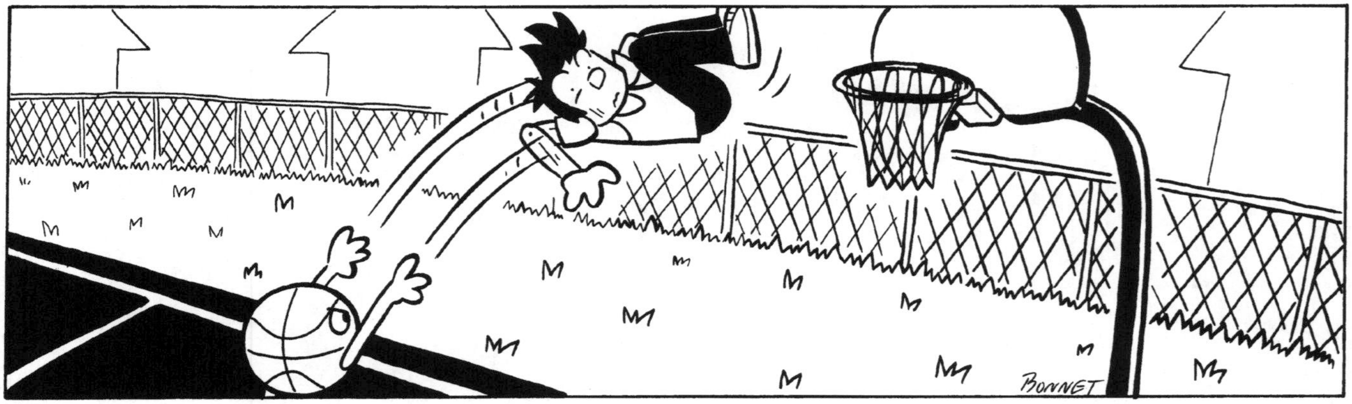
BONNET

May 1, 4, 6, 2009

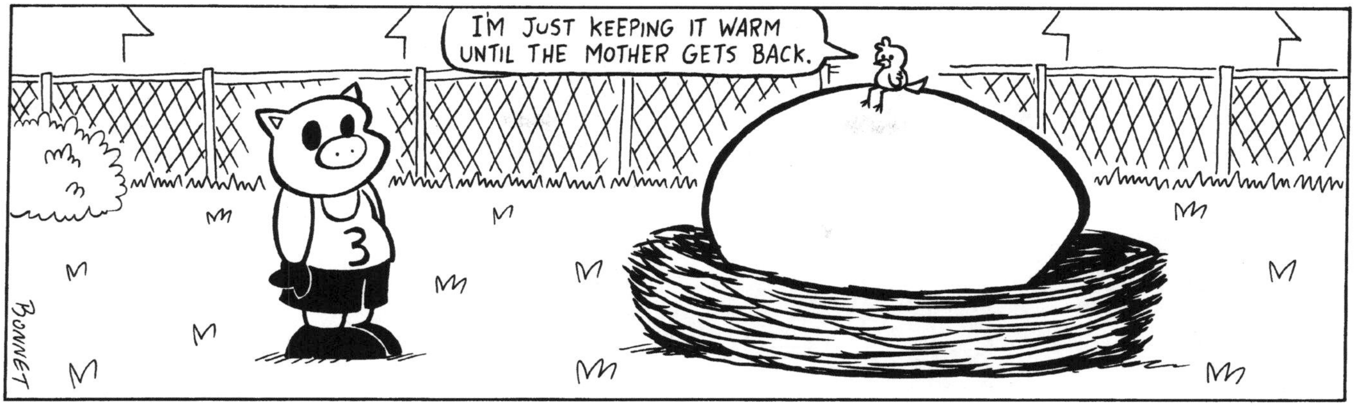
I'M JUST KEEPING IT WARM UNTIL THE MOTHER GETS BACK.
3
BONNET

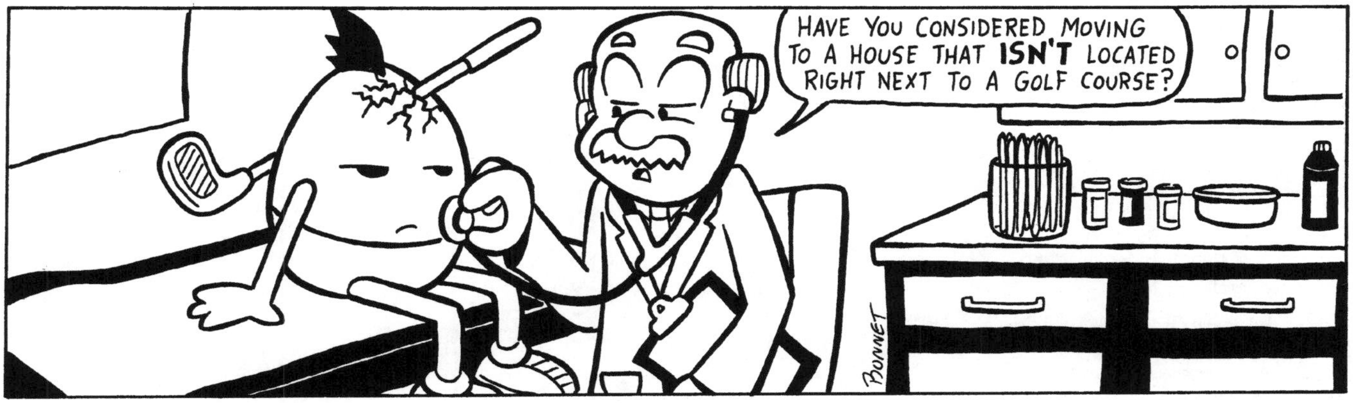
HAVE YOU CONSIDERED MOVING TO A HOUSE THAT **ISN'T** LOCATED RIGHT NEXT TO A GOLF COURSE?
BONNET

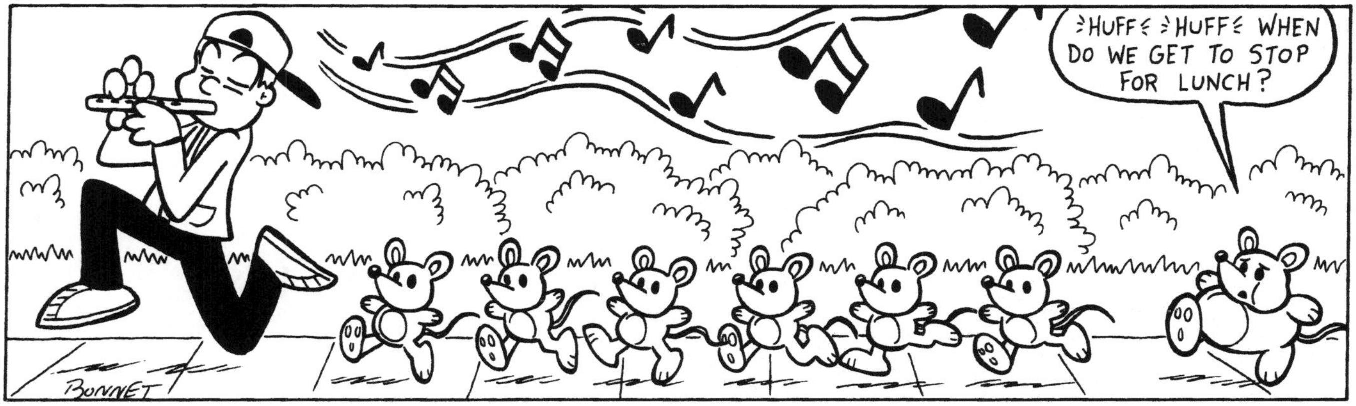
HUFF HUFF WHEN DO WE GET TO STOP FOR LUNCH?
BONNET

May 8, 11, 13, 2009

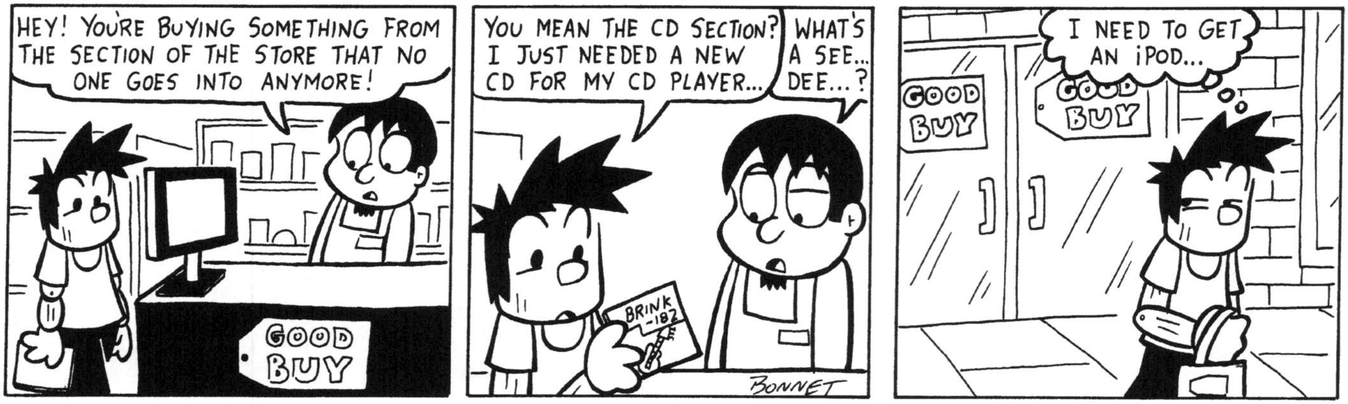
HEY! YOU'RE BUYING SOMETHING FROM THE SECTION OF THE STORE THAT NO ONE GOES INTO ANYMORE!
GOOD BUY
YOU MEAN THE CD SECTION? I JUST NEEDED A NEW CD FOR MY CD PLAYER...
WHAT'S A SEE... DEE...?
BRINK -182
BONNET
GOOD BUY
GOOD BUY
I NEED TO GET AN iPOD...

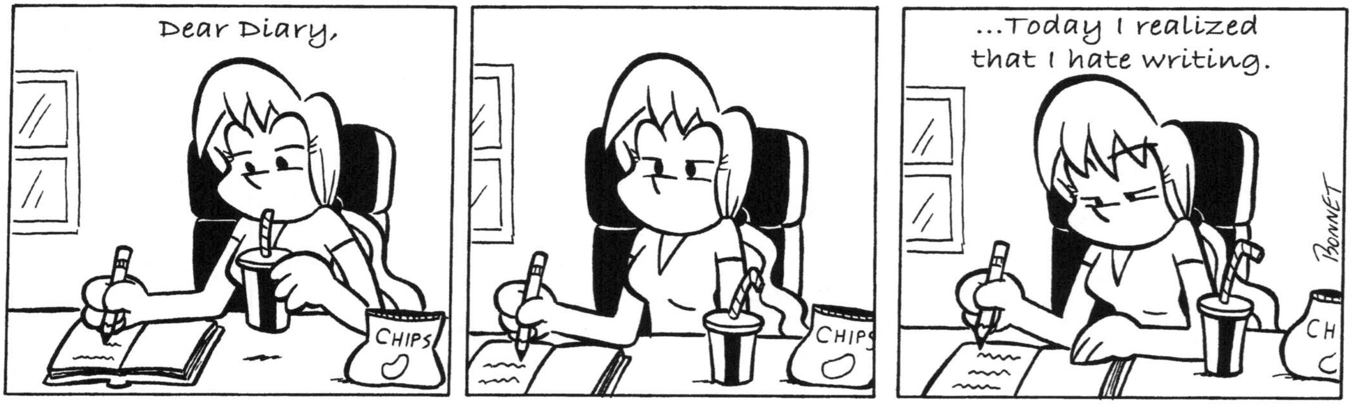
Dear Diary,
CHIPS
CHIPS
...Today I realized that I hate writing.
BONNET

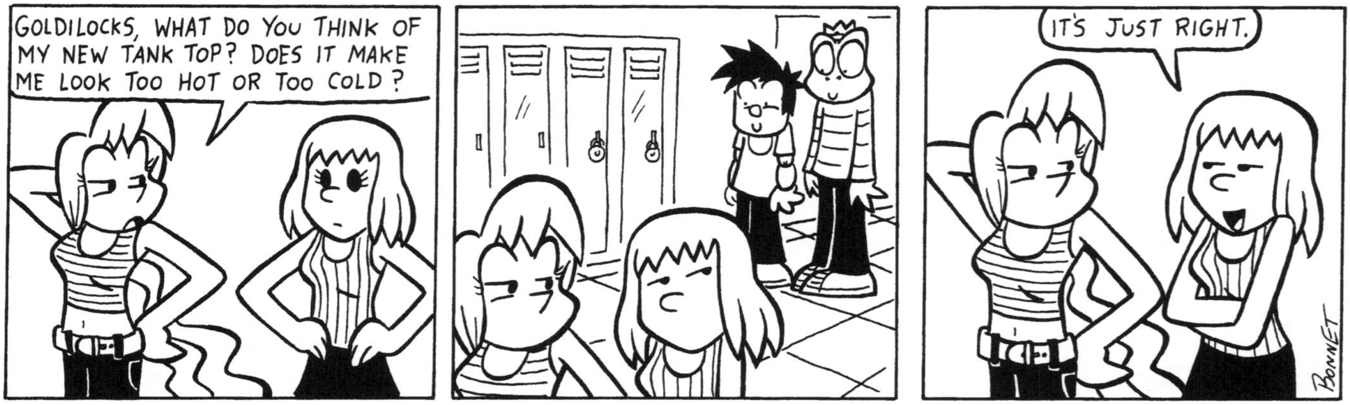
GOLDILOCKS, WHAT DO YOU THINK OF MY NEW TANK TOP? DOES IT MAKE ME LOOK TOO HOT OR TOO COLD?
IT'S JUST RIGHT.
BONNET

May 15, 18, 20, 2009

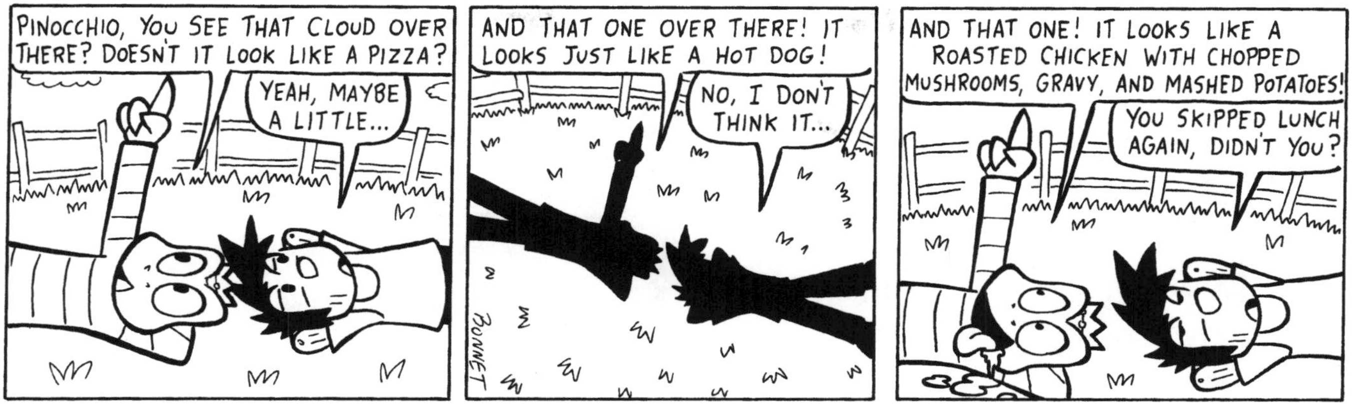
PINOCCHIO, YOU SEE THAT CLOUD OVER THERE? DOESN'T IT LOOK LIKE A PIZZA?
YEAH, MAYBE A LITTLE...
AND THAT ONE OVER THERE! IT LOOKS JUST LIKE A HOT DOG!
NO, I DON'T THINK IT...
AND THAT ONE! IT LOOKS LIKE A ROASTED CHICKEN WITH CHOPPED MUSHROOMS, GRAVY, AND MASHED POTATOES!
YOU SKIPPED LUNCH AGAIN, DIDN'T YOU?

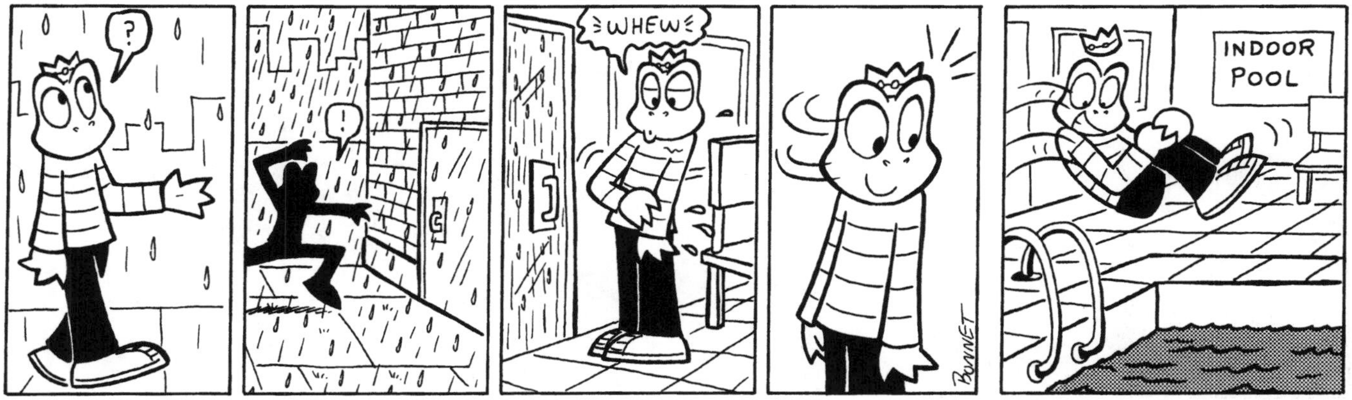
?
!
WHEW
INDOOR POOL

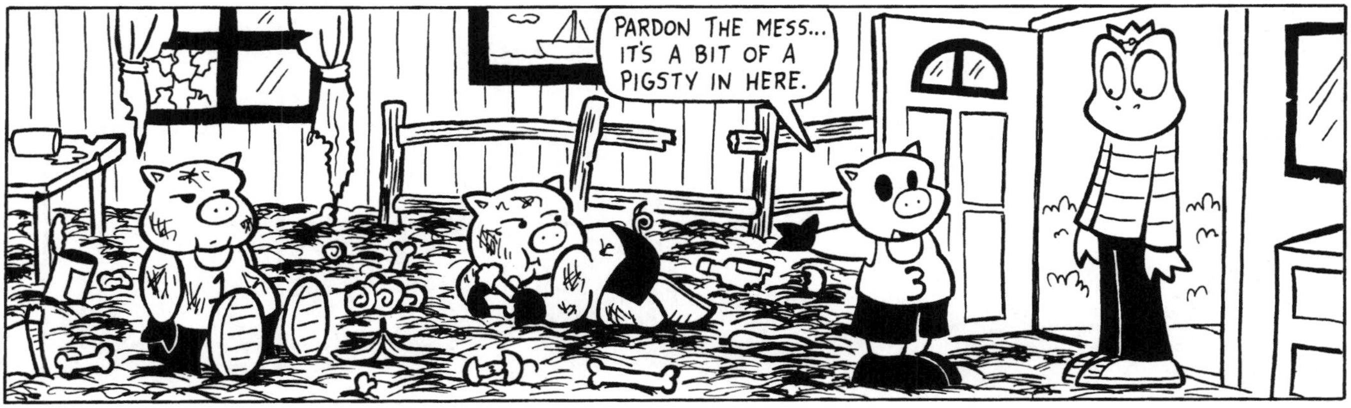
PARDON THE MESS... IT'S A BIT OF A PIGSTY IN HERE.

May 22, 25, 27, 2009

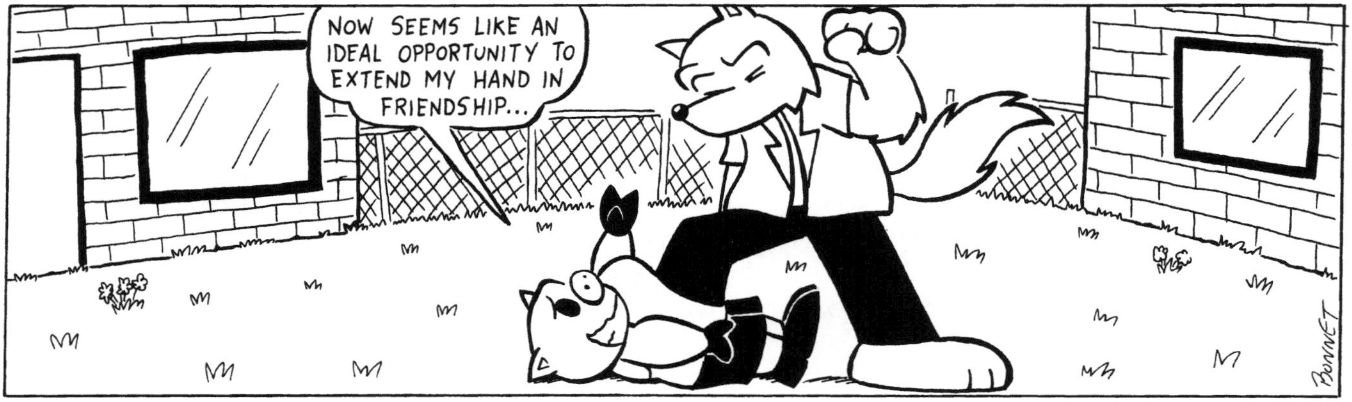
NOW SEEMS LIKE AN IDEAL OPPORTUNITY TO EXTEND MY HAND IN FRIENDSHIP...
BONNET

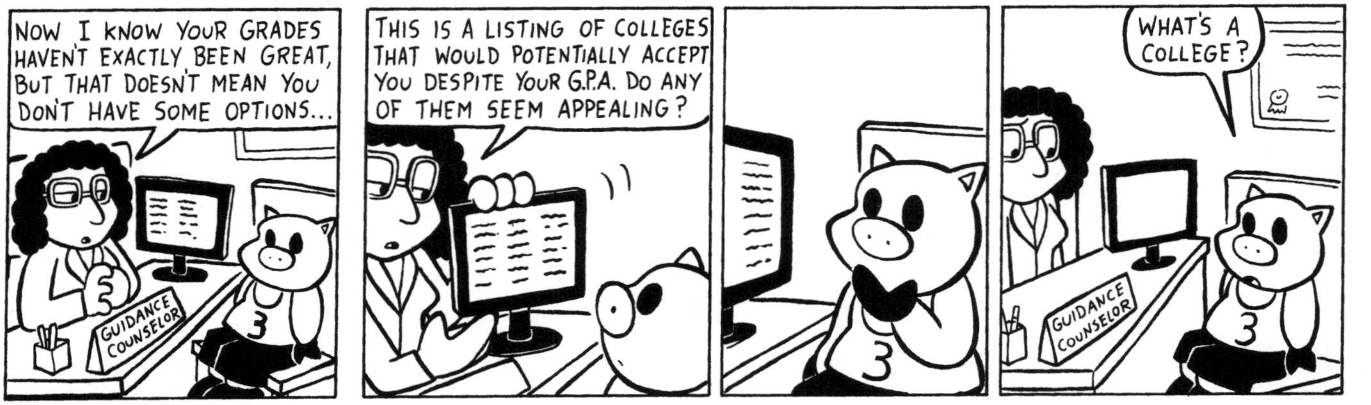
NOW I KNOW YOUR GRADES HAVEN'T EXACTLY BEEN GREAT, BUT THAT DOESN'T MEAN YOU DON'T HAVE SOME OPTIONS...
GUIDANCE COUNSELOR
THIS IS A LISTING OF COLLEGES THAT WOULD POTENTIALLY ACCEPT YOU DESPITE YOUR G.P.A. DO ANY OF THEM SEEM APPEALING?
WHAT'S A COLLEGE?
GUIDANCE COUNSELOR

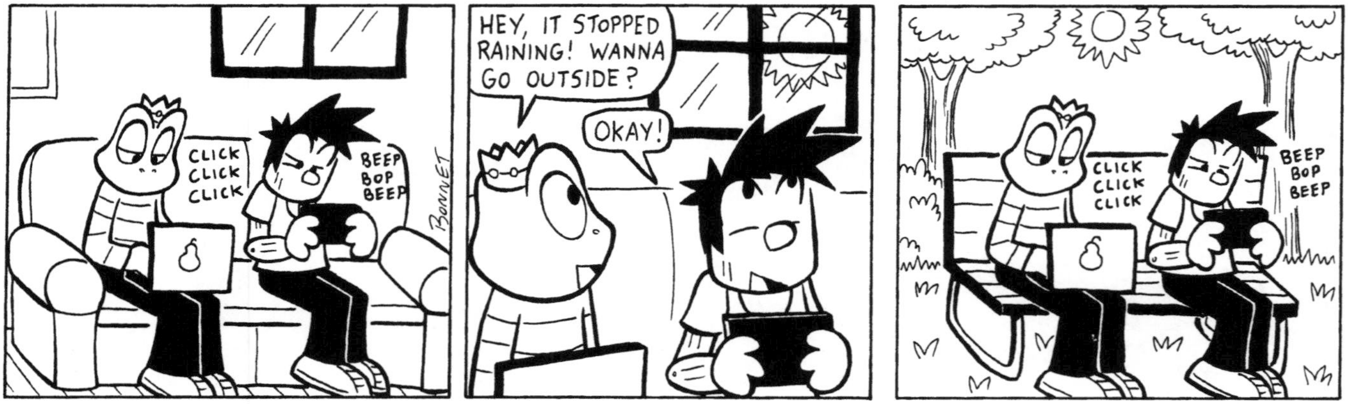
CLICK CLICK CLICK
BEEP BOP BEEP
BONNET
HEY, IT STOPPED RAINING! WANNA GO OUTSIDE?
OKAY!
CLICK CLICK CLICK
BEEP BOP BEEP

May 29, June 1, 3, 2009

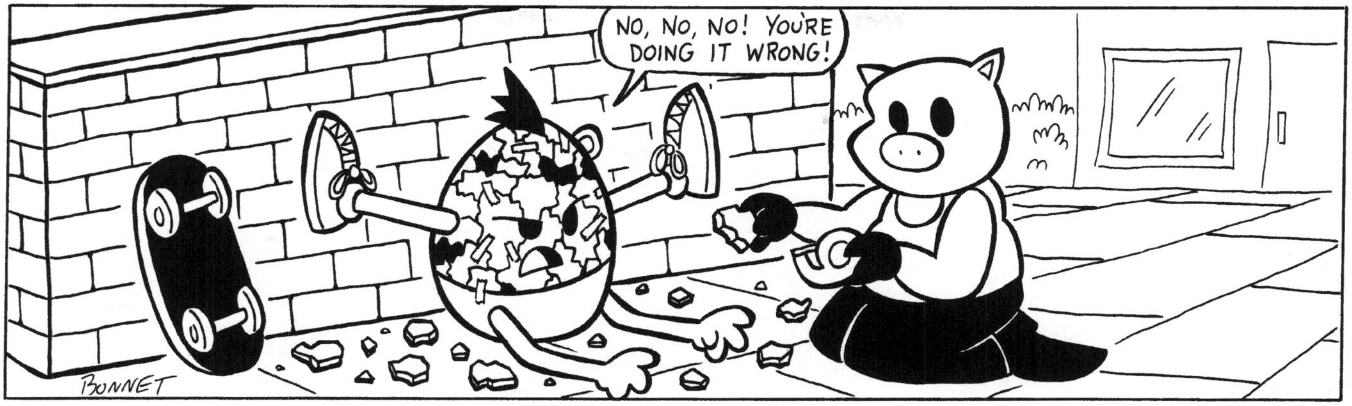
NO, NO, NO! YOU'RE DOING IT WRONG!

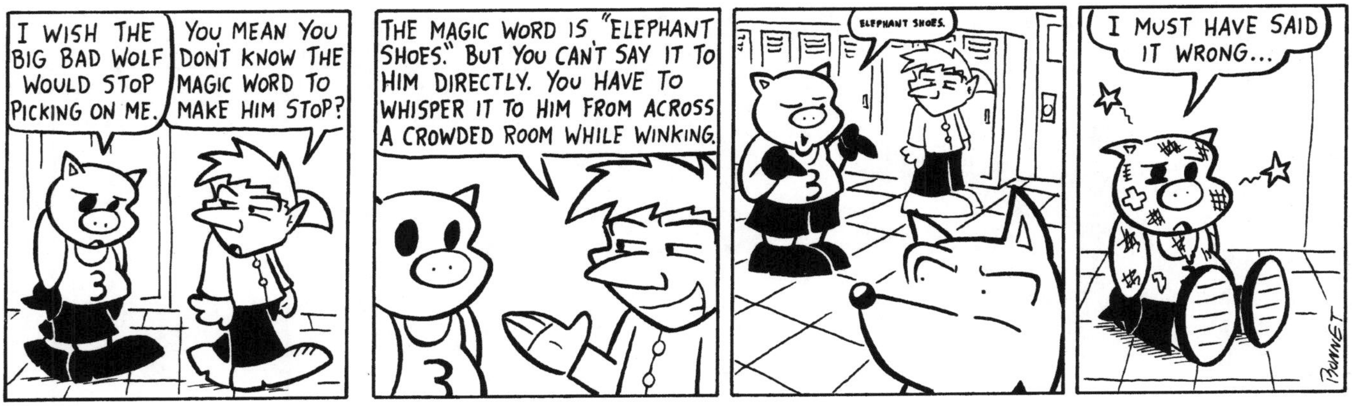
I WISH THE BIG BAD WOLF WOULD STOP PICKING ON ME.
YOU MEAN YOU DON'T KNOW THE MAGIC WORD TO MAKE HIM STOP?
THE MAGIC WORD IS "ELEPHANT SHOES." BUT YOU CAN'T SAY IT TO HIM DIRECTLY. YOU HAVE TO WHISPER IT TO HIM FROM ACROSS A CROWDED ROOM WHILE WINKING.
ELEPHANT SHOES.
I MUST HAVE SAID IT WRONG...

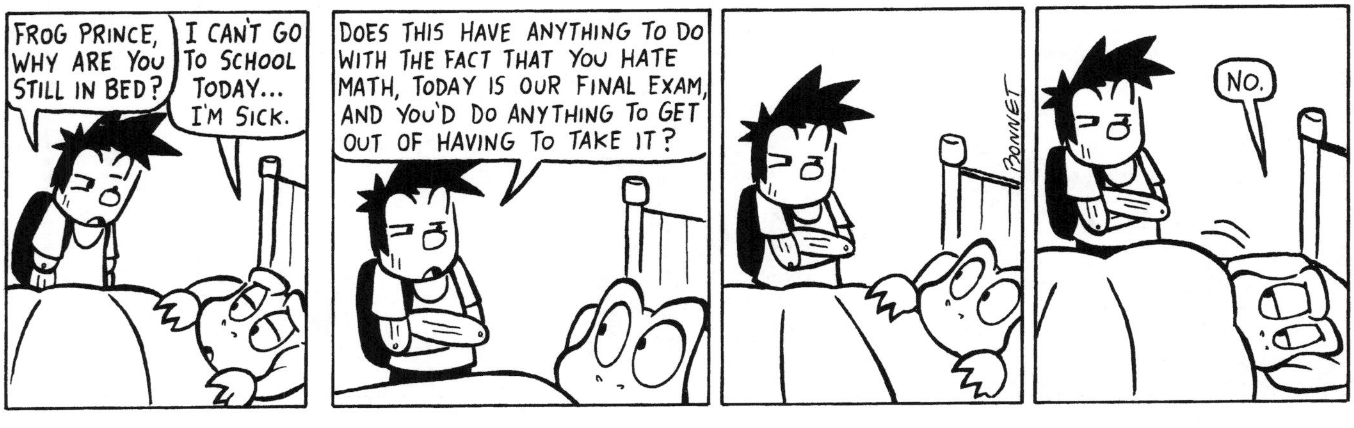
FROG PRINCE, WHY ARE YOU STILL IN BED?
I CAN'T GO TO SCHOOL TODAY... I'M SICK.
DOES THIS HAVE ANYTHING TO DO WITH THE FACT THAT YOU HATE MATH, TODAY IS OUR FINAL EXAM, AND YOU'D DO ANYTHING TO GET OUT OF HAVING TO TAKE IT?
NO.

June 5, 8, 10, 2009

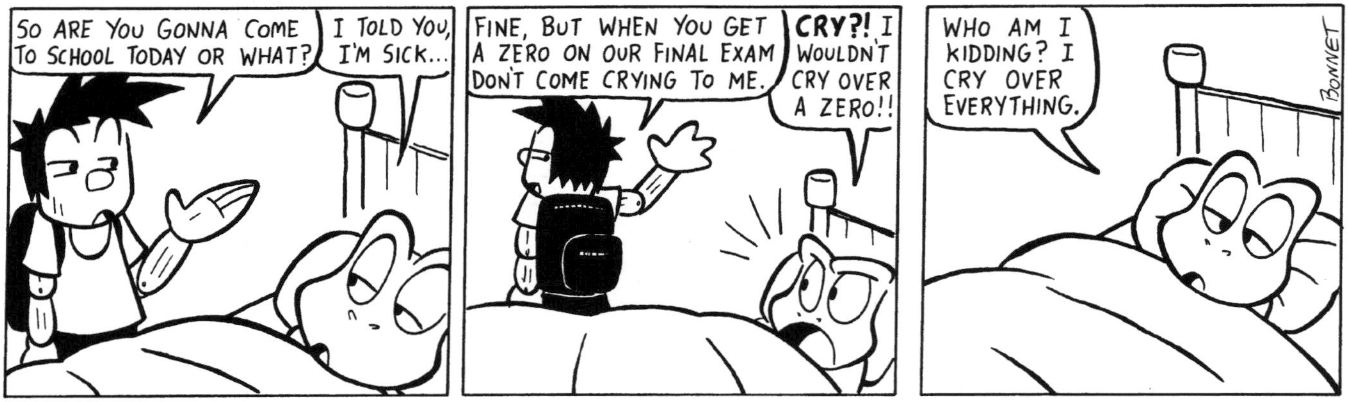
SO ARE YOU GONNA COME TO SCHOOL TODAY OR WHAT?
I TOLD YOU, I'M SICK...
FINE, BUT WHEN YOU GET A ZERO ON OUR FINAL EXAM DON'T COME CRYING TO ME.
CRY?! I WOULDN'T CRY OVER A ZERO!!
WHO AM I KIDDING? I CRY OVER EVERYTHING.
BONNET

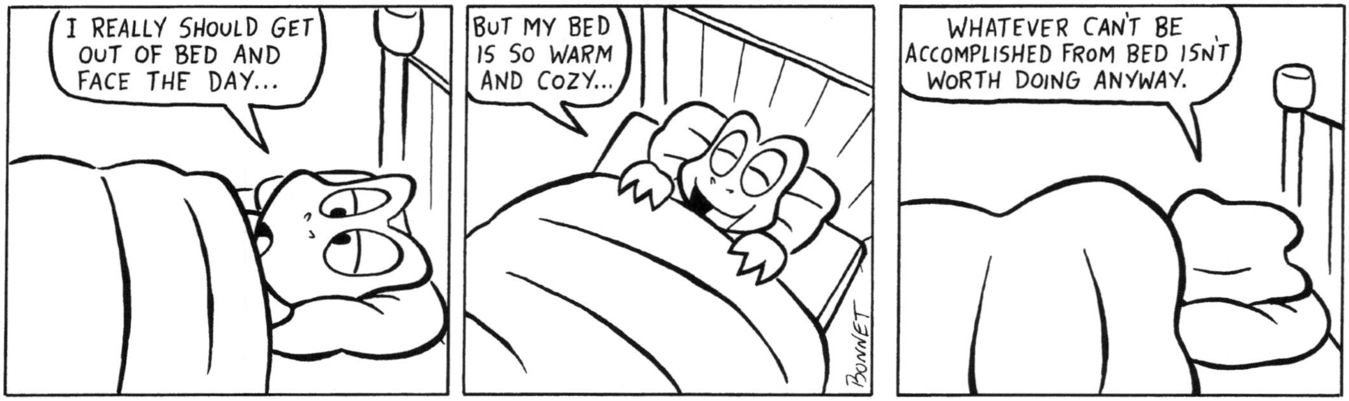
I REALLY SHOULD GET OUT OF BED AND FACE THE DAY...
BUT MY BED IS SO WARM AND COZY...
WHATEVER CAN'T BE ACCOMPLISHED FROM BED ISN'T WORTH DOING ANYWAY.
BONNET

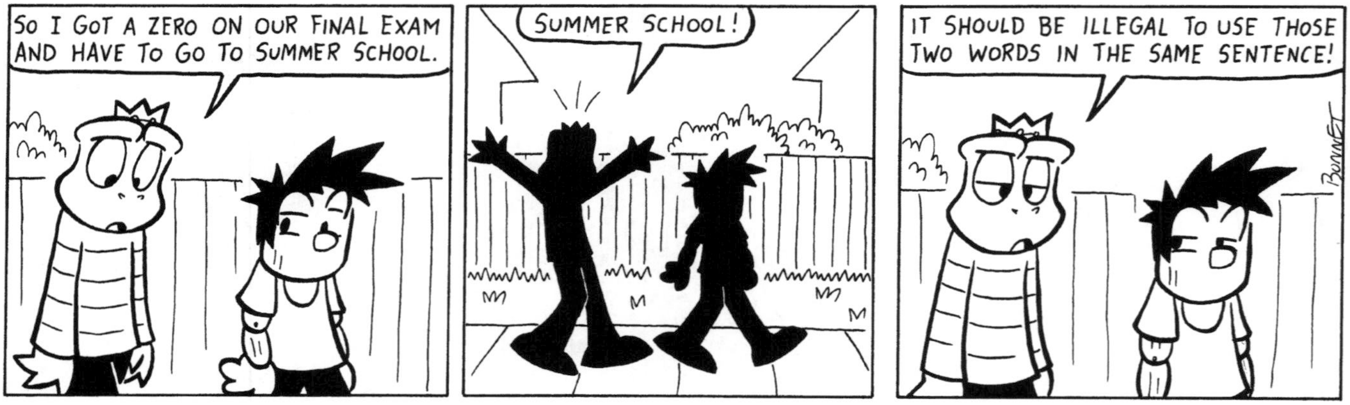
SO I GOT A ZERO ON OUR FINAL EXAM AND HAVE TO GO TO SUMMER SCHOOL.
SUMMER SCHOOL!
IT SHOULD BE ILLEGAL TO USE THOSE TWO WORDS IN THE SAME SENTENCE!
BONNET

June 12, 15, 17, 2009

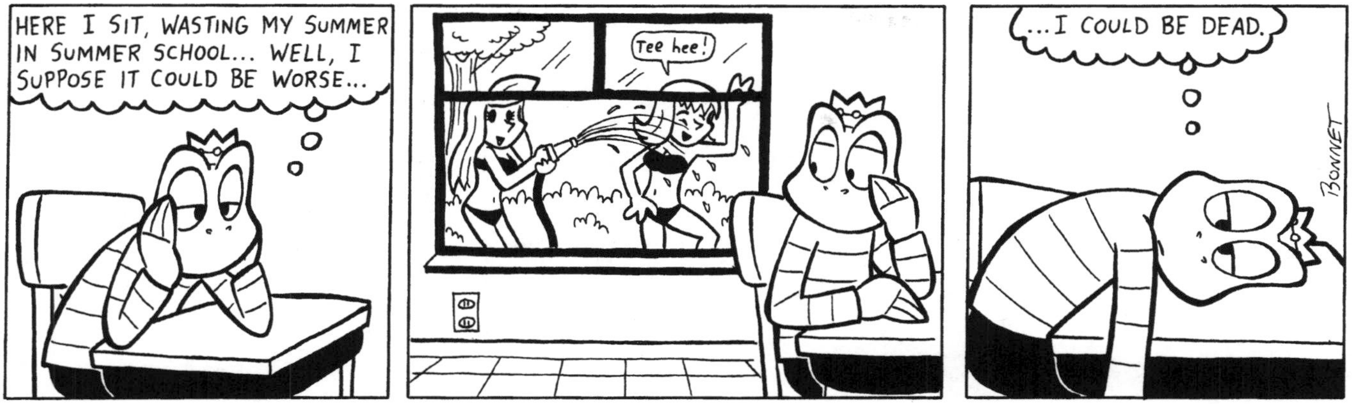
HERE I SIT, WASTING MY SUMMER IN SUMMER SCHOOL... WELL, I SUPPOSE IT COULD BE WORSE...
Tee hee!
...I COULD BE DEAD.
BONNET

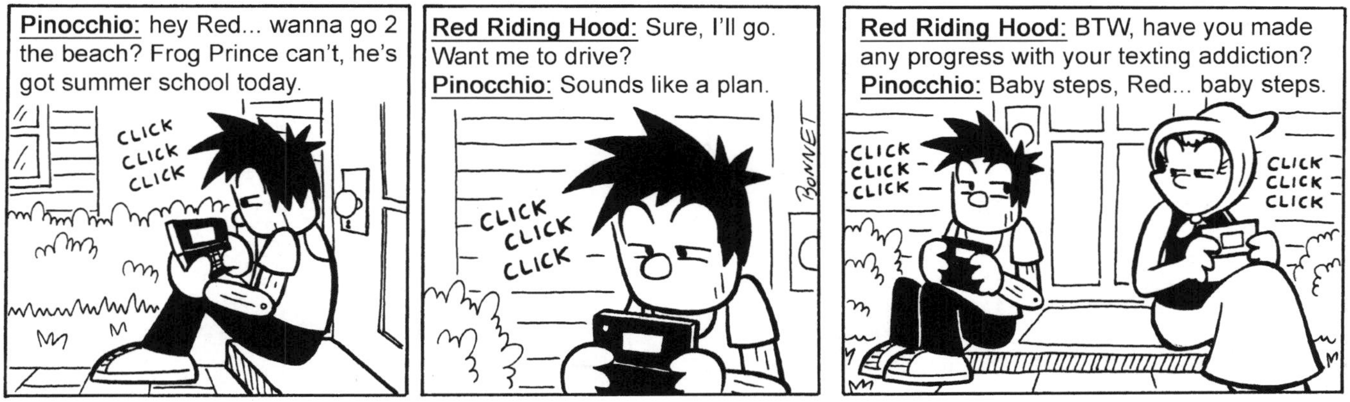
Pinocchio: hey Red... wanna go 2 the beach? Frog Prince can't, he's got summer school today.
CLICK CLICK CLICK
Red Riding Hood: Sure, I'll go. Want me to drive?
Pinocchio: Sounds like a plan.
CLICK CLICK CLICK
BONNET
Red Riding Hood: BTW, have you made any progress with your texting addiction?
Pinocchio: Baby steps, Red... baby steps.
CLICK CLICK CLICK
CLICK CLICK CLICK

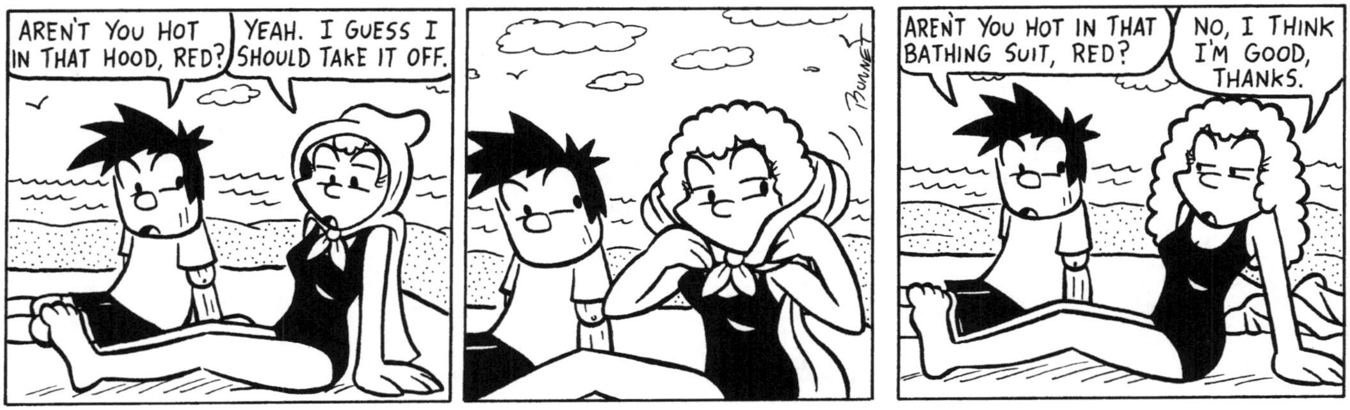
AREN'T YOU HOT IN THAT HOOD, RED?
YEAH. I GUESS I SHOULD TAKE IT OFF.
BONNET
AREN'T YOU HOT IN THAT BATHING SUIT, RED?
NO, I THINK I'M GOOD, THANKS.

June 19, 22, 24, 2009

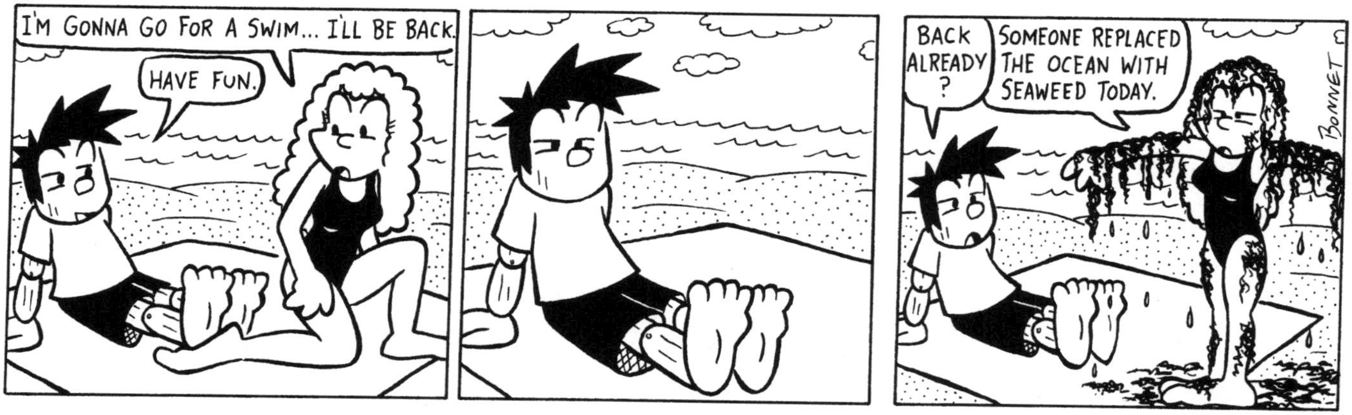
I'M GONNA GO FOR A SWIM... I'LL BE BACK.
HAVE FUN.
BACK ALREADY ?
SOMEONE REPLACED THE OCEAN WITH SEAWEED TODAY.
BONNET

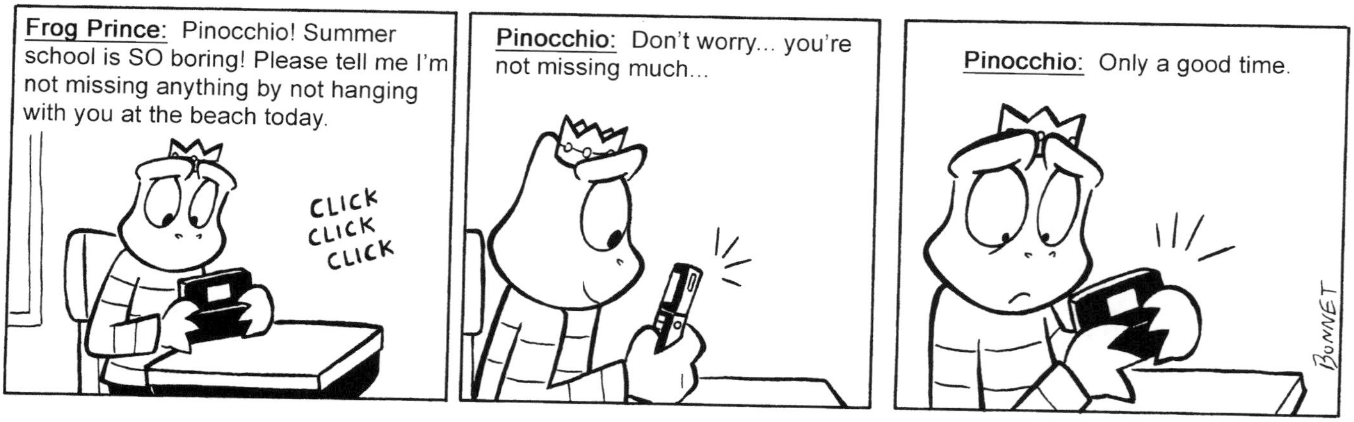
Frog Prince: Pinocchio! Summer school is SO boring! Please tell me I'm not missing anything by not hanging with you at the beach today.
CLICK CLICK CLICK
Pinocchio: Don't worry... you're not missing much...
Pinocchio: Only a good time.
BONNET

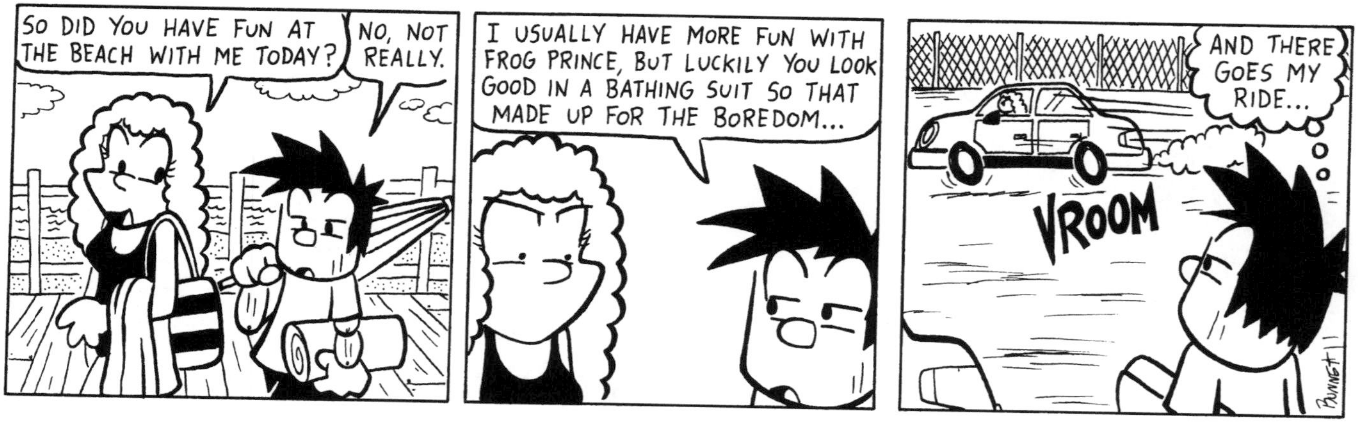
SO DID YOU HAVE FUN AT THE BEACH WITH ME TODAY?
NO, NOT REALLY.
I USUALLY HAVE MORE FUN WITH FROG PRINCE, BUT LUCKILY YOU LOOK GOOD IN A BATHING SUIT SO THAT MADE UP FOR THE BOREDOM...
AND THERE GOES MY RIDE...
VROOM
BONNET

June 26, 29, July 1, 2009

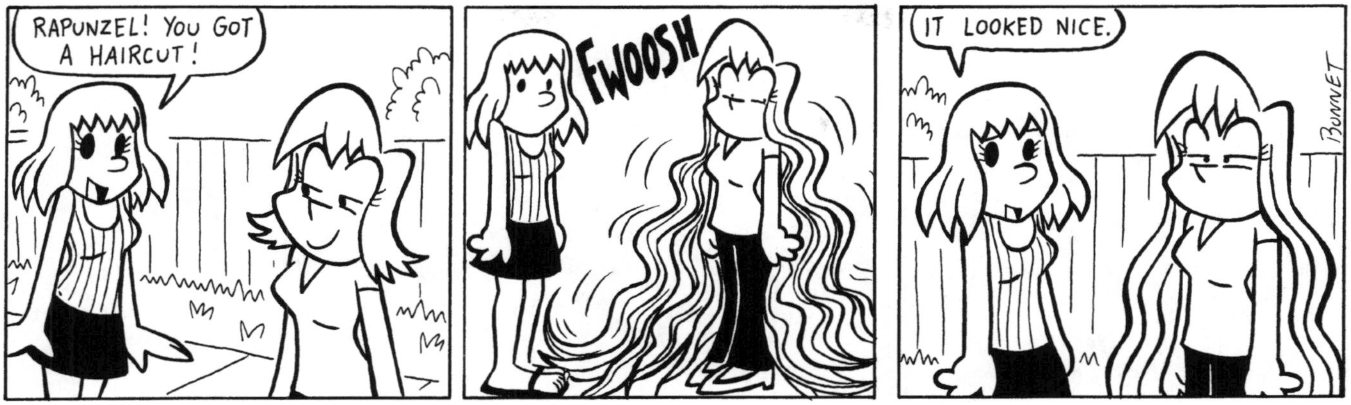
RAPUNZEL! YOU GOT A HAIRCUT!
FWOOSH
IT LOOKED NICE.
BONNET

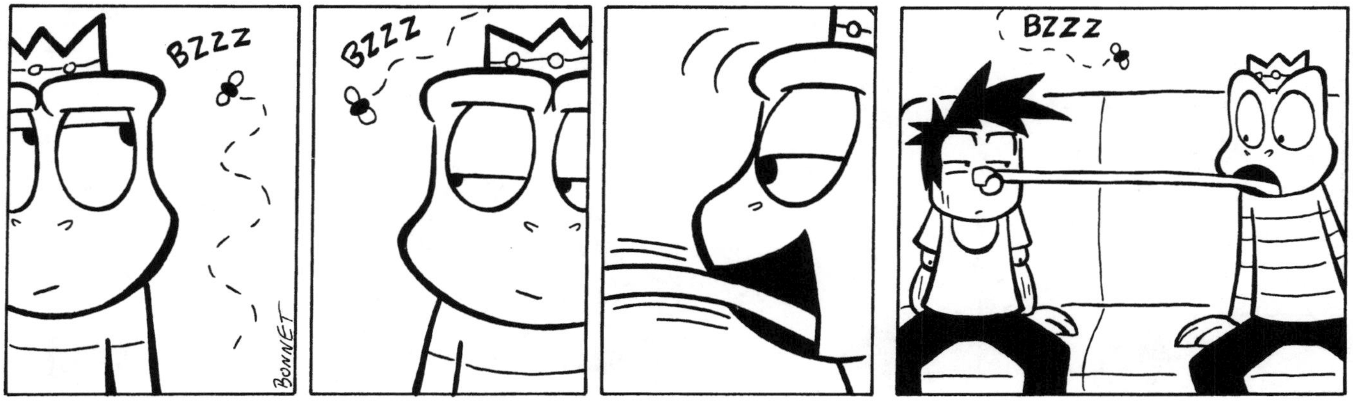
BZZZ
BONNET
BZZZ
BZZZ

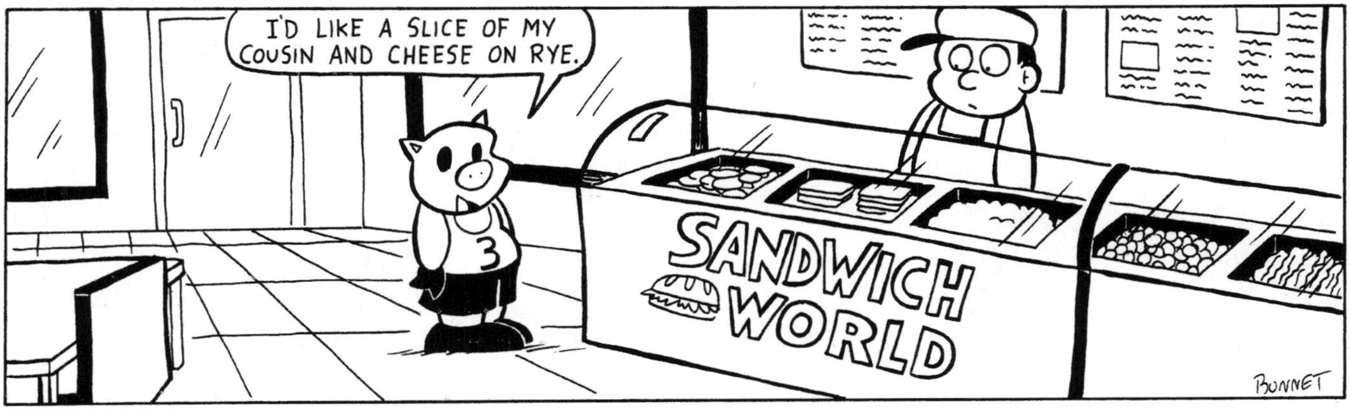
I'D LIKE A SLICE OF MY COUSIN AND CHEESE ON RYE.
3
SANDWICH WORLD
BONNET

July 3, 6, 8, 2009

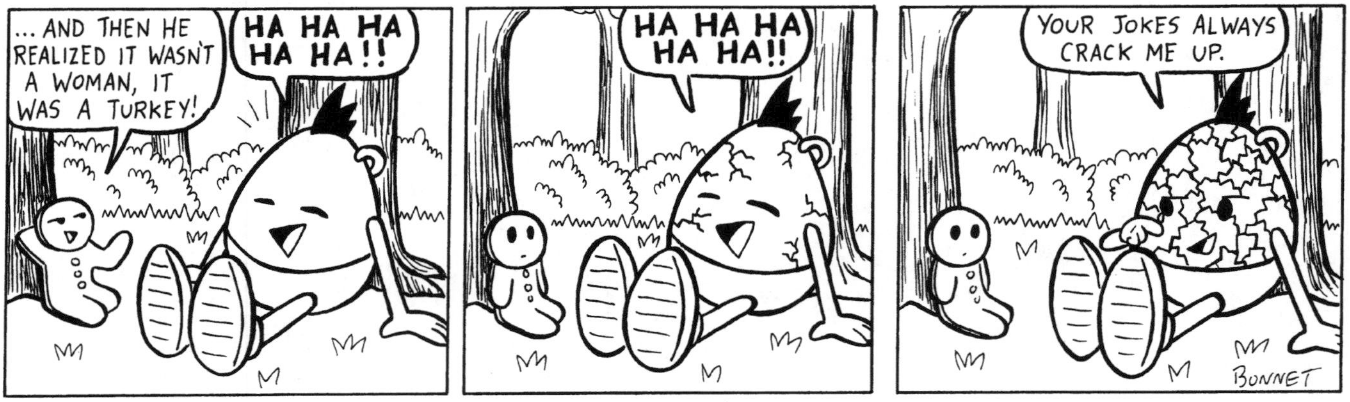

... AND THEN HE REALIZED IT WASN'T A WOMAN, IT WAS A TURKEY!
HA HA HA HA HA!!
HA HA HA HA HA!!
YOUR JOKES ALWAYS CRACK ME UP.
BONNET

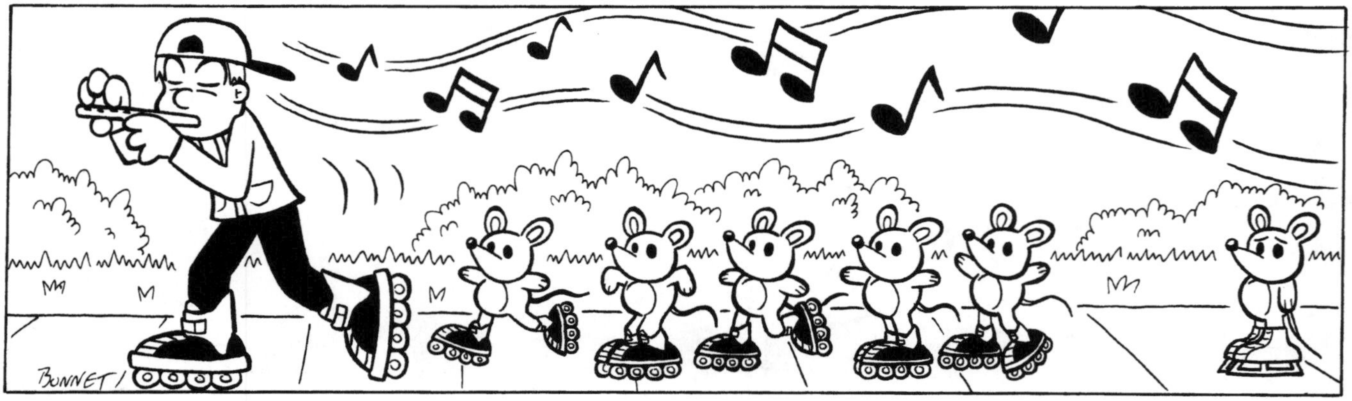

BONNET!

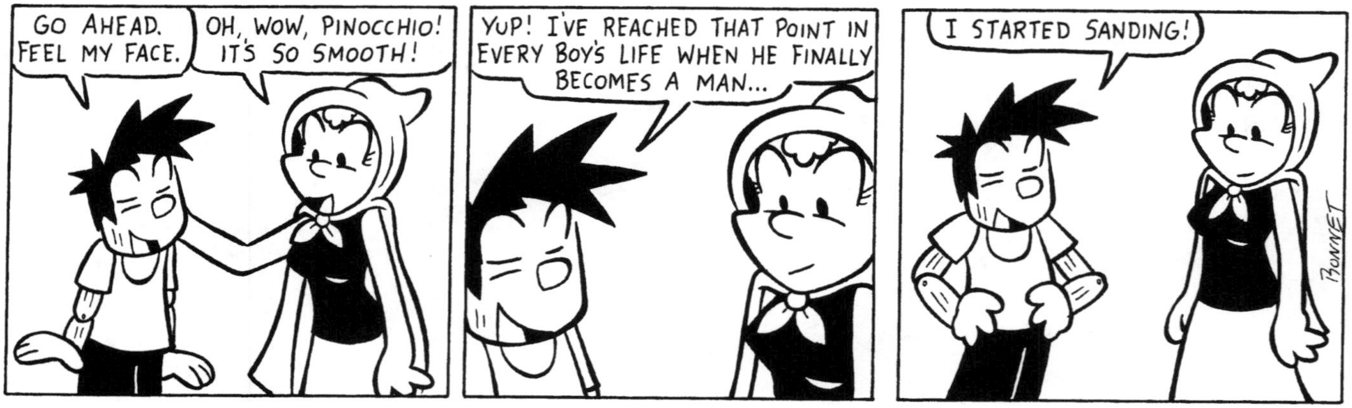

GO AHEAD. FEEL MY FACE.
OH, WOW, PINOCCHIO! IT'S SO SMOOTH!
YUP! I'VE REACHED THAT POINT IN EVERY BOY'S LIFE WHEN HE FINALLY BECOMES A MAN...
I STARTED SANDING!
BONNET

July 10, 13, 15, 2009

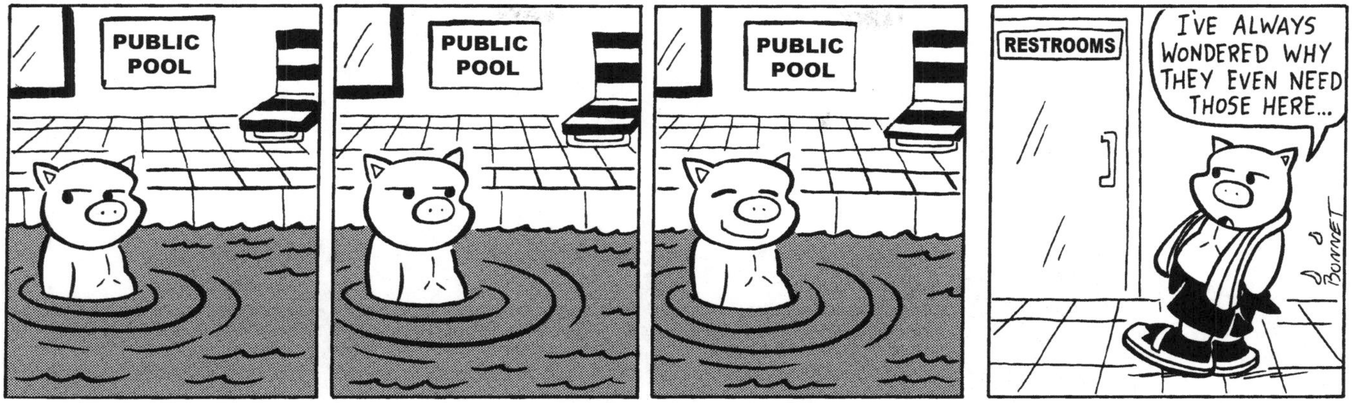
PUBLIC POOL
PUBLIC POOL
PUBLIC POOL
RESTROOMS
I'VE ALWAYS WONDERED WHY THEY EVEN NEED THOSE HERE...

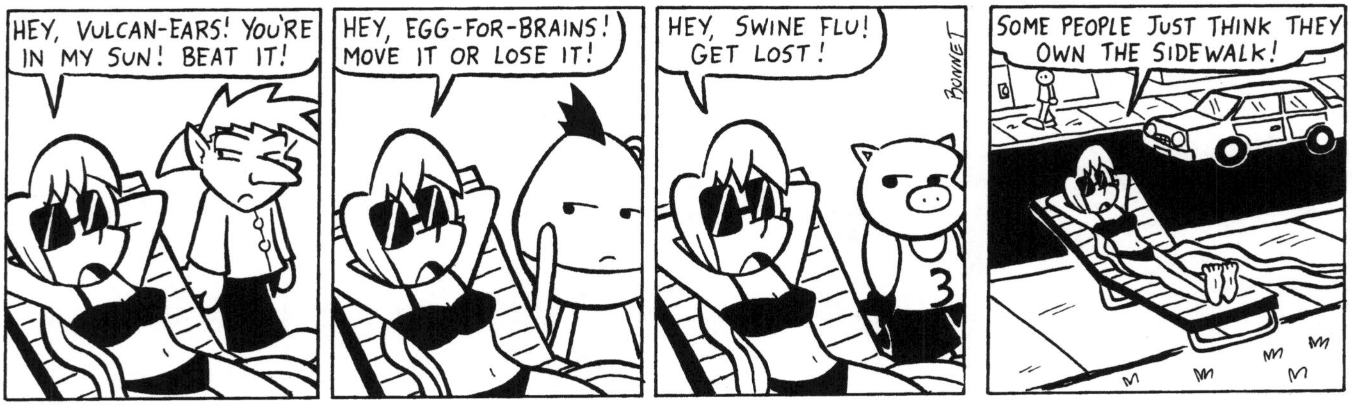
HEY, VULCAN-EARS! YOU'RE IN MY SUN! BEAT IT!
HEY, EGG-FOR-BRAINS! MOVE IT OR LOSE IT!
HEY, SWINE FLU! GET LOST!
SOME PEOPLE JUST THINK THEY OWN THE SIDEWALK!

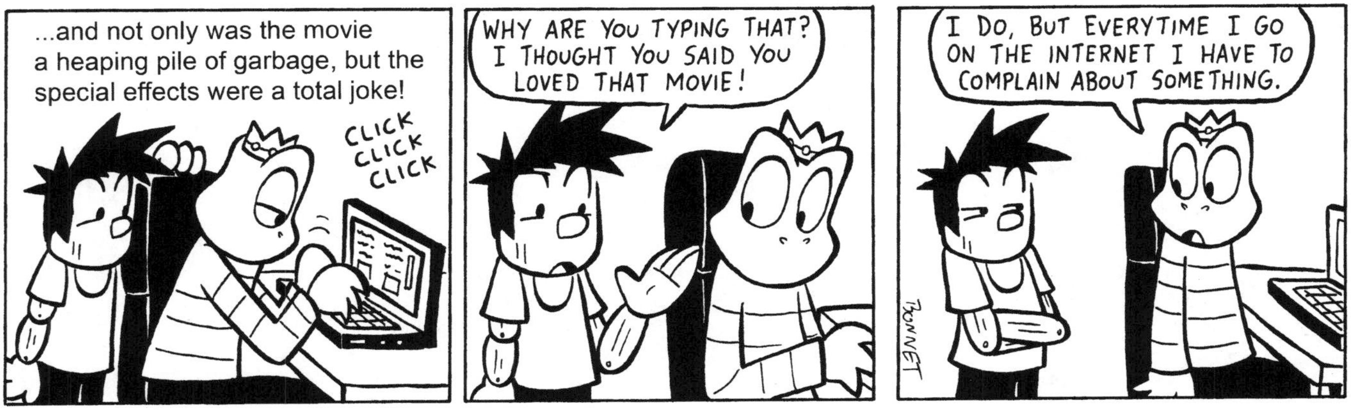
...and not only was the movie a heaping pile of garbage, but the special effects were a total joke!
CLICK CLICK CLICK
WHY ARE YOU TYPING THAT? I THOUGHT YOU SAID YOU LOVED THAT MOVIE!
I DO, BUT EVERYTIME I GO ON THE INTERNET I HAVE TO COMPLAIN ABOUT SOMETHING.

July 17, 20, 22, 2009

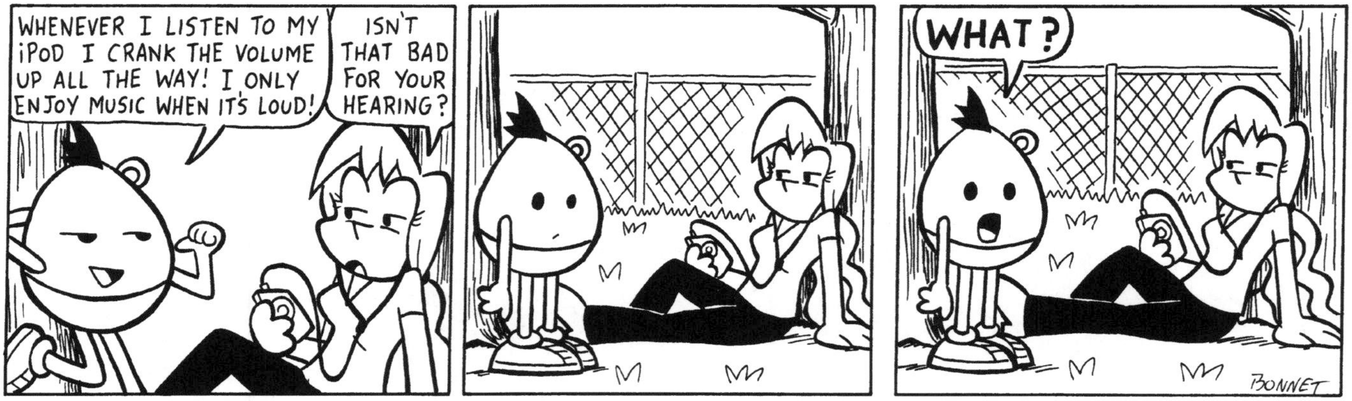
WHENEVER I LISTEN TO MY iPOD I CRANK THE VOLUME UP ALL THE WAY! I ONLY ENJOY MUSIC WHEN IT'S LOUD!
ISN'T THAT BAD FOR YOUR HEARING?
WHAT?
BONNET

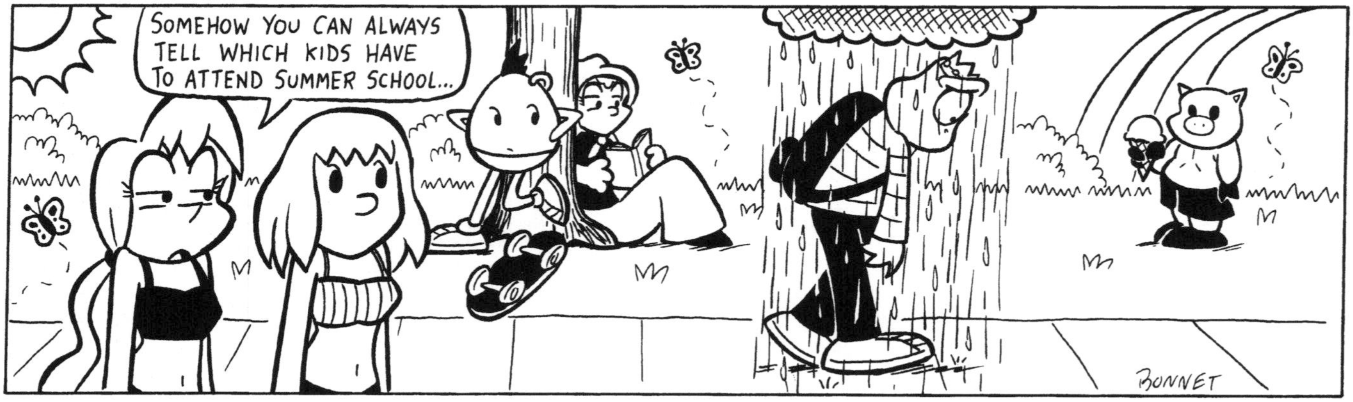
SOMEHOW YOU CAN ALWAYS TELL WHICH KIDS HAVE TO ATTEND SUMMER SCHOOL...
BONNET

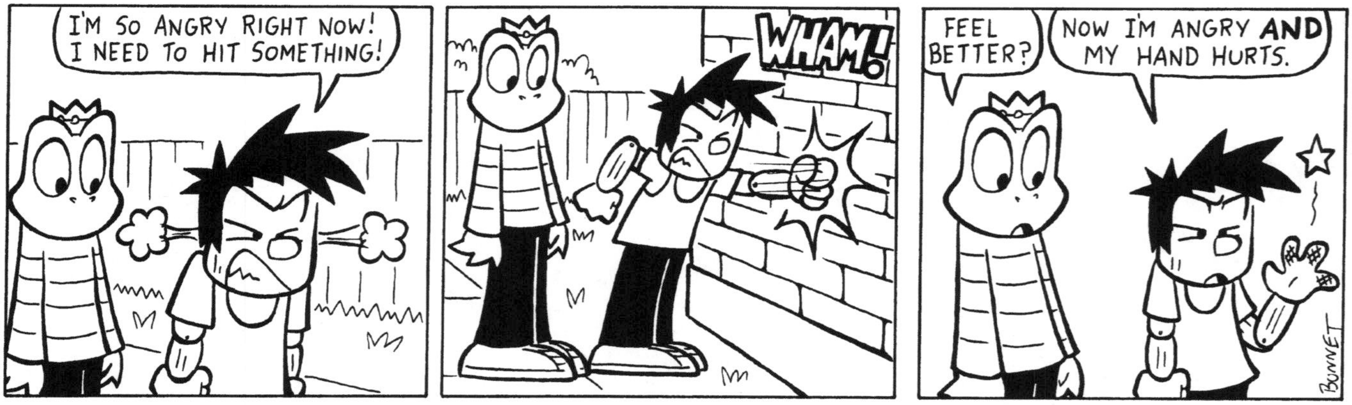
I'M SO ANGRY RIGHT NOW! I NEED TO HIT SOMETHING!
WHAM!
FEEL BETTER?
NOW I'M ANGRY **AND** MY HAND HURTS.
BONNET

July 24, 27, 29, 2009

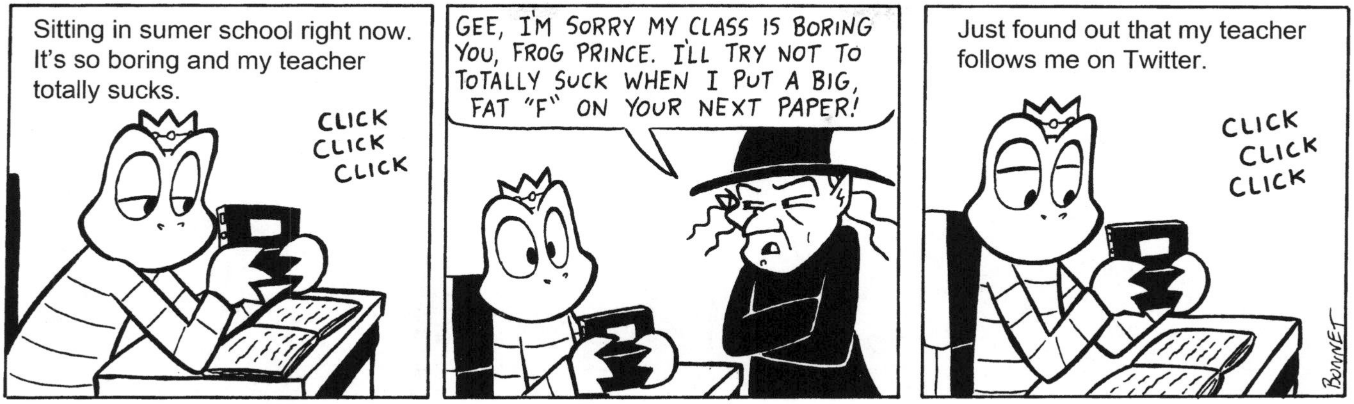
Sitting in sumer school right now. It's so boring and my teacher totally sucks.
CLICK CLICK CLICK
GEE, I'M SORRY MY CLASS IS BORING YOU, FROG PRINCE. I'LL TRY NOT TO TOTALLY SUCK WHEN I PUT A BIG, FAT "F" ON YOUR NEXT PAPER!
Just found out that my teacher follows me on Twitter.
CLICK CLICK CLICK
BONNET

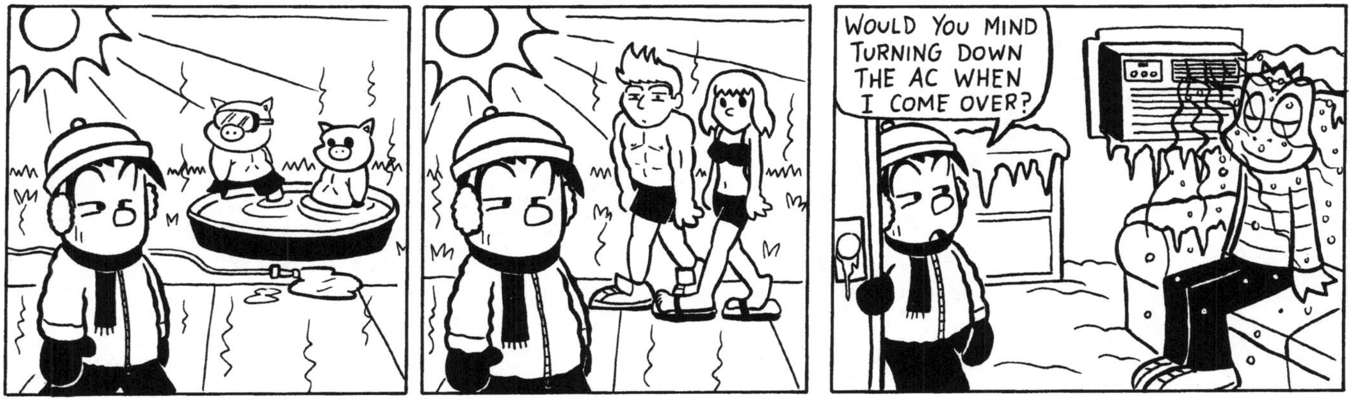
WOULD YOU MIND TURNING DOWN THE AC WHEN I COME OVER?

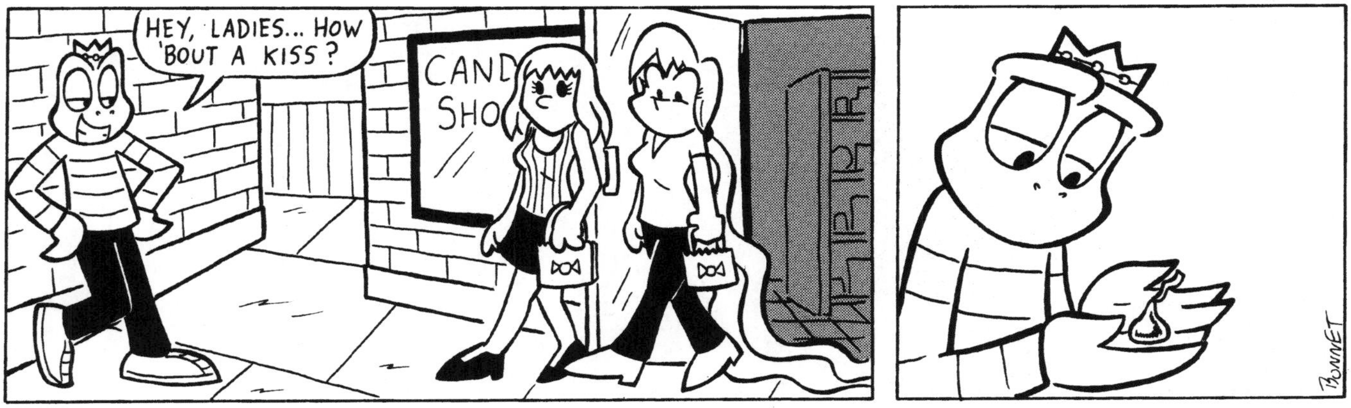
HEY, LADIES... HOW 'BOUT A KISS?
CAND
SHO
BONNET

July 31, Aug. 3, 5, 2009

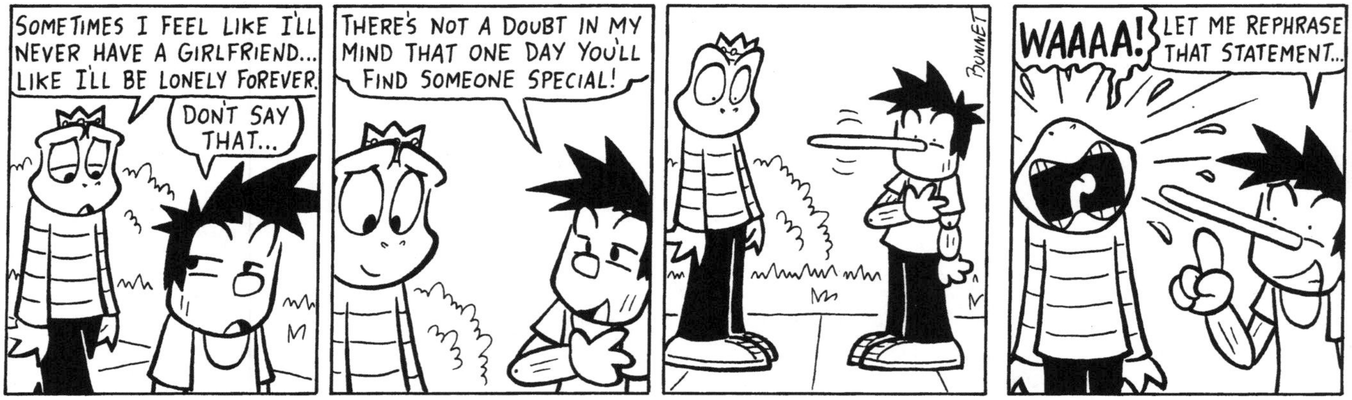
SOMETIMES I FEEL LIKE I'LL NEVER HAVE A GIRLFRIEND... LIKE I'LL BE LONELY FOREVER.
DON'T SAY THAT...
THERE'S NOT A DOUBT IN MY MIND THAT ONE DAY YOU'LL FIND SOMEONE SPECIAL!
BONNET
WAAAA!
LET ME REPHRASE THAT STATEMENT...

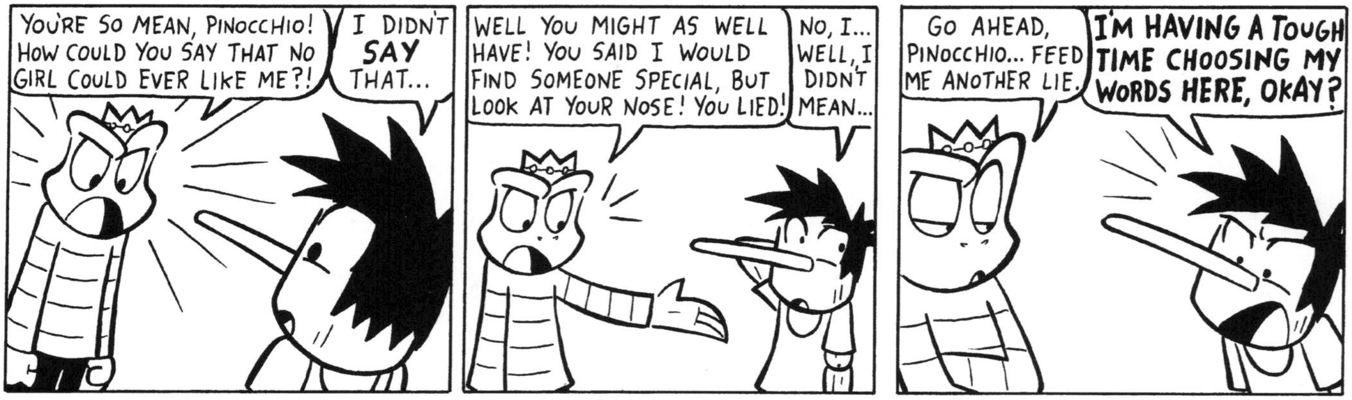
YOU'RE SO MEAN, PINOCCHIO! HOW COULD YOU SAY THAT NO GIRL COULD EVER LIKE ME?!
I DIDN'T SAY THAT...
WELL YOU MIGHT AS WELL HAVE! YOU SAID I WOULD FIND SOMEONE SPECIAL, BUT LOOK AT YOUR NOSE! YOU LIED!
NO, I... WELL, I DIDN'T MEAN...
GO AHEAD, PINOCCHIO... FEED ME ANOTHER LIE.
I'M HAVING A TOUGH TIME CHOOSING MY WORDS HERE, OKAY?

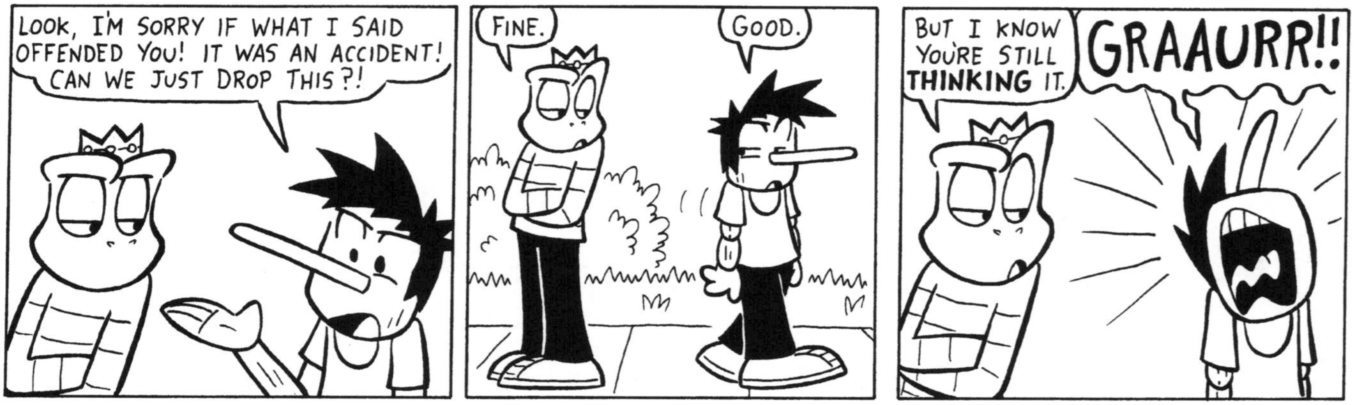
LOOK, I'M SORRY IF WHAT I SAID OFFENDED YOU! IT WAS AN ACCIDENT! CAN WE JUST DROP THIS?!
FINE.
GOOD.
BUT I KNOW YOU'RE STILL THINKING IT.
GRAAURR!!

Aug. 7, 10, 12, 2009

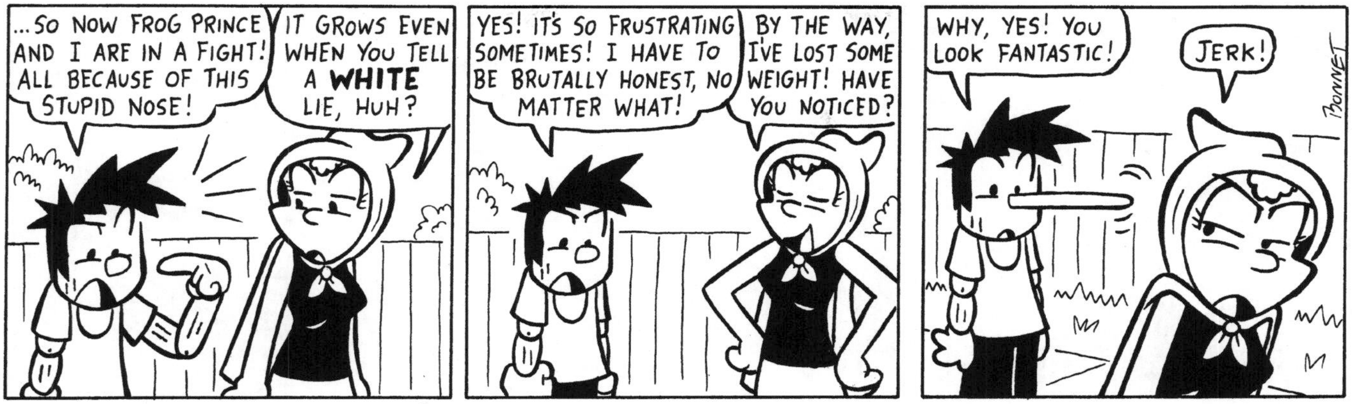
...SO NOW FROG PRINCE AND I ARE IN A FIGHT! ALL BECAUSE OF THIS STUPID NOSE!
IT GROWS EVEN WHEN YOU TELL A **WHITE** LIE, HUH?
YES! IT'S SO FRUSTRATING SOMETIMES! I HAVE TO BE BRUTALLY HONEST, NO MATTER WHAT!
BY THE WAY, I'VE LOST SOME WEIGHT! HAVE YOU NOTICED?
WHY, YES! YOU LOOK FANTASTIC!
JERK!
BONNET

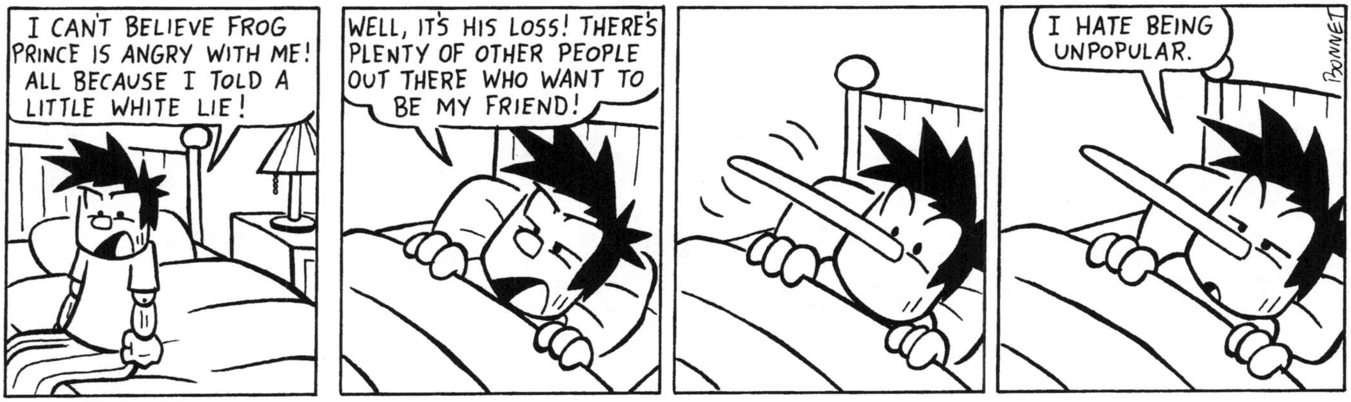
I CAN'T BELIEVE FROG PRINCE IS ANGRY WITH ME! ALL BECAUSE I TOLD A LITTLE WHITE LIE!
WELL, IT'S HIS LOSS! THERE'S PLENTY OF OTHER PEOPLE OUT THERE WHO WANT TO BE MY FRIEND!
I HATE BEING UNPOPULAR.
BONNET

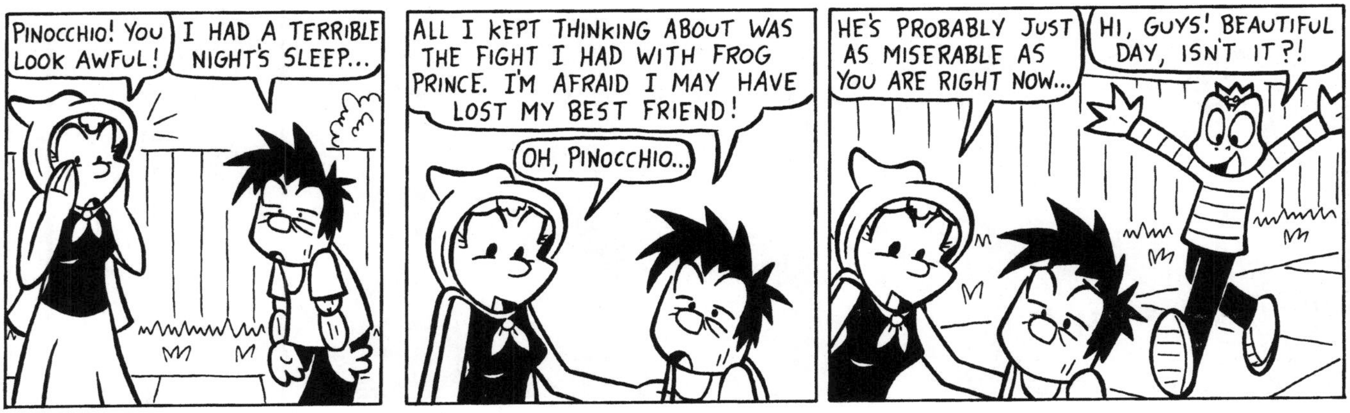
PINOCCHIO! YOU LOOK AWFUL!
I HAD A TERRIBLE NIGHT'S SLEEP...
ALL I KEPT THINKING ABOUT WAS THE FIGHT I HAD WITH FROG PRINCE. I'M AFRAID I MAY HAVE LOST MY BEST FRIEND!
OH, PINOCCHIO...
HE'S PROBABLY JUST AS MISERABLE AS YOU ARE RIGHT NOW...
HI, GUYS! BEAUTIFUL DAY, ISN'T IT?!

Aug. 14, 17, 19, 2009

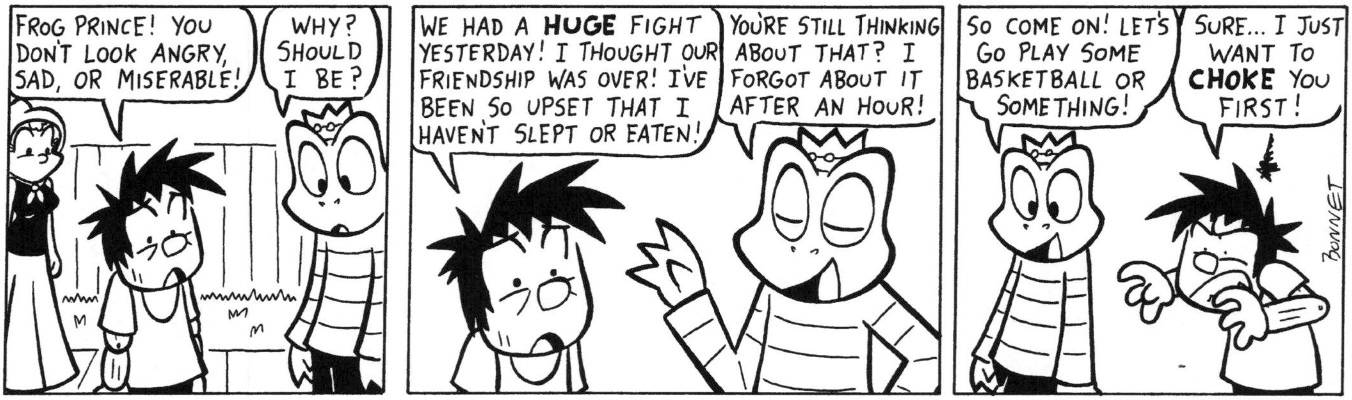
FROG PRINCE! YOU DON'T LOOK ANGRY, SAD, OR MISERABLE!
WHY? SHOULD I BE?
WE HAD A **HUGE** FIGHT YESTERDAY! I THOUGHT OUR FRIENDSHIP WAS OVER! I'VE BEEN SO UPSET THAT I HAVEN'T SLEPT OR EATEN!
YOU'RE STILL THINKING ABOUT THAT? I FORGOT ABOUT IT AFTER AN HOUR!
SO COME ON! LET'S GO PLAY SOME BASKETBALL OR SOMETHING!
SURE... I JUST WANT TO **CHOKE** YOU FIRST!
BONNET

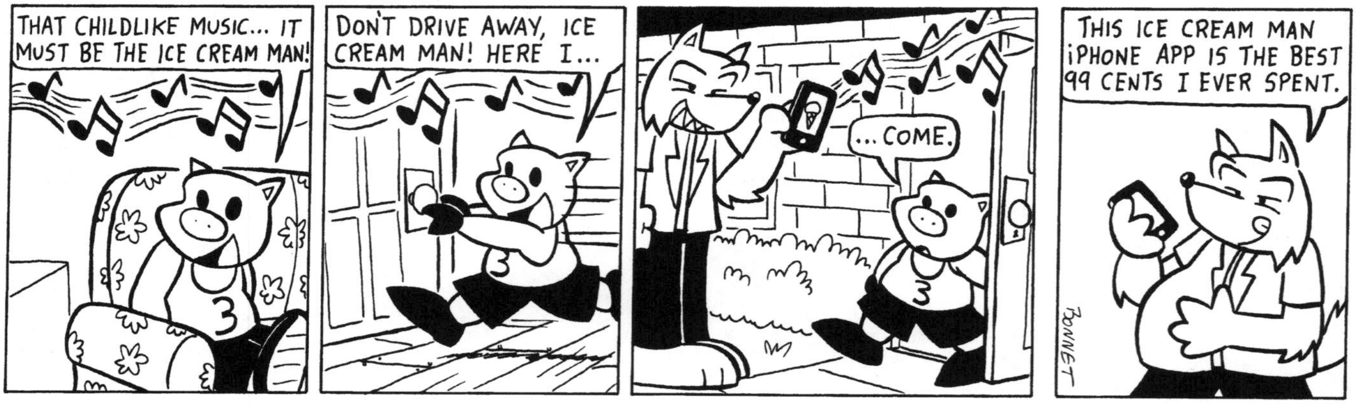
THAT CHILDLIKE MUSIC... IT MUST BE THE ICE CREAM MAN!
DON'T DRIVE AWAY, ICE CREAM MAN! HERE I...
...COME.
BONNET
THIS ICE CREAM MAN iPHONE APP IS THE BEST 99 CENTS I EVER SPENT.

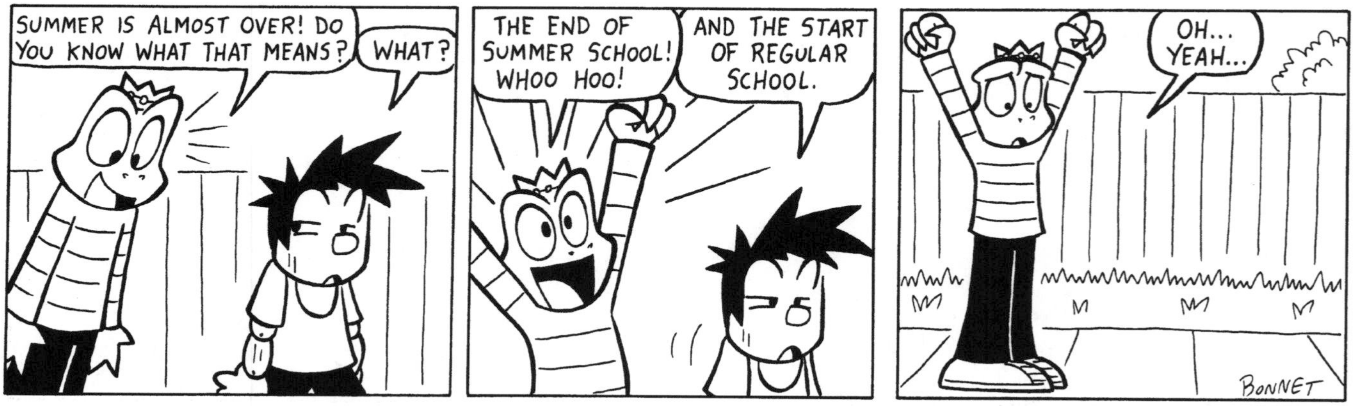
SUMMER IS ALMOST OVER! DO YOU KNOW WHAT THAT MEANS?
WHAT?
THE END OF SUMMER SCHOOL! WHOO HOO!
AND THE START OF REGULAR SCHOOL.
OH... YEAH...
BONNET

Aug. 21, 24, 26, 2009

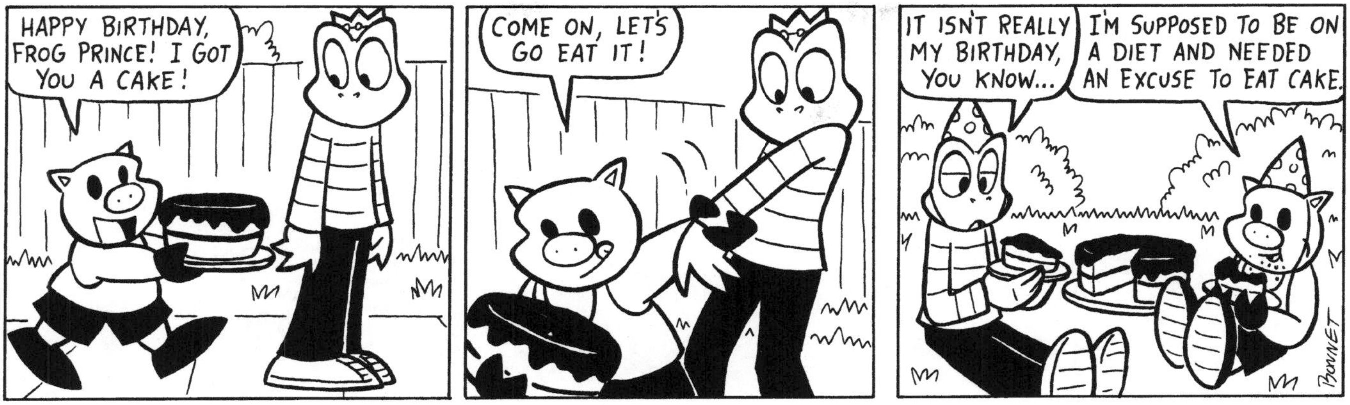
HAPPY BIRTHDAY, FROG PRINCE! I GOT YOU A CAKE!
COME ON, LET'S GO EAT IT!
IT ISN'T REALLY MY BIRTHDAY, YOU KNOW...
I'M SUPPOSED TO BE ON A DIET AND NEEDED AN EXCUSE TO EAT CAKE.
BONNET

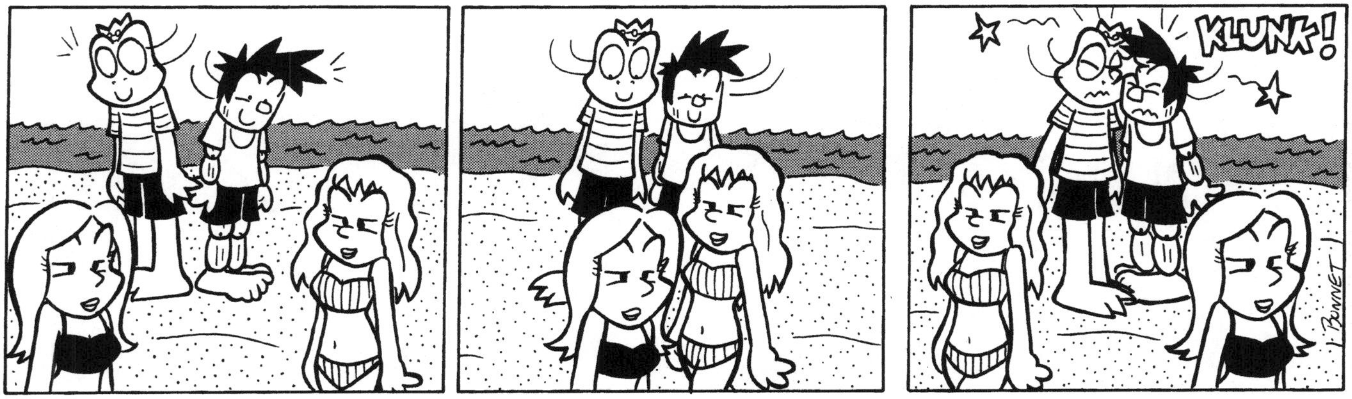
KLUNK!
BONNET

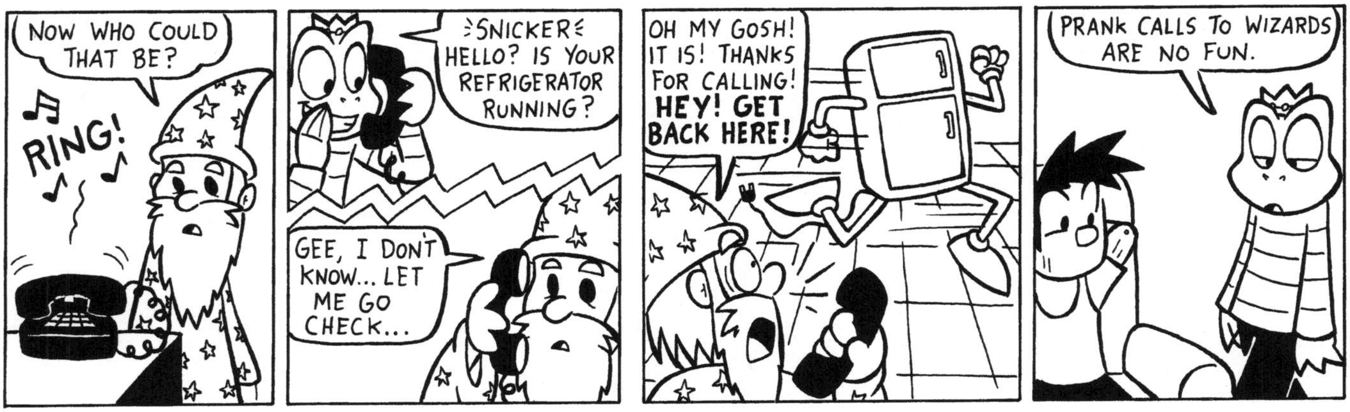
NOW WHO COULD THAT BE?
RING!
SNICKER
HELLO? IS YOUR REFRIGERATOR RUNNING?
GEE, I DON'T KNOW... LET ME GO CHECK...
OH MY GOSH! IT IS! THANKS FOR CALLING! HEY! GET BACK HERE!
PRANK CALLS TO WIZARDS ARE NO FUN.

Aug. 28, 31, Sept. 2, 2009

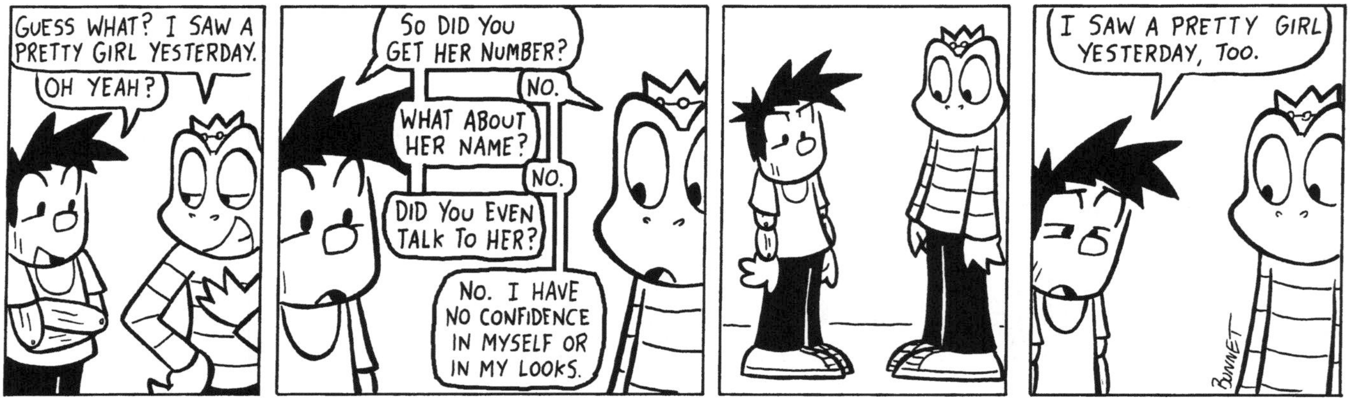
GUESS WHAT? I SAW A PRETTY GIRL YESTERDAY.
OH YEAH?
SO DID YOU GET HER NUMBER?
NO.
WHAT ABOUT HER NAME?
NO.
DID YOU EVEN TALK TO HER?
NO. I HAVE NO CONFIDENCE IN MYSELF OR IN MY LOOKS.
I SAW A PRETTY GIRL YESTERDAY, TOO.
BONNET

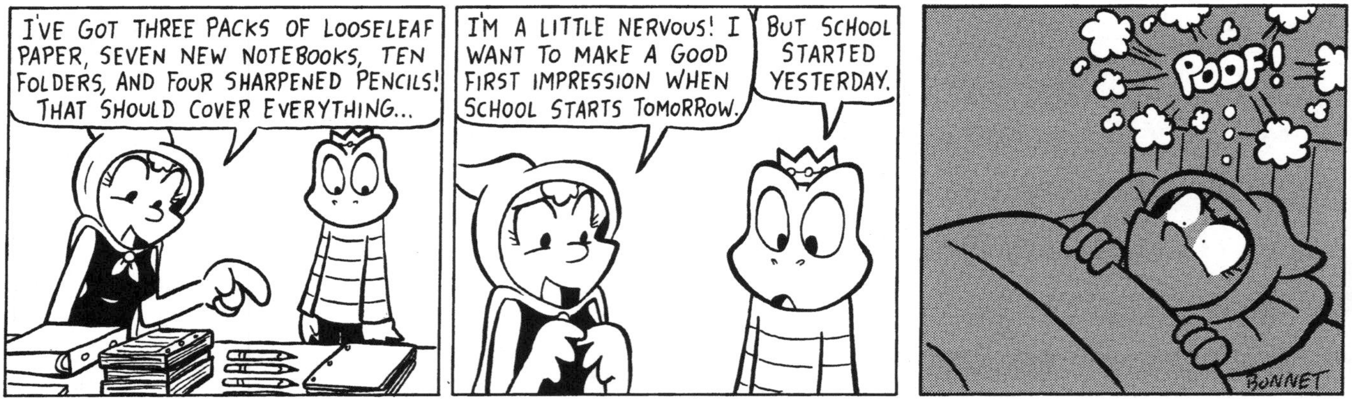
I'VE GOT THREE PACKS OF LOOSELEAF PAPER, SEVEN NEW NOTEBOOKS, TEN FOLDERS, AND FOUR SHARPENED PENCILS! THAT SHOULD COVER EVERYTHING...
I'M A LITTLE NERVOUS! I WANT TO MAKE A GOOD FIRST IMPRESSION WHEN SCHOOL STARTS TOMORROW.
BUT SCHOOL STARTED YESTERDAY.
POOF!
BONNET

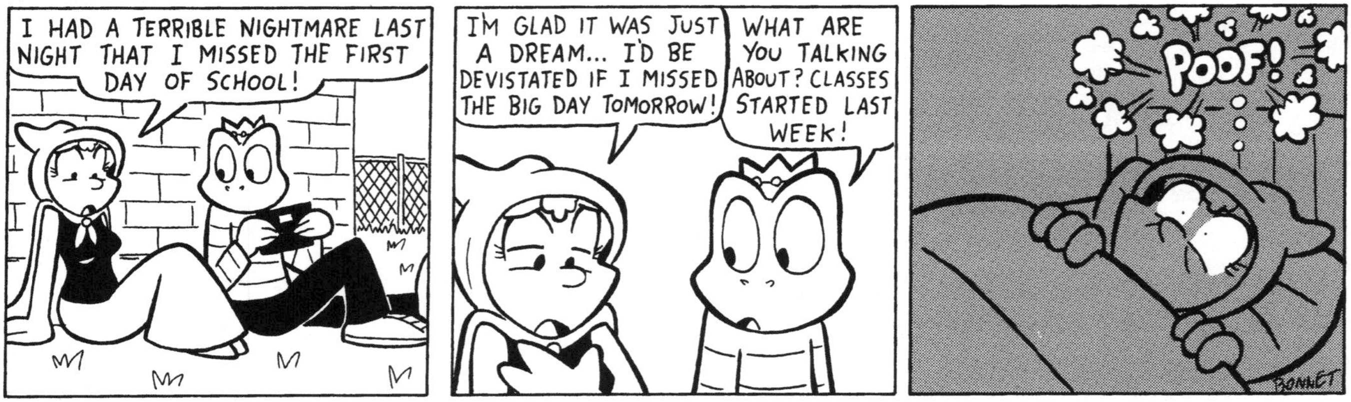
I HAD A TERRIBLE NIGHTMARE LAST NIGHT THAT I MISSED THE FIRST DAY OF SCHOOL!
I'M GLAD IT WAS JUST A DREAM... I'D BE DEVISTATED IF I MISSED THE BIG DAY TOMORROW!
WHAT ARE YOU TALKING ABOUT? CLASSES STARTED LAST WEEK!
POOF!
BONNET

Sept. 4, 7, 9, 2009

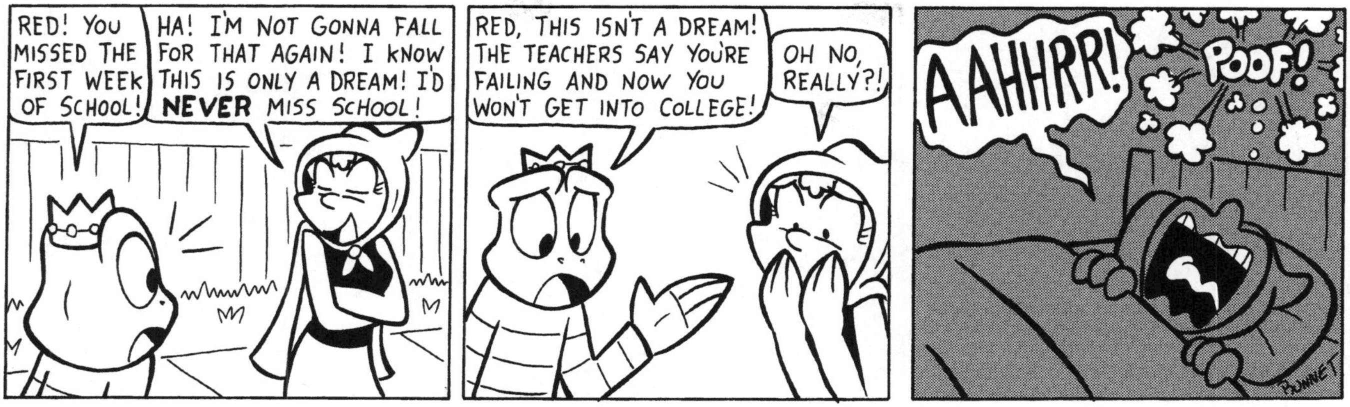
RED! YOU MISSED THE FIRST WEEK OF SCHOOL!
HA! I'M NOT GONNA FALL FOR THAT AGAIN! I KNOW THIS IS ONLY A DREAM! I'D **NEVER** MISS SCHOOL!
RED, THIS ISN'T A DREAM! THE TEACHERS SAY YOU'RE FAILING AND NOW YOU WON'T GET INTO COLLEGE!
OH NO, REALLY?!
AAHHRR!
POOF!
BONNET

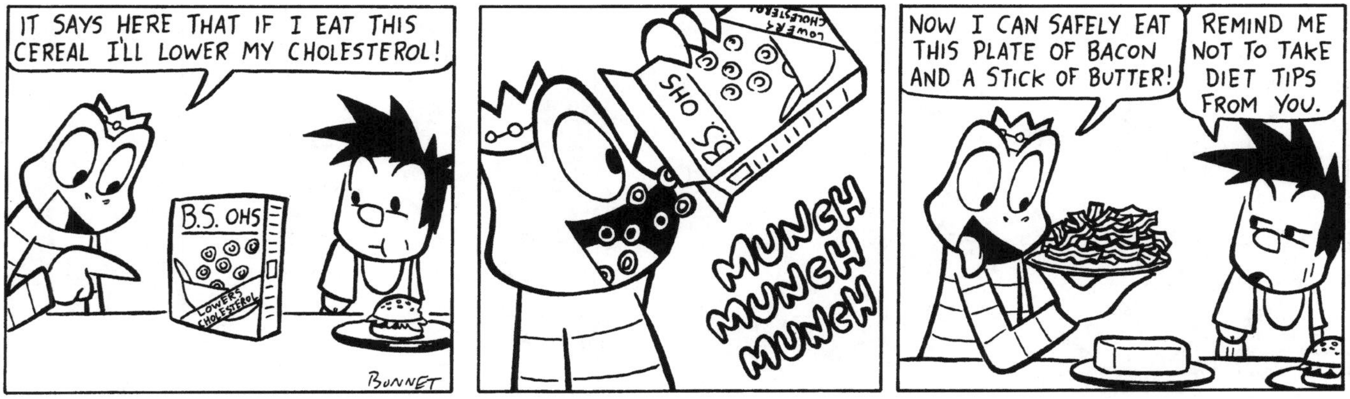
IT SAYS HERE THAT IF I EAT THIS CEREAL I'LL LOWER MY CHOLESTEROL!
B.S. OHS
LOWERS CHOLESTEROL
BONNET
MUNCH MUNCH MUNCH
NOW I CAN SAFELY EAT THIS PLATE OF BACON AND A STICK OF BUTTER!
REMIND ME NOT TO TAKE DIET TIPS FROM YOU.

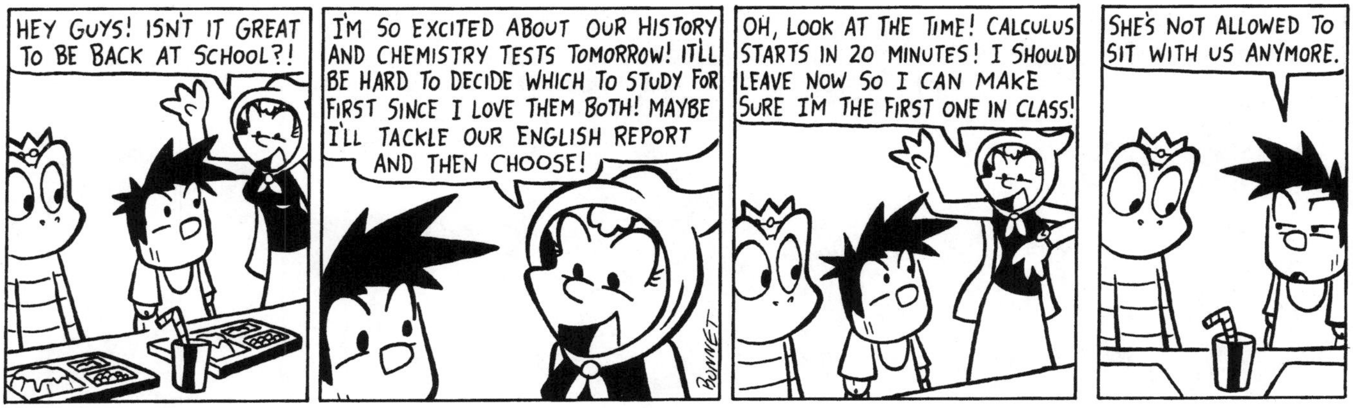
HEY GUYS! ISN'T IT GREAT TO BE BACK AT SCHOOL?!
I'M SO EXCITED ABOUT OUR HISTORY AND CHEMISTRY TESTS TOMORROW! IT'LL BE HARD TO DECIDE WHICH TO STUDY FOR FIRST SINCE I LOVE THEM BOTH! MAYBE I'LL TACKLE OUR ENGLISH REPORT AND THEN CHOOSE!
BONNET
OH, LOOK AT THE TIME! CALCULUS STARTS IN 20 MINUTES! I SHOULD LEAVE NOW SO I CAN MAKE SURE I'M THE FIRST ONE IN CLASS!
SHE'S NOT ALLOWED TO SIT WITH US ANYMORE.

Sept. 11, 14, 16, 2009

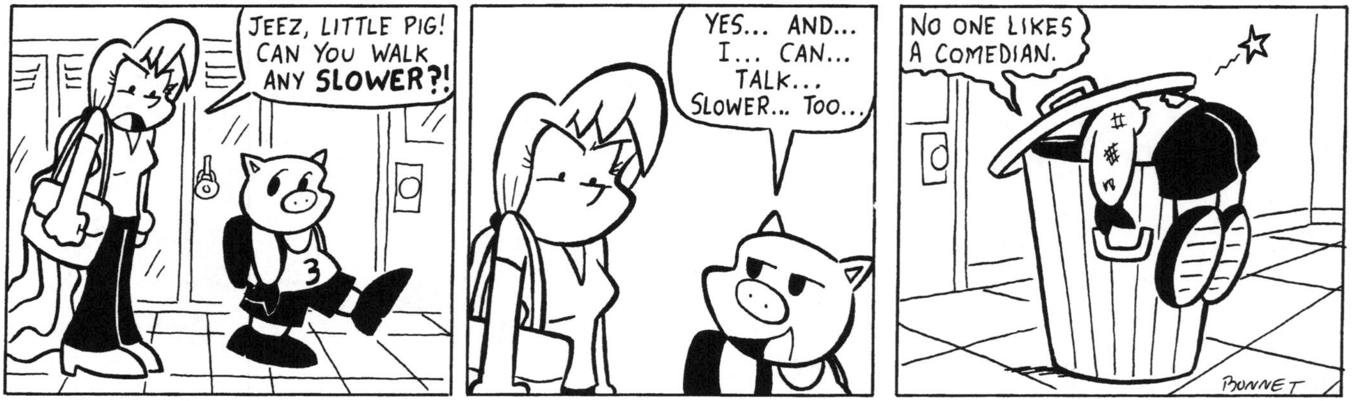
JEEZ, LITTLE PIG! CAN YOU WALK ANY SLOWER?!
YES... AND... I... CAN... TALK... SLOWER... TOO...
NO ONE LIKES A COMEDIAN.
BONNET

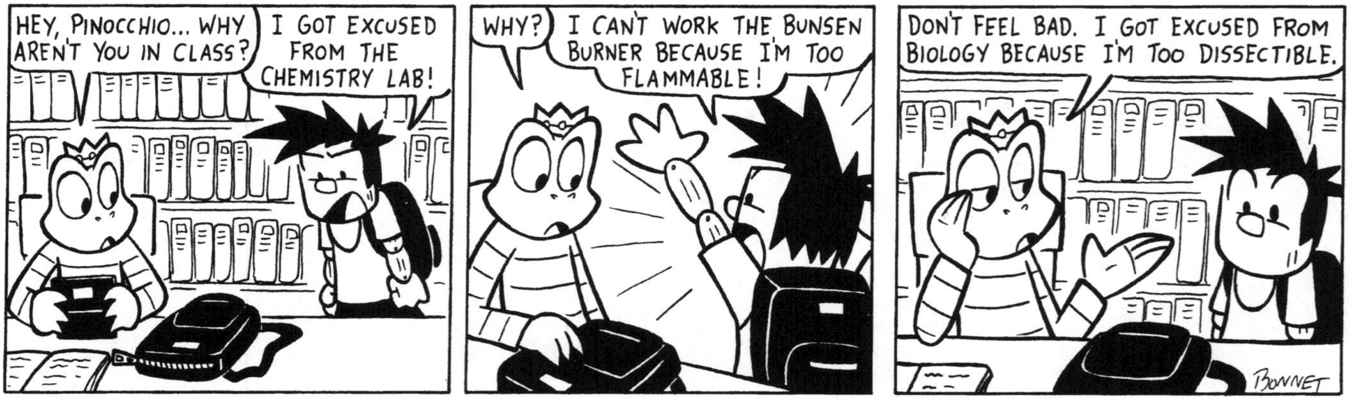
HEY, PINOCCHIO... WHY AREN'T YOU IN CLASS?
I GOT EXCUSED FROM THE CHEMISTRY LAB!
WHY?
I CAN'T WORK THE BUNSEN BURNER BECAUSE I'M TOO FLAMMABLE!
DON'T FEEL BAD. I GOT EXCUSED FROM BIOLOGY BECAUSE I'M TOO DISSECTIBLE.
BONNET

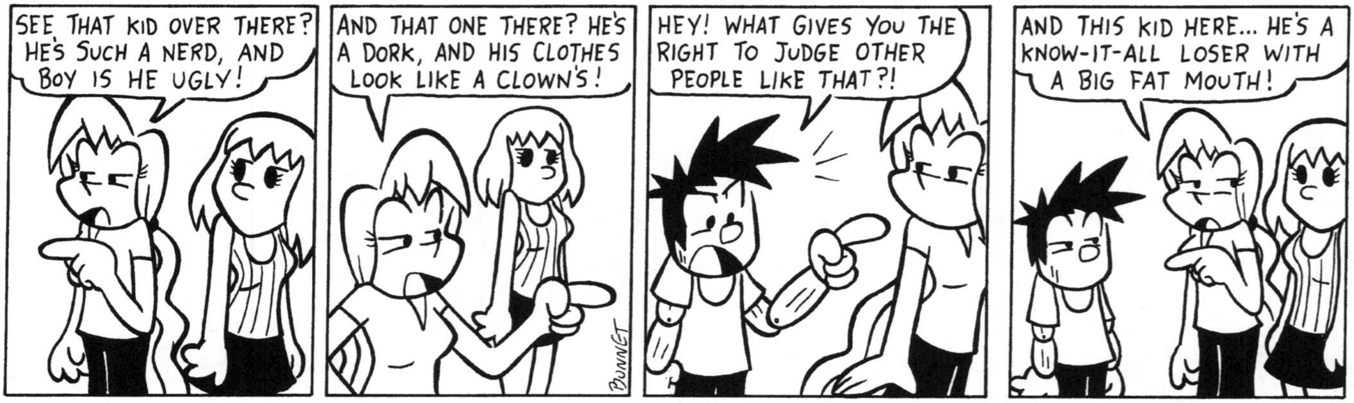
SEE THAT KID OVER THERE? HE'S SUCH A NERD, AND BOY IS HE UGLY!
AND THAT ONE THERE? HE'S A DORK, AND HIS CLOTHES LOOK LIKE A CLOWN'S!
BONNET
HEY! WHAT GIVES YOU THE RIGHT TO JUDGE OTHER PEOPLE LIKE THAT?!
AND THIS KID HERE... HE'S A KNOW-IT-ALL LOSER WITH A BIG FAT MOUTH!

Sept. 18, 21, 23, 2009

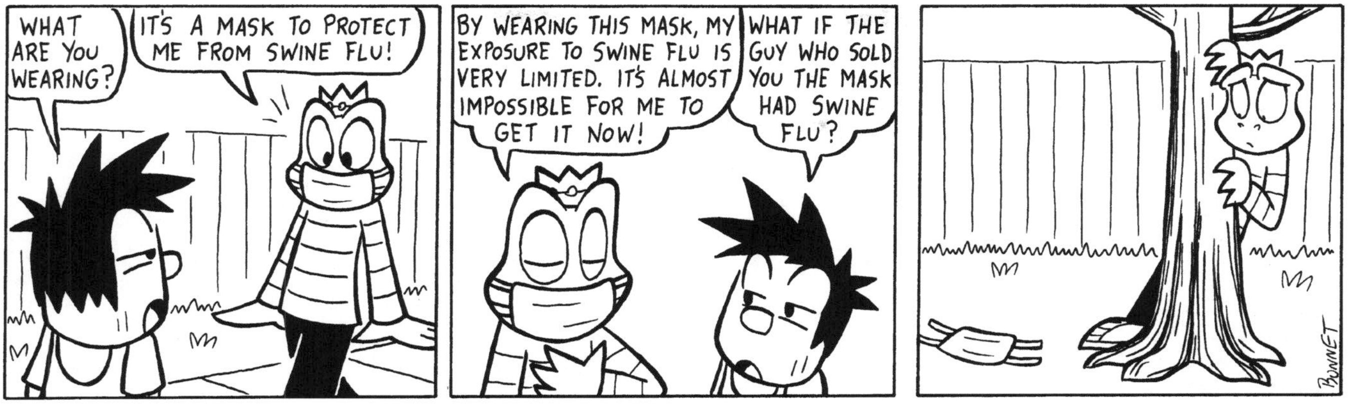
WHAT ARE YOU WEARING?
IT'S A MASK TO PROTECT ME FROM SWINE FLU!
BY WEARING THIS MASK, MY EXPOSURE TO SWINE FLU IS VERY LIMITED. IT'S ALMOST IMPOSSIBLE FOR ME TO GET IT NOW!
WHAT IF THE GUY WHO SOLD YOU THE MASK HAD SWINE FLU?
BONNET

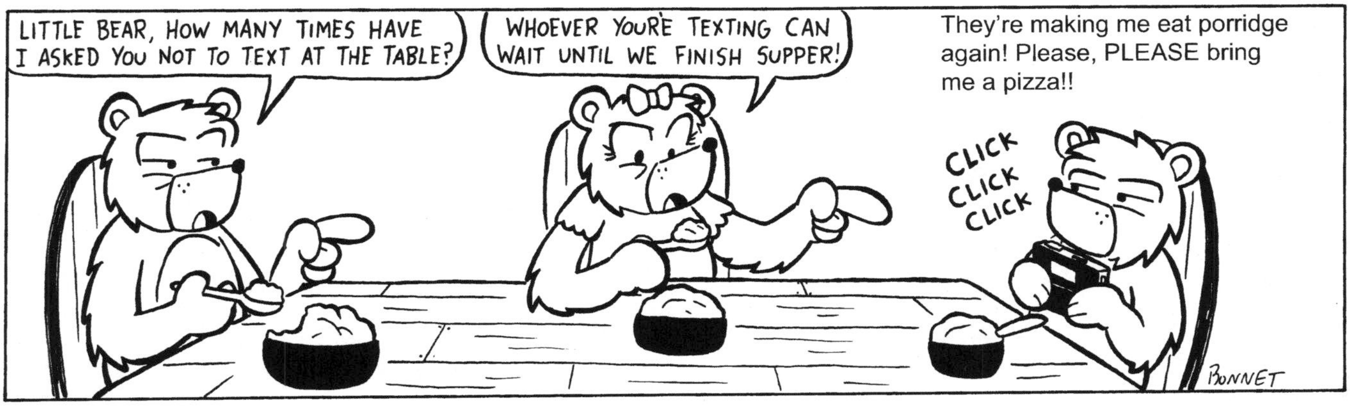
LITTLE BEAR, HOW MANY TIMES HAVE I ASKED YOU NOT TO TEXT AT THE TABLE?
WHOEVER YOU'RE TEXTING CAN WAIT UNTIL WE FINISH SUPPER!
They're making me eat porridge again! Please, PLEASE bring me a pizza!!
CLICK CLICK CLICK
BONNET

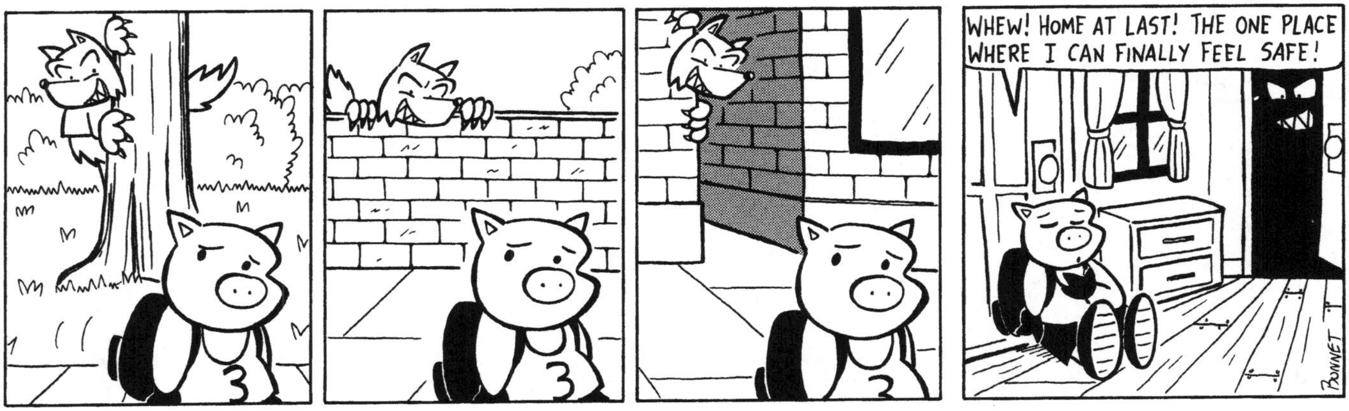
WHEW! HOME AT LAST! THE ONE PLACE WHERE I CAN FINALLY FEEL SAFE!
BONNET

Sept. 25, 28, 30, 2009

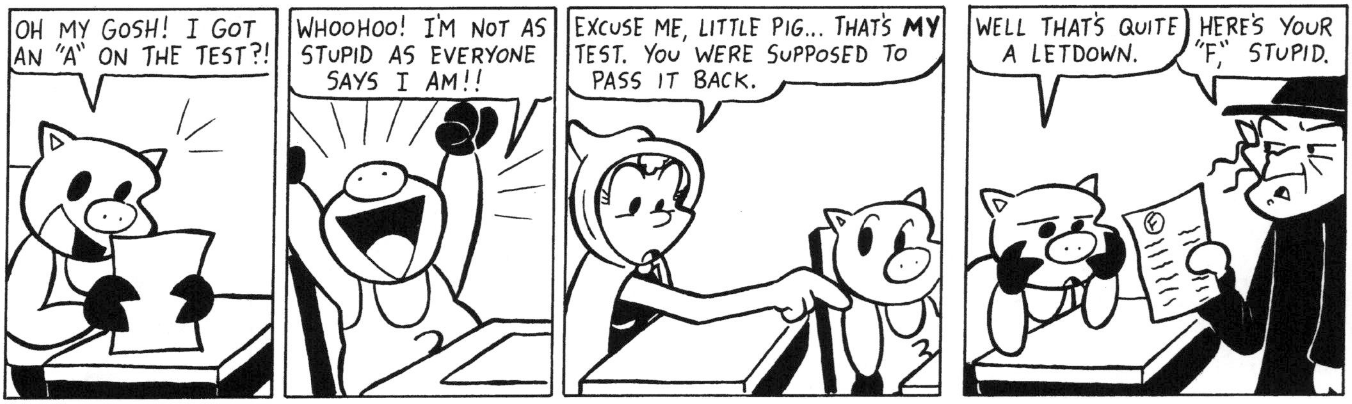
OH MY GOSH! I GOT AN "A" ON THE TEST?!
WHOOHOO! I'M NOT AS STUPID AS EVERYONE SAYS I AM!!
EXCUSE ME, LITTLE PIG... THAT'S **MY** TEST. YOU WERE SUPPOSED TO PASS IT BACK.
WELL THAT'S QUITE A LETDOWN.
HERE'S YOUR "F," STUPID.

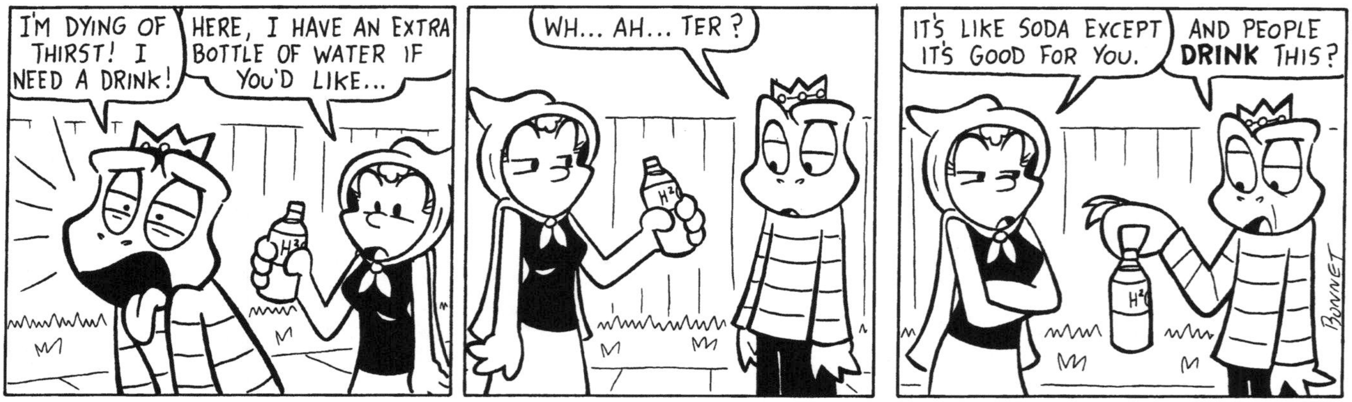
I'M DYING OF THIRST! I NEED A DRINK!
HERE, I HAVE AN EXTRA BOTTLE OF WATER IF YOU'D LIKE...
WH... AH... TER?
IT'S LIKE SODA EXCEPT IT'S GOOD FOR YOU.
AND PEOPLE **DRINK** THIS?
BONNET

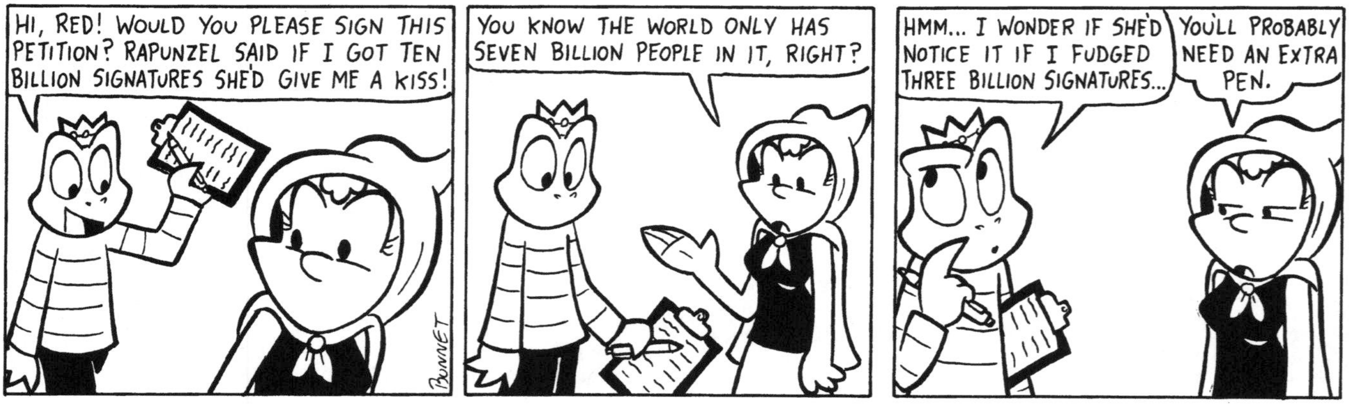
HI, RED! WOULD YOU PLEASE SIGN THIS PETITION? RAPUNZEL SAID IF I GOT TEN BILLION SIGNATURES SHE'D GIVE ME A KISS!
BONNET
YOU KNOW THE WORLD ONLY HAS SEVEN BILLION PEOPLE IN IT, RIGHT?
HMM... I WONDER IF SHE'D NOTICE IT IF I FUDGED THREE BILLION SIGNATURES...
YOU'LL PROBABLY NEED AN EXTRA PEN.

Oct. 2, 5, 7, 2009

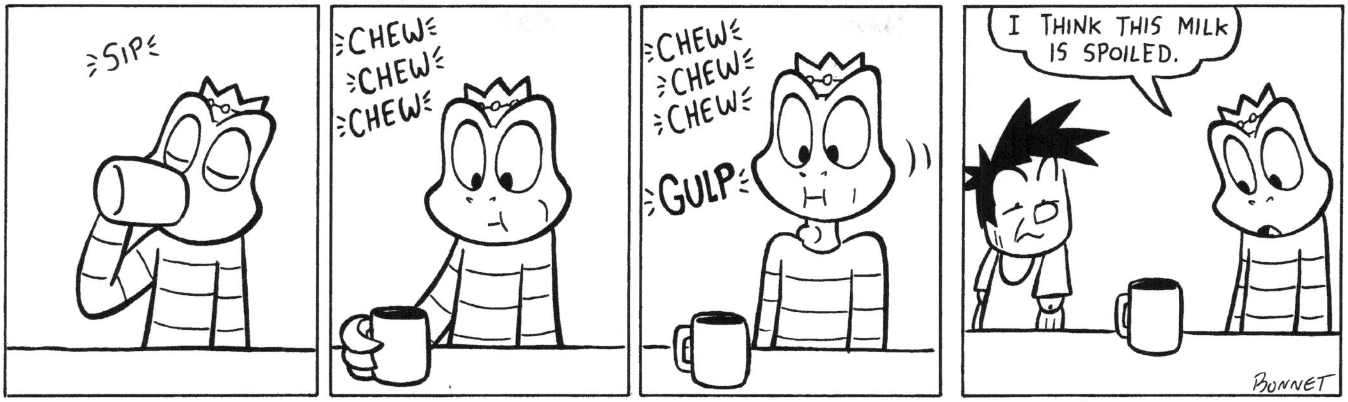
SIP
CHEW CHEW CHEW
CHEW CHEW CHEW
GULP
I THINK THIS MILK IS SPOILED.
BONNET

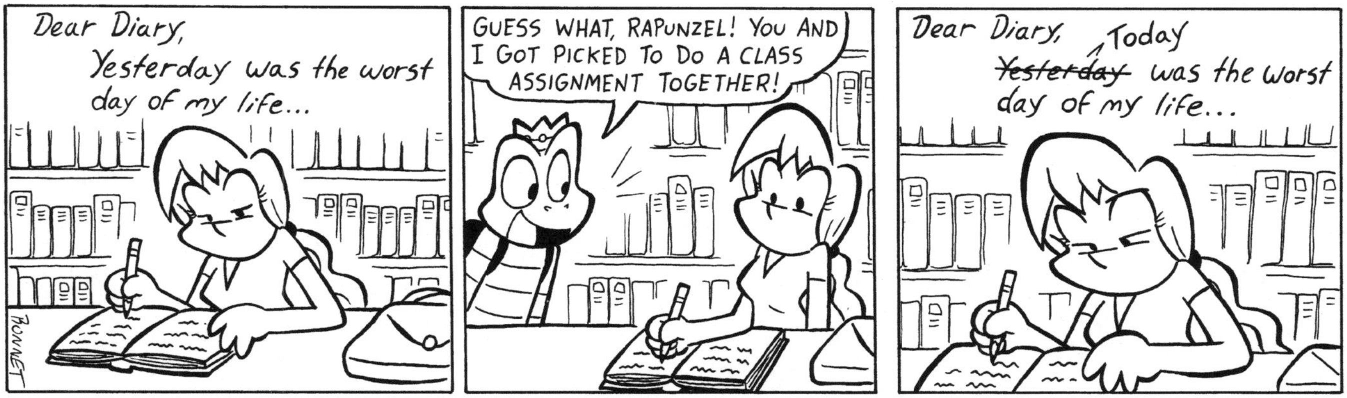
Dear Diary,
Yesterday was the worst day of my life...
BONNET
GUESS WHAT, RAPUNZEL! YOU AND I GOT PICKED TO DO A CLASS ASSIGNMENT TOGETHER!
Dear Diary,
~~Yesterday~~ Today was the worst day of my life...

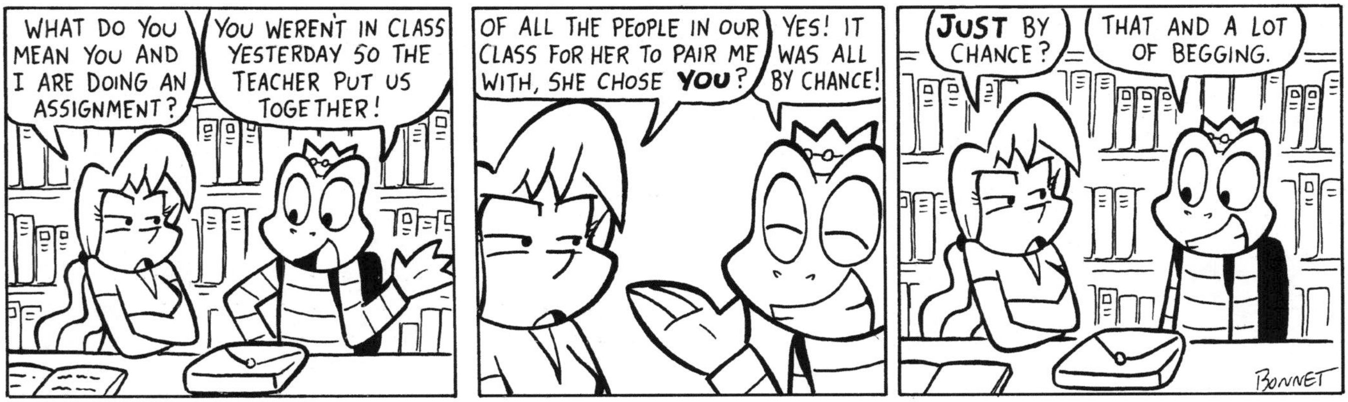
WHAT DO YOU MEAN YOU AND I ARE DOING AN ASSIGNMENT?
YOU WEREN'T IN CLASS YESTERDAY SO THE TEACHER PUT US TOGETHER!
OF ALL THE PEOPLE IN OUR CLASS FOR HER TO PAIR ME WITH, SHE CHOSE **YOU**?
YES! IT WAS ALL BY CHANCE!
JUST BY CHANCE?
THAT AND A LOT OF BEGGING.
BONNET

Oct. 9, 12, 14, 2009

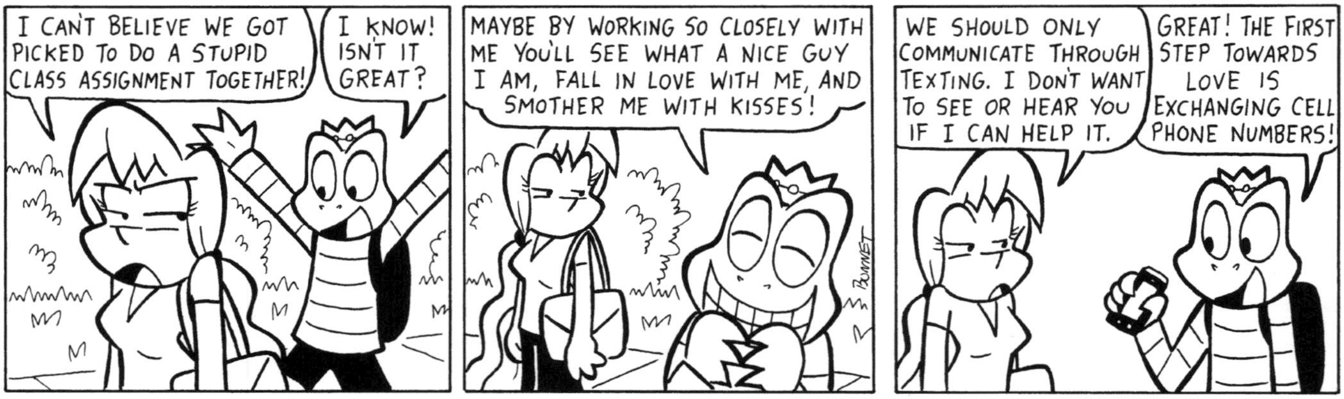
I CAN'T BELIEVE WE GOT PICKED TO DO A STUPID CLASS ASSIGNMENT TOGETHER!
I KNOW! ISN'T IT GREAT?
MAYBE BY WORKING SO CLOSELY WITH ME YOU'LL SEE WHAT A NICE GUY I AM, FALL IN LOVE WITH ME, AND SMOTHER ME WITH KISSES!
WE SHOULD ONLY COMMUNICATE THROUGH TEXTING. I DON'T WANT TO SEE OR HEAR YOU IF I CAN HELP IT.
GREAT! THE FIRST STEP TOWARDS LOVE IS EXCHANGING CELL PHONE NUMBERS!

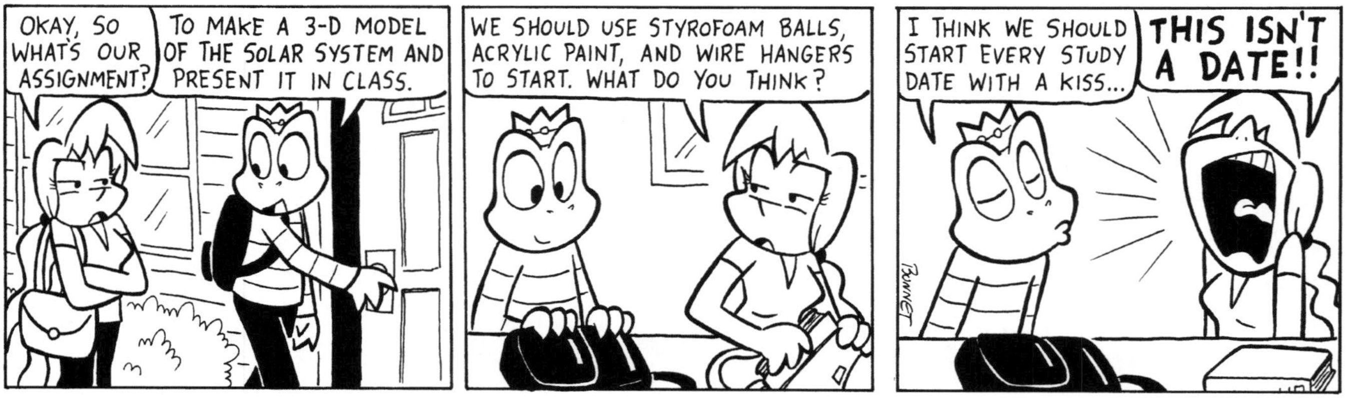
OKAY, SO WHAT'S OUR ASSIGNMENT?
TO MAKE A 3-D MODEL OF THE SOLAR SYSTEM AND PRESENT IT IN CLASS.
WE SHOULD USE STYROFOAM BALLS, ACRYLIC PAINT, AND WIRE HANGERS TO START. WHAT DO YOU THINK?
I THINK WE SHOULD START EVERY STUDY DATE WITH A KISS...
THIS ISN'T A DATE!!

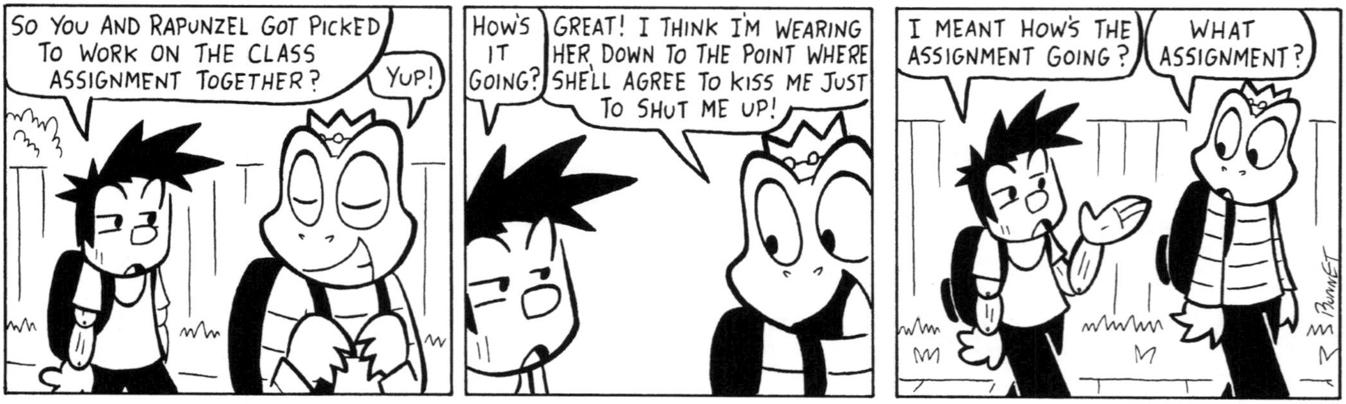
SO YOU AND RAPUNZEL GOT PICKED TO WORK ON THE CLASS ASSIGNMENT TOGETHER?
YUP!
HOW'S IT GOING?
GREAT! I THINK I'M WEARING HER DOWN TO THE POINT WHERE SHE'LL AGREE TO KISS ME JUST TO SHUT ME UP!
I MEANT HOW'S THE ASSIGNMENT GOING?
WHAT ASSIGNMENT?

Oct. 16, 19, 21, 2009

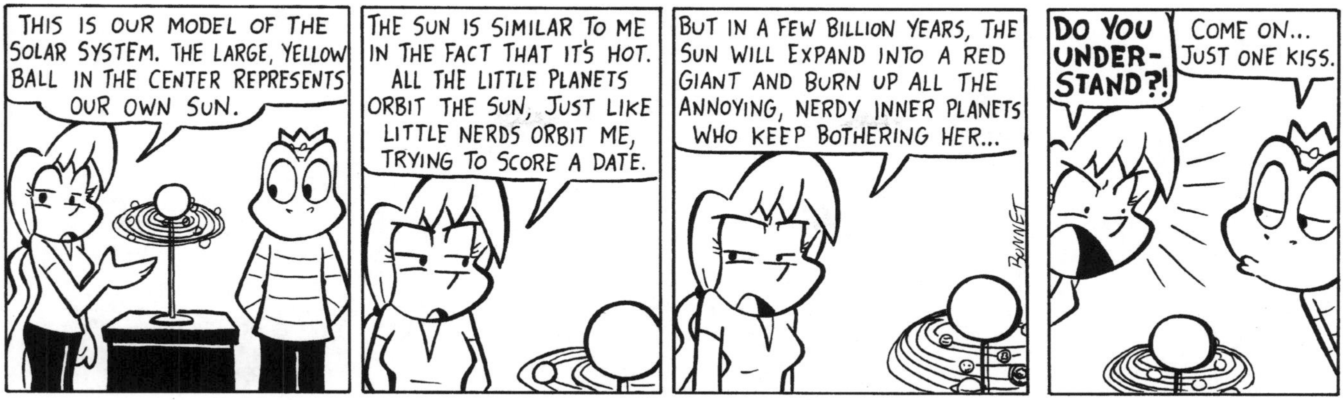
THIS IS OUR MODEL OF THE SOLAR SYSTEM. THE LARGE, YELLOW BALL IN THE CENTER REPRESENTS OUR OWN SUN.
THE SUN IS SIMILAR TO ME IN THE FACT THAT IT'S HOT. ALL THE LITTLE PLANETS ORBIT THE SUN, JUST LIKE LITTLE NERDS ORBIT ME, TRYING TO SCORE A DATE.
BUT IN A FEW BILLION YEARS, THE SUN WILL EXPAND INTO A RED GIANT AND BURN UP ALL THE ANNOYING, NERDY INNER PLANETS WHO KEEP BOTHERING HER...
BONNET
DO YOU UNDER-STAND?!
COME ON... JUST ONE KISS.

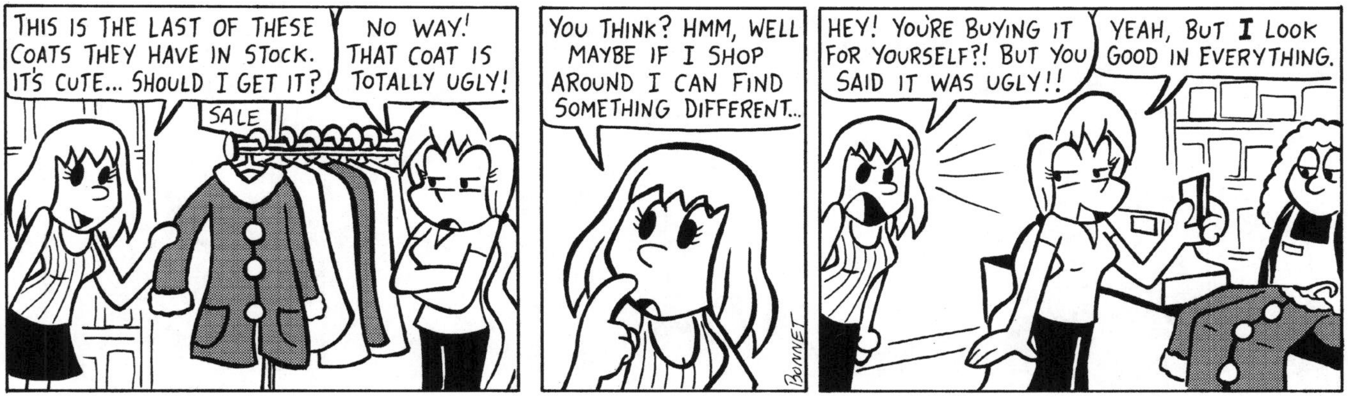
THIS IS THE LAST OF THESE COATS THEY HAVE IN STOCK. IT'S CUTE... SHOULD I GET IT?
NO WAY! THAT COAT IS TOTALLY UGLY!
SALE
YOU THINK? HMM, WELL MAYBE IF I SHOP AROUND I CAN FIND SOMETHING DIFFERENT...
BONNET
HEY! YOU'RE BUYING IT FOR YOURSELF?! BUT YOU SAID IT WAS UGLY!!
YEAH, BUT I LOOK GOOD IN EVERYTHING.

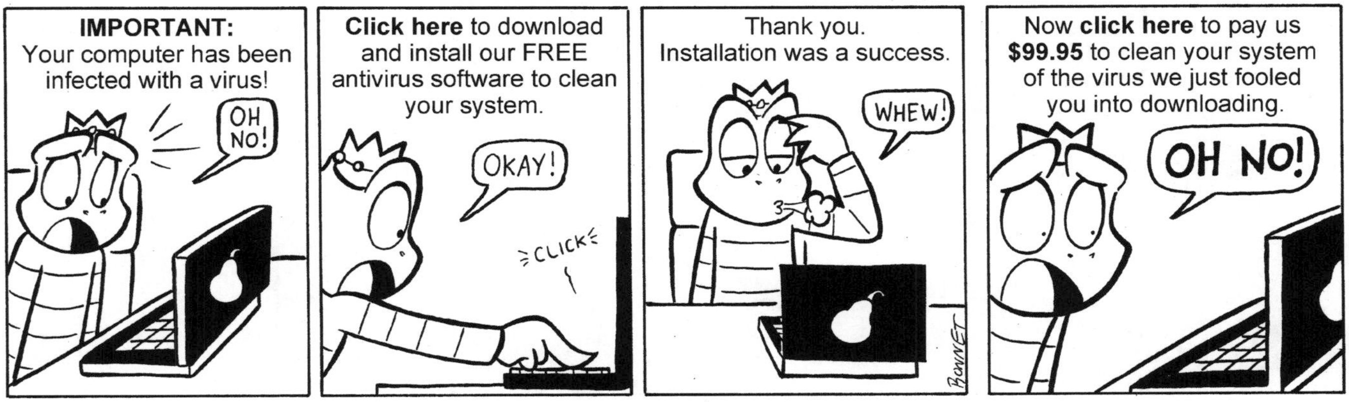
IMPORTANT: Your computer has been infected with a virus!
OH NO!
Click here to download and install our FREE antivirus software to clean your system.
OKAY!
CLICK
Thank you. Installation was a success.
WHEW!
BONNET
Now click here to pay us $99.95 to clean your system of the virus we just fooled you into downloading.
OH NO!

Oct. 23, 26, 28, 2009

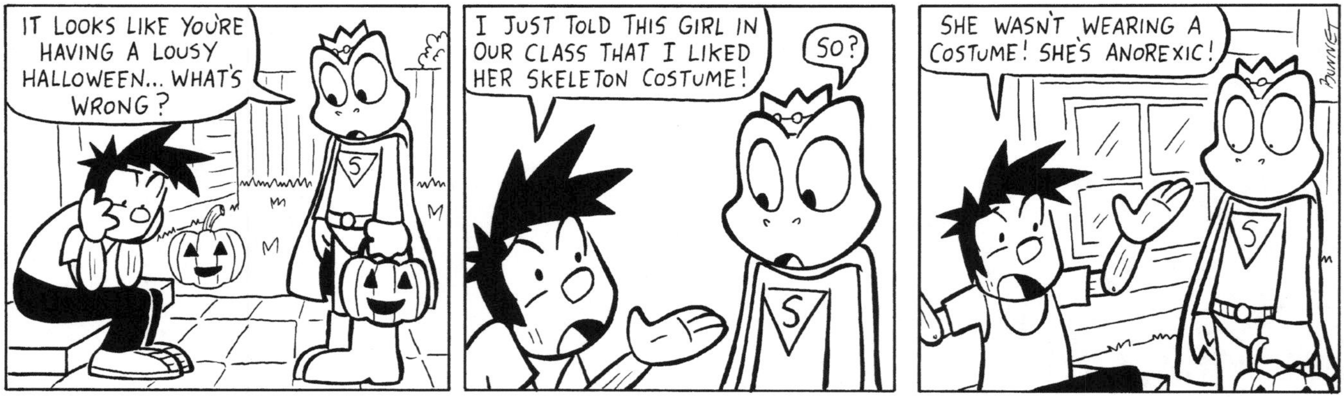

IT LOOKS LIKE YOU'RE HAVING A LOUSY HALLOWEEN... WHAT'S WRONG?
I JUST TOLD THIS GIRL IN OUR CLASS THAT I LIKED HER SKELETON COSTUME!
SO?
SHE WASN'T WEARING A COSTUME! SHE'S ANOREXIC!
BONNET

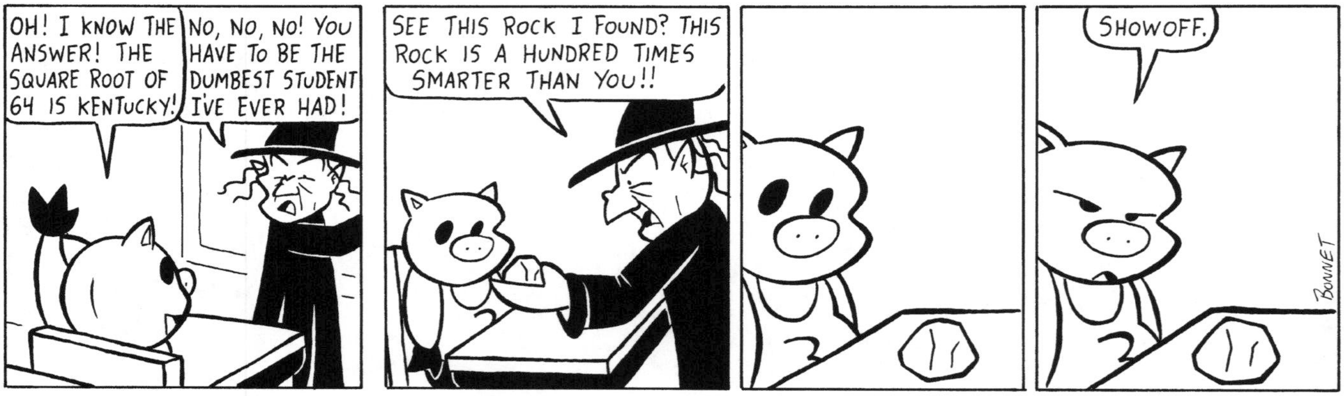

OH! I KNOW THE ANSWER! THE SQUARE ROOT OF 64 IS KENTUCKY!
NO, NO, NO! YOU HAVE TO BE THE DUMBEST STUDENT I'VE EVER HAD!
SEE THIS ROCK I FOUND? THIS ROCK IS A HUNDRED TIMES SMARTER THAN YOU!!
SHOWOFF.
BONNET

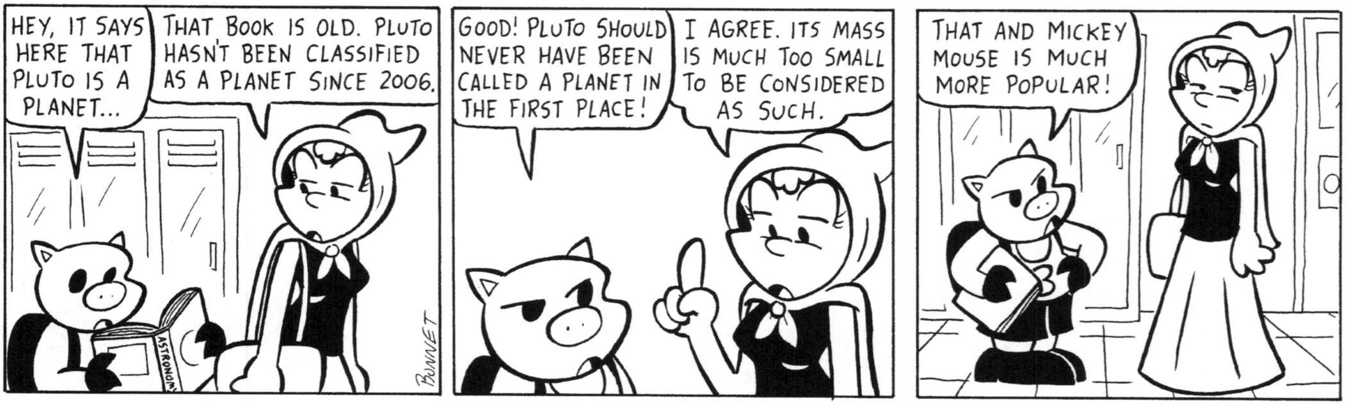

HEY, IT SAYS HERE THAT PLUTO IS A PLANET...
THAT BOOK IS OLD. PLUTO HASN'T BEEN CLASSIFIED AS A PLANET SINCE 2006.
ASTRONOMY
BONNET
GOOD! PLUTO SHOULD NEVER HAVE BEEN CALLED A PLANET IN THE FIRST PLACE!
I AGREE. ITS MASS IS MUCH TOO SMALL TO BE CONSIDERED AS SUCH.
THAT AND MICKEY MOUSE IS MUCH MORE POPULAR!

Oct. 30, Nov. 2, 4, 2009

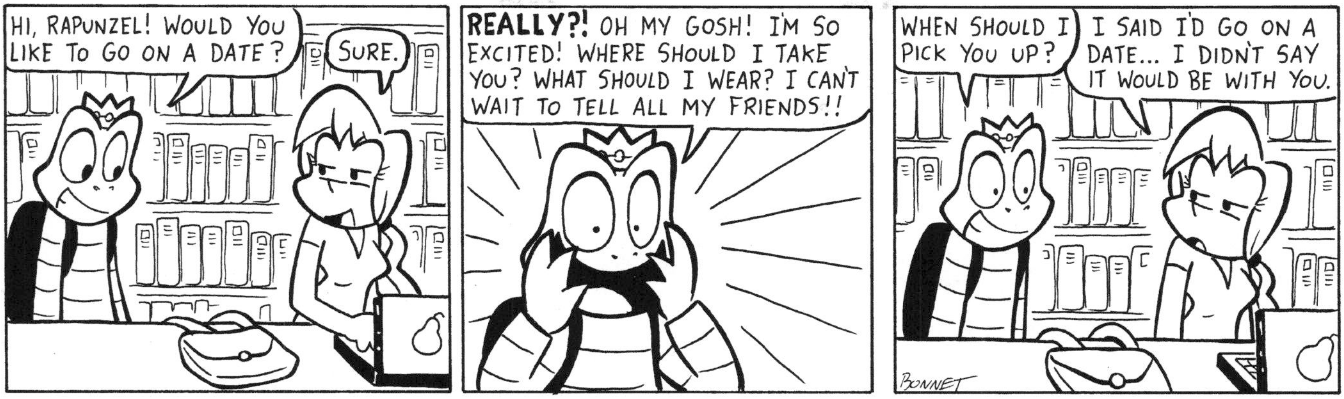
HI, RAPUNZEL! WOULD YOU LIKE TO GO ON A DATE?
SURE.
REALLY?! OH MY GOSH! I'M SO EXCITED! WHERE SHOULD I TAKE YOU? WHAT SHOULD I WEAR? I CAN'T WAIT TO TELL ALL MY FRIENDS!!
WHEN SHOULD I PICK YOU UP?
I SAID I'D GO ON A DATE... I DIDN'T SAY IT WOULD BE WITH YOU.
BONNET

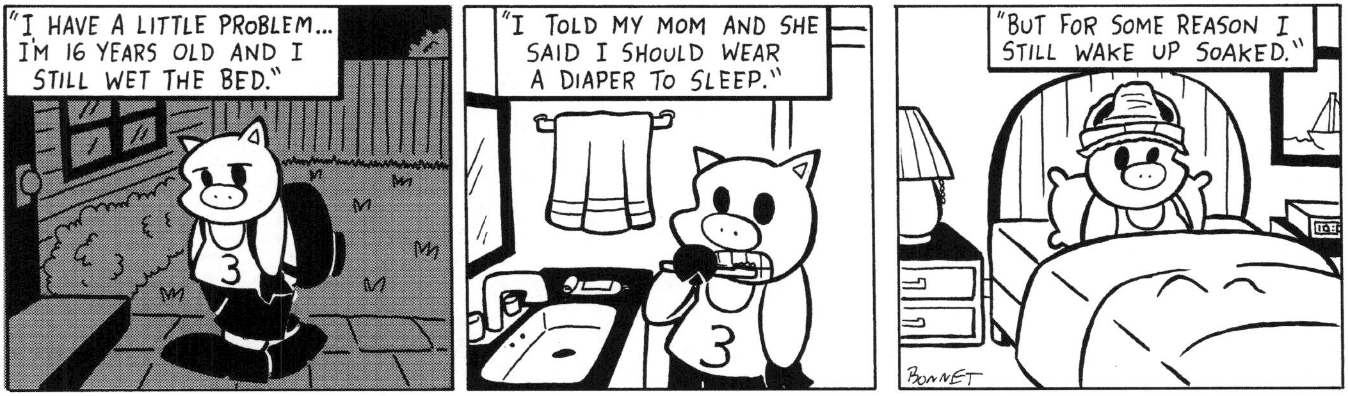
"I HAVE A LITTLE PROBLEM... I'M 16 YEARS OLD AND I STILL WET THE BED."
"I TOLD MY MOM AND SHE SAID I SHOULD WEAR A DIAPER TO SLEEP."
"BUT FOR SOME REASON I STILL WAKE UP SOAKED."
BONNET

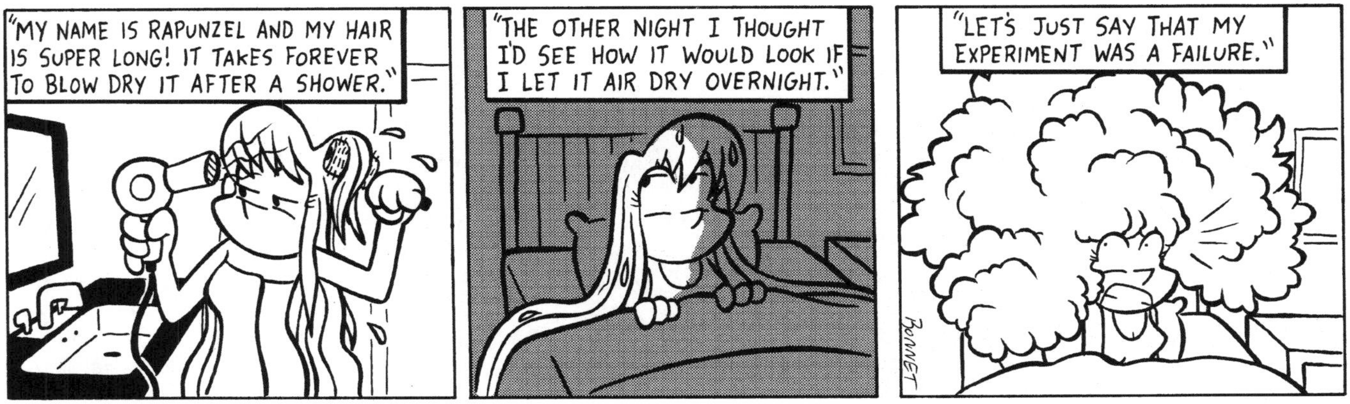
"MY NAME IS RAPUNZEL AND MY HAIR IS SUPER LONG! IT TAKES FOREVER TO BLOW DRY IT AFTER A SHOWER."
"THE OTHER NIGHT I THOUGHT I'D SEE HOW IT WOULD LOOK IF I LET IT AIR DRY OVERNIGHT."
"LET'S JUST SAY THAT MY EXPERIMENT WAS A FAILURE."
BONNET

Nov. 6, 9, 11, 2009

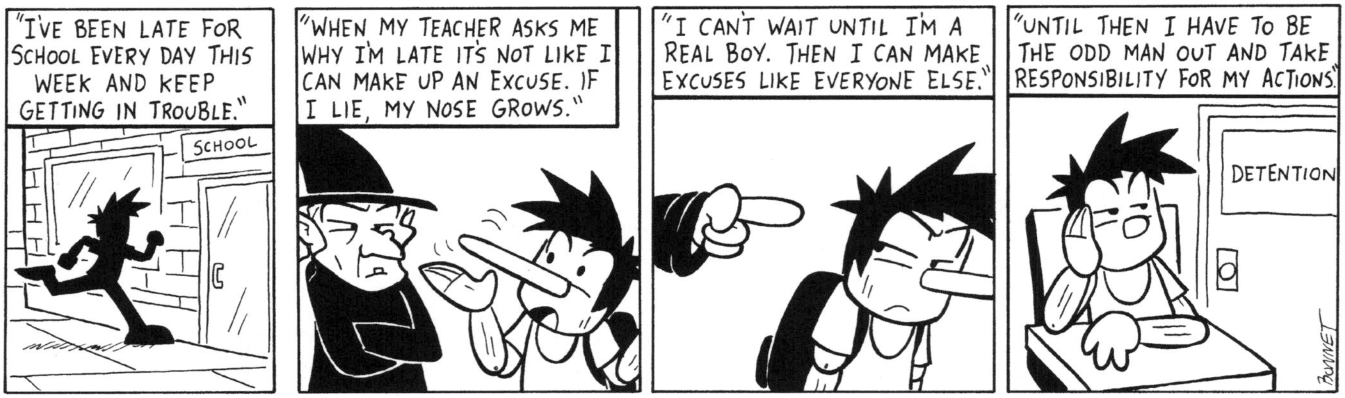
"I'VE BEEN LATE FOR SCHOOL EVERY DAY THIS WEEK AND KEEP GETTING IN TROUBLE."
SCHOOL
"WHEN MY TEACHER ASKS ME WHY I'M LATE IT'S NOT LIKE I CAN MAKE UP AN EXCUSE. IF I LIE, MY NOSE GROWS."
"I CAN'T WAIT UNTIL I'M A REAL BOY. THEN I CAN MAKE EXCUSES LIKE EVERYONE ELSE."
"UNTIL THEN I HAVE TO BE THE ODD MAN OUT AND TAKE RESPONSIBILITY FOR MY ACTIONS."
DETENTION
BONNET

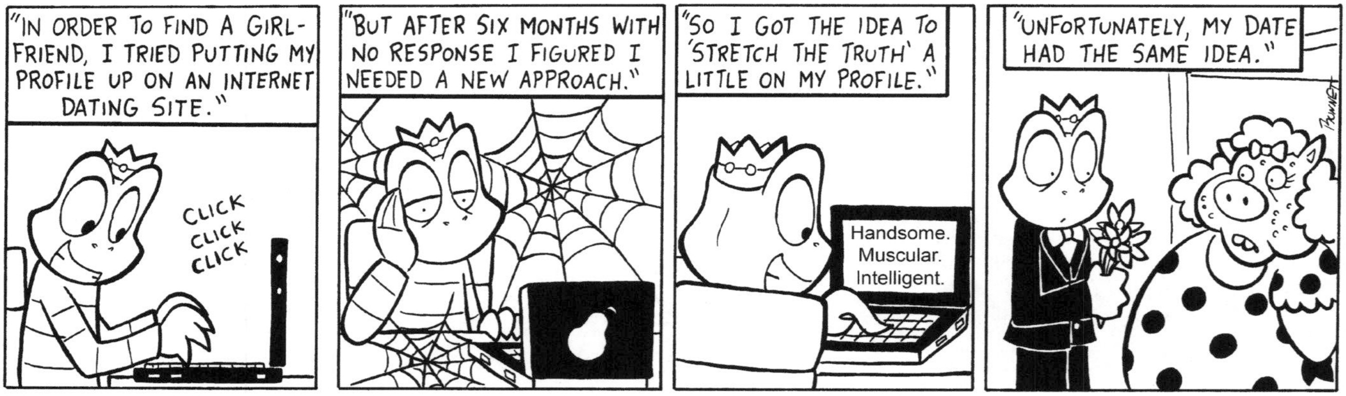
"IN ORDER TO FIND A GIRL-FRIEND, I TRIED PUTTING MY PROFILE UP ON AN INTERNET DATING SITE."
CLICK CLICK CLICK
"BUT AFTER SIX MONTHS WITH NO RESPONSE I FIGURED I NEEDED A NEW APPROACH."
"SO I GOT THE IDEA TO 'STRETCH THE TRUTH' A LITTLE ON MY PROFILE."
Handsome. Muscular. Intelligent.
"UNFORTUNATELY, MY DATE HAD THE SAME IDEA."
BONNET

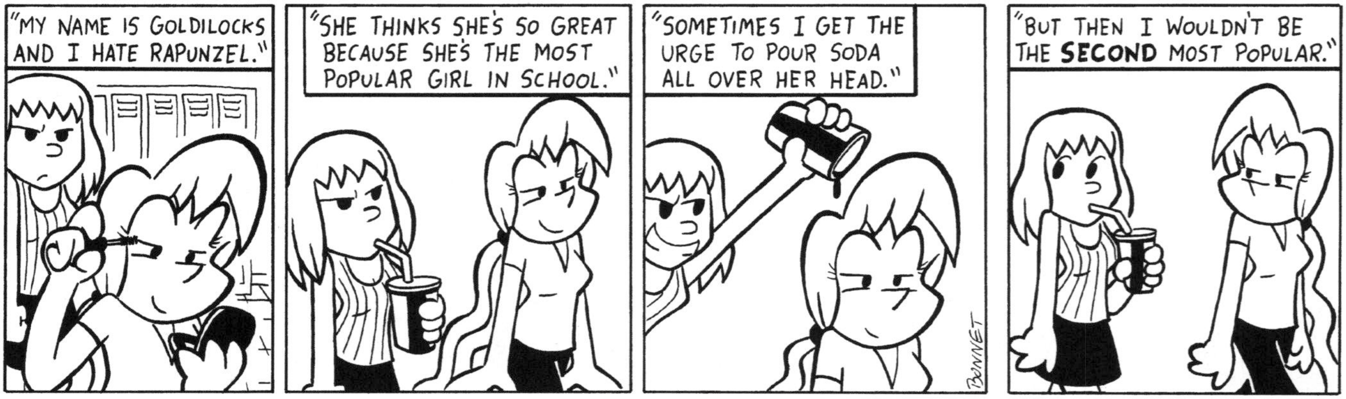
"MY NAME IS GOLDILOCKS AND I HATE RAPUNZEL."
"SHE THINKS SHE'S SO GREAT BECAUSE SHE'S THE MOST POPULAR GIRL IN SCHOOL."
"SOMETIMES I GET THE URGE TO POUR SODA ALL OVER HER HEAD."
BONNET
"BUT THEN I WOULDN'T BE THE **SECOND** MOST POPULAR."

Nov. 13, 16, 18, 2009

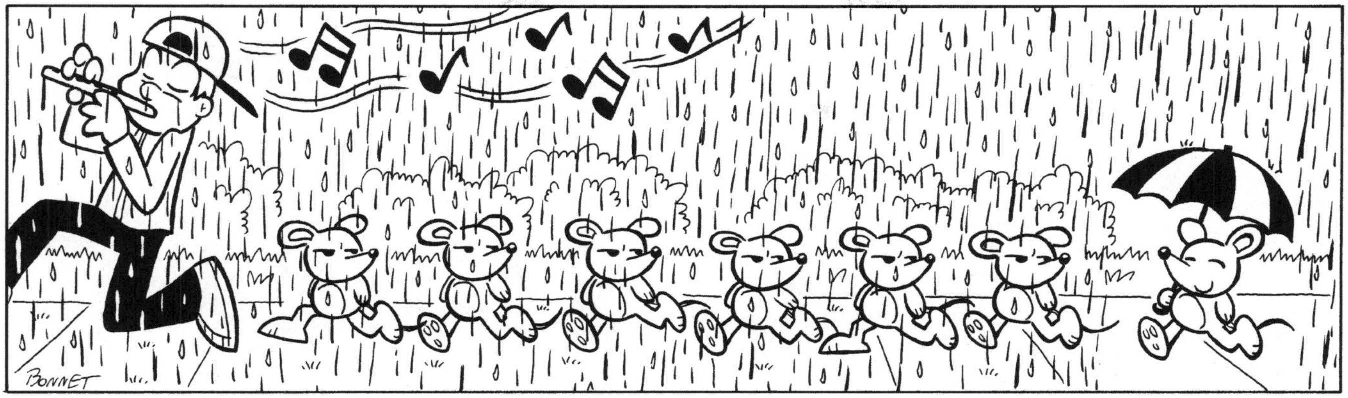
BONNET

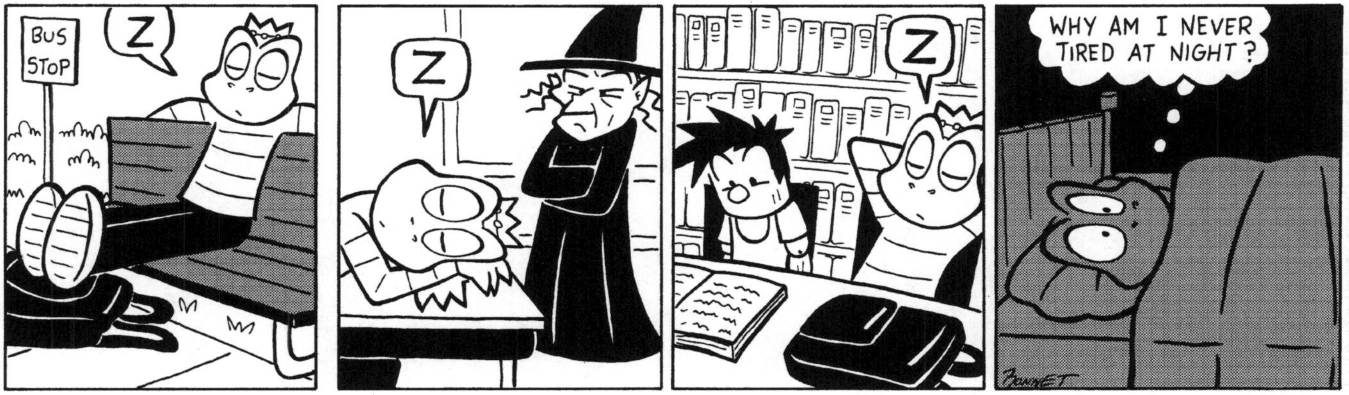
BUS STOP
Z
Z
Z
WHY AM I NEVER TIRED AT NIGHT?
BONNET

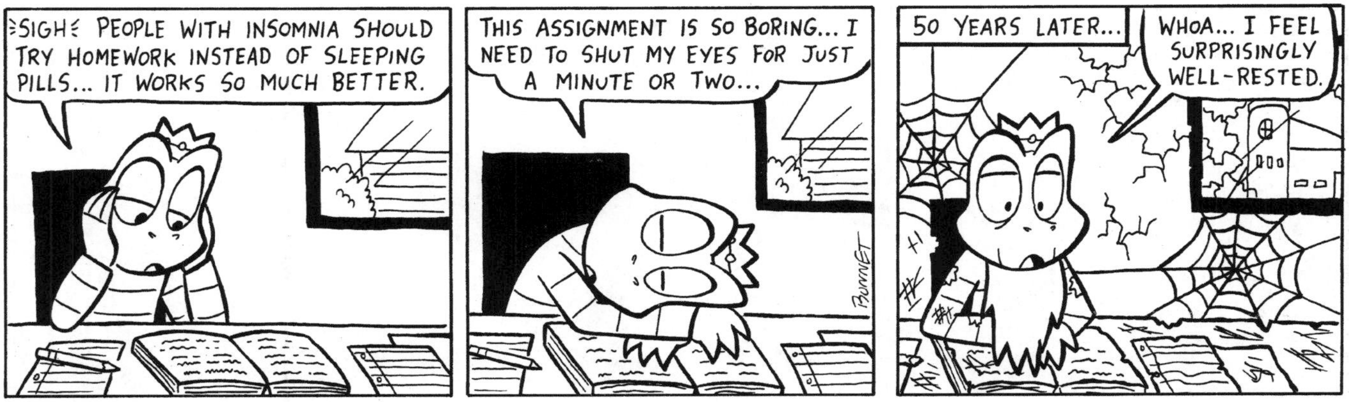
≷SIGH≷ PEOPLE WITH INSOMNIA SHOULD TRY HOMEWORK INSTEAD OF SLEEPING PILLS... IT WORKS SO MUCH BETTER.
THIS ASSIGNMENT IS SO BORING... I NEED TO SHUT MY EYES FOR JUST A MINUTE OR TWO...
BONNET
50 YEARS LATER...
WHOA... I FEEL SURPRISINGLY WELL-RESTED.

Nov. 20, 23, 25, 2009

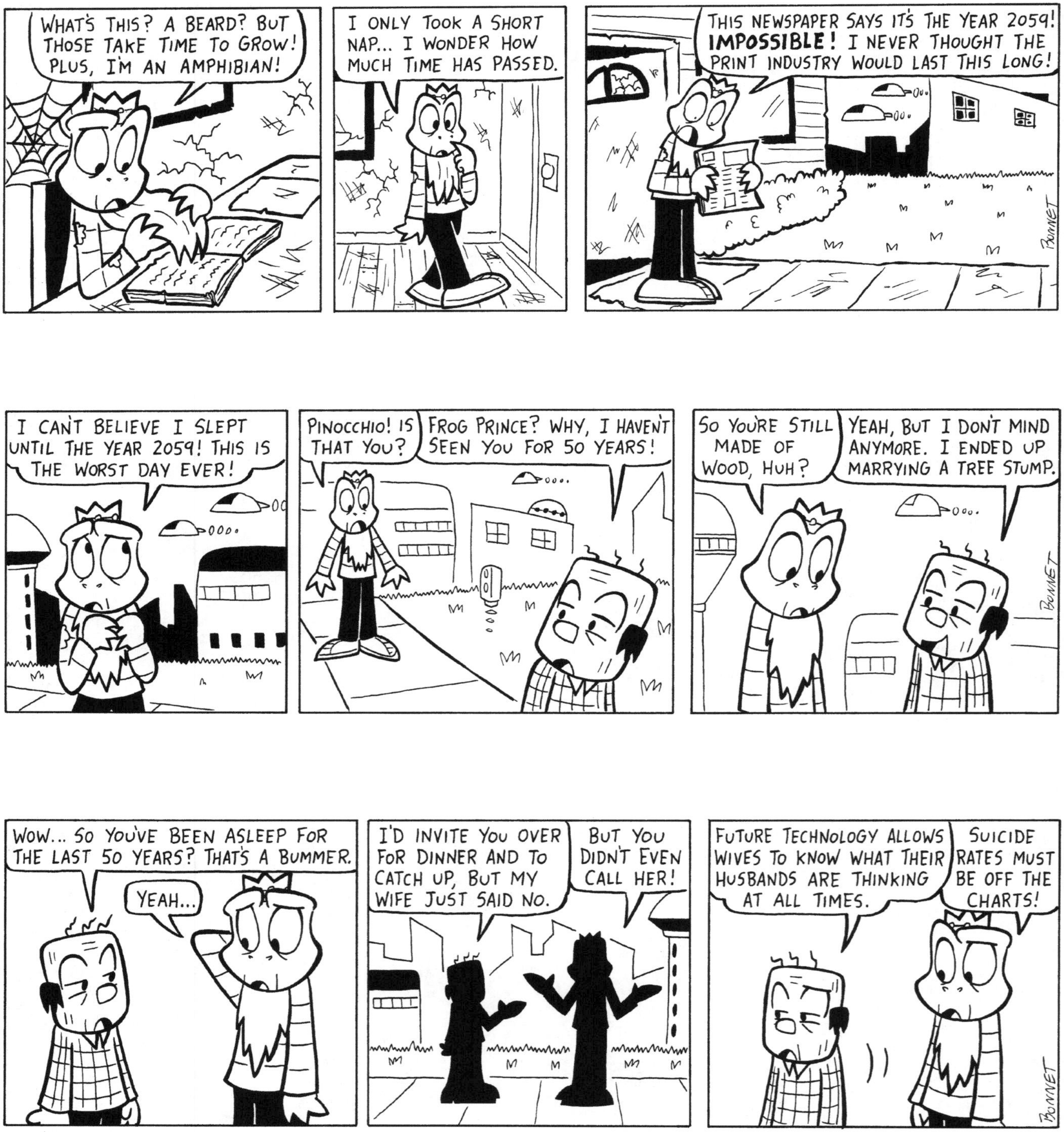
WHAT'S THIS? A BEARD? BUT THOSE TAKE TIME TO GROW! PLUS, I'M AN AMPHIBIAN!
I ONLY TOOK A SHORT NAP... I WONDER HOW MUCH TIME HAS PASSED.
THIS NEWSPAPER SAYS IT'S THE YEAR 2059! IMPOSSIBLE! I NEVER THOUGHT THE PRINT INDUSTRY WOULD LAST THIS LONG!
BONNET
I CAN'T BELIEVE I SLEPT UNTIL THE YEAR 2059! THIS IS THE WORST DAY EVER!
PINOCCHIO! IS THAT YOU?
FROG PRINCE? WHY, I HAVEN'T SEEN YOU FOR 50 YEARS!
SO YOU'RE STILL MADE OF WOOD, HUH?
YEAH, BUT I DON'T MIND ANYMORE. I ENDED UP MARRYING A TREE STUMP.
BONNET
WOW... SO YOU'VE BEEN ASLEEP FOR THE LAST 50 YEARS? THAT'S A BUMMER.
YEAH...
I'D INVITE YOU OVER FOR DINNER AND TO CATCH UP, BUT MY WIFE JUST SAID NO.
BUT YOU DIDN'T EVEN CALL HER!
FUTURE TECHNOLOGY ALLOWS WIVES TO KNOW WHAT THEIR HUSBANDS ARE THINKING AT ALL TIMES.
SUICIDE RATES MUST BE OFF THE CHARTS!
BONNET

Nov. 27, 30, Dec.2, 2009

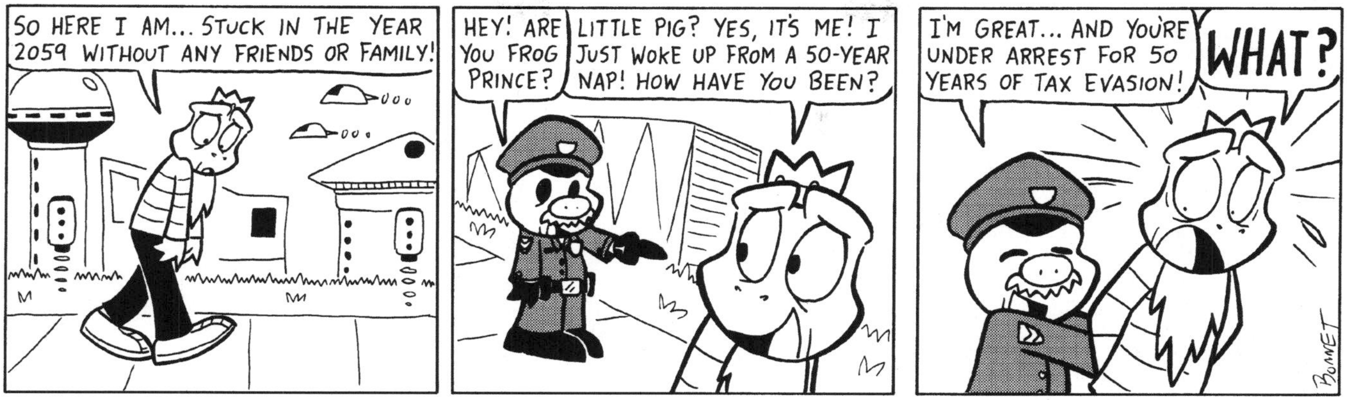
SO HERE I AM... STUCK IN THE YEAR 2059 WITHOUT ANY FRIENDS OR FAMILY!
HEY! ARE YOU FROG PRINCE?
LITTLE PIG? YES, IT'S ME! I JUST WOKE UP FROM A 50-YEAR NAP! HOW HAVE YOU BEEN?
I'M GREAT... AND YOU'RE UNDER ARREST FOR 50 YEARS OF TAX EVASION!
WHAT?
BONNET

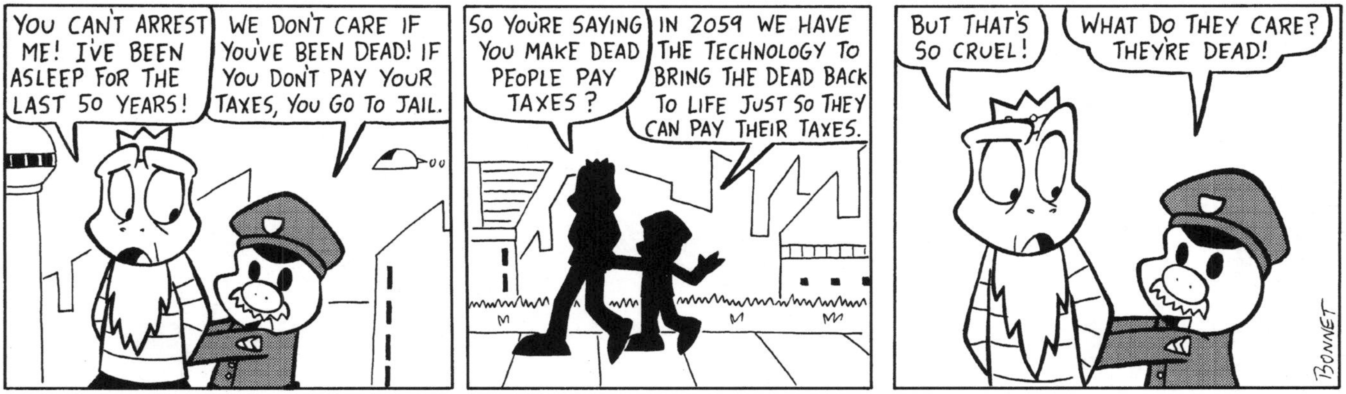
YOU CAN'T ARREST ME! I'VE BEEN ASLEEP FOR THE LAST 50 YEARS!
WE DON'T CARE IF YOU'VE BEEN DEAD! IF YOU DON'T PAY YOUR TAXES, YOU GO TO JAIL.
SO YOU'RE SAYING YOU MAKE DEAD PEOPLE PAY TAXES?
IN 2059 WE HAVE THE TECHNOLOGY TO BRING THE DEAD BACK TO LIFE JUST SO THEY CAN PAY THEIR TAXES.
BUT THAT'S SO CRUEL!
WHAT DO THEY CARE? THEY'RE DEAD!
BONNET

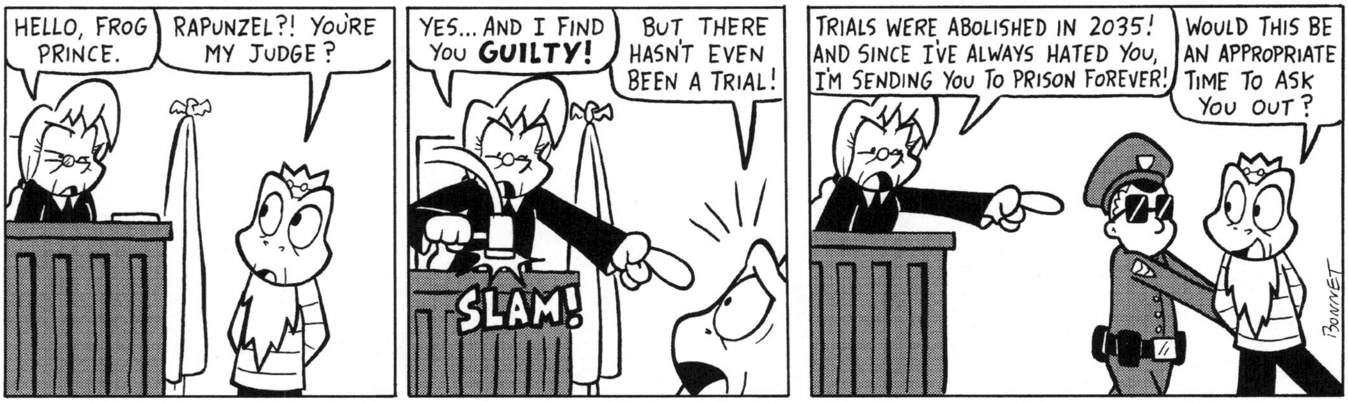
HELLO, FROG PRINCE.
RAPUNZEL?! YOU'RE MY JUDGE?
YES... AND I FIND YOU GUILTY!
BUT THERE HASN'T EVEN BEEN A TRIAL!
SLAM!
TRIALS WERE ABOLISHED IN 2035! AND SINCE I'VE ALWAYS HATED YOU, I'M SENDING YOU TO PRISON FOREVER!
WOULD THIS BE AN APPROPRIATE TIME TO ASK YOU OUT?
BONNET

Dec. 4, 7, 9, 2009

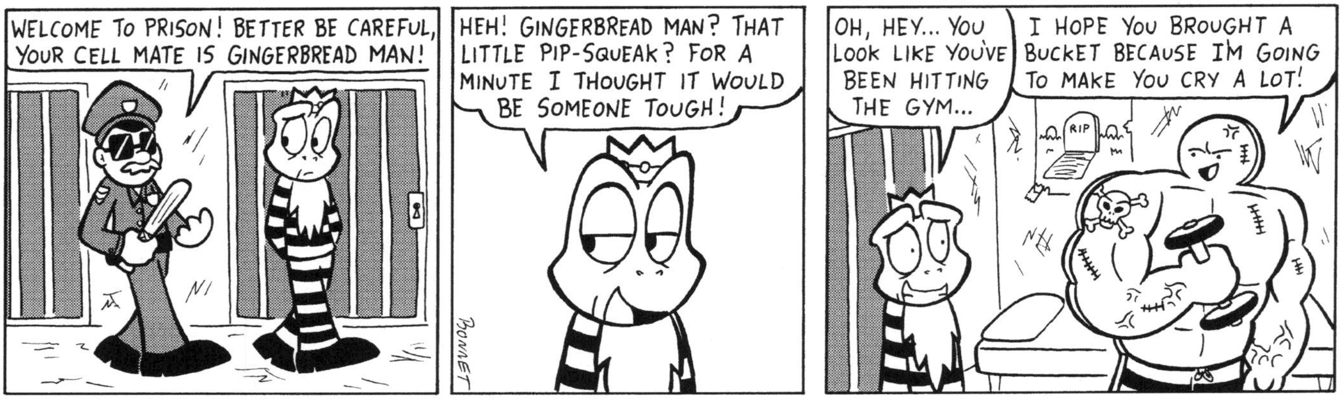
WELCOME TO PRISON! BETTER BE CAREFUL, YOUR CELL MATE IS GINGERBREAD MAN!
HEH! GINGERBREAD MAN? THAT LITTLE PIP-SQUEAK? FOR A MINUTE I THOUGHT IT WOULD BE SOMEONE TOUGH!
BONNET
OH, HEY... YOU LOOK LIKE YOU'VE BEEN HITTING THE GYM...
I HOPE YOU BROUGHT A BUCKET BECAUSE I'M GOING TO MAKE YOU CRY A LOT!
RIP

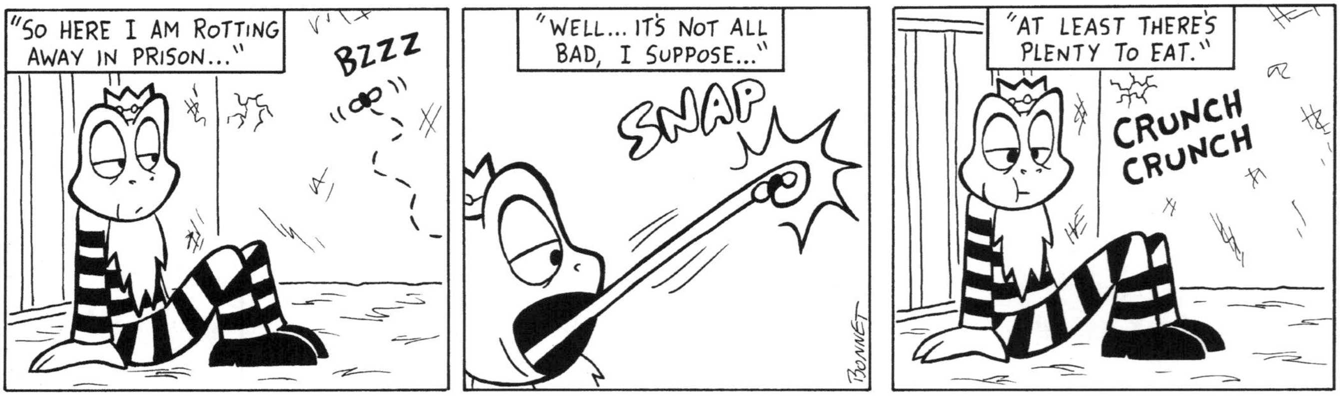
"SO HERE I AM ROTTING AWAY IN PRISON..."
BZZZ
"WELL... IT'S NOT ALL BAD, I SUPPOSE..."
SNAP
BONNET
"AT LEAST THERE'S PLENTY TO EAT."
CRUNCH CRUNCH

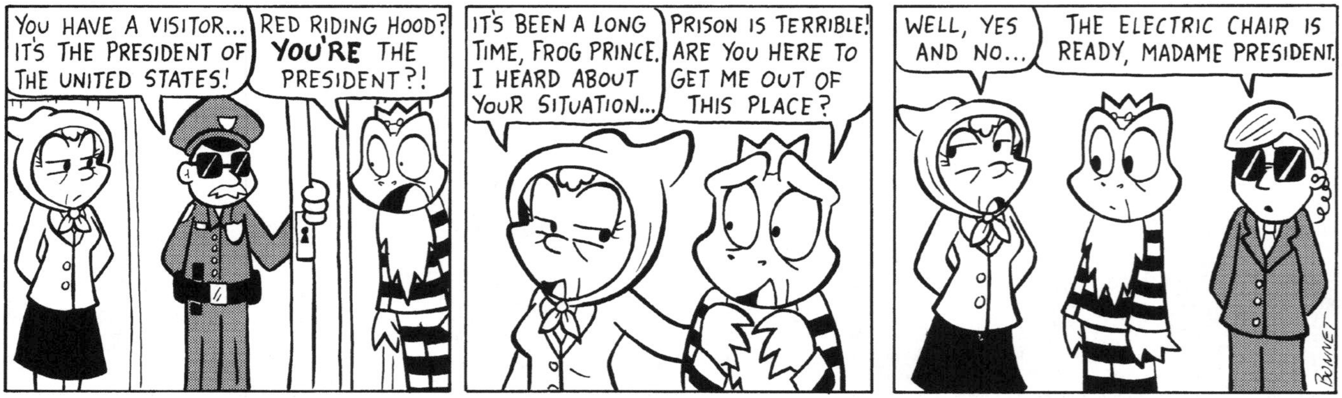
YOU HAVE A VISITOR... IT'S THE PRESIDENT OF THE UNITED STATES!
RED RIDING HOOD? YOU'RE THE PRESIDENT?!
IT'S BEEN A LONG TIME, FROG PRINCE. I HEARD ABOUT YOUR SITUATION...
PRISON IS TERRIBLE! ARE YOU HERE TO GET ME OUT OF THIS PLACE?
WELL, YES AND NO...
THE ELECTRIC CHAIR IS READY, MADAME PRESIDENT.
BONNET

Dec. 11, 14, 16, 2009

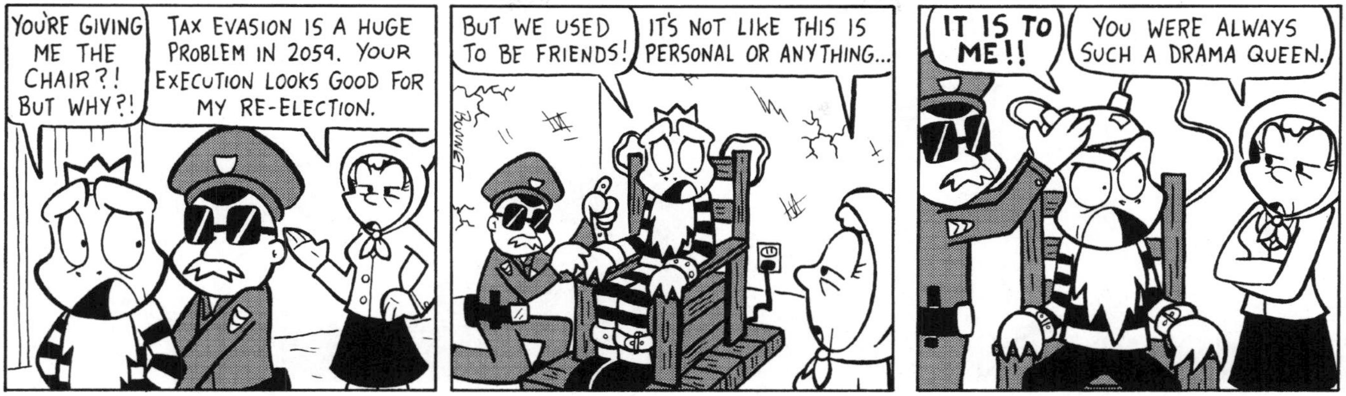
YOU'RE GIVING ME THE CHAIR?! BUT WHY?!
TAX EVASION IS A HUGE PROBLEM IN 2059. YOUR EXECUTION LOOKS GOOD FOR MY RE-ELECTION.
BUT WE USED TO BE FRIENDS!
IT'S NOT LIKE THIS IS PERSONAL OR ANYTHING...
BONNET
IT IS TO ME!!
YOU WERE ALWAYS SUCH A DRAMA QUEEN.

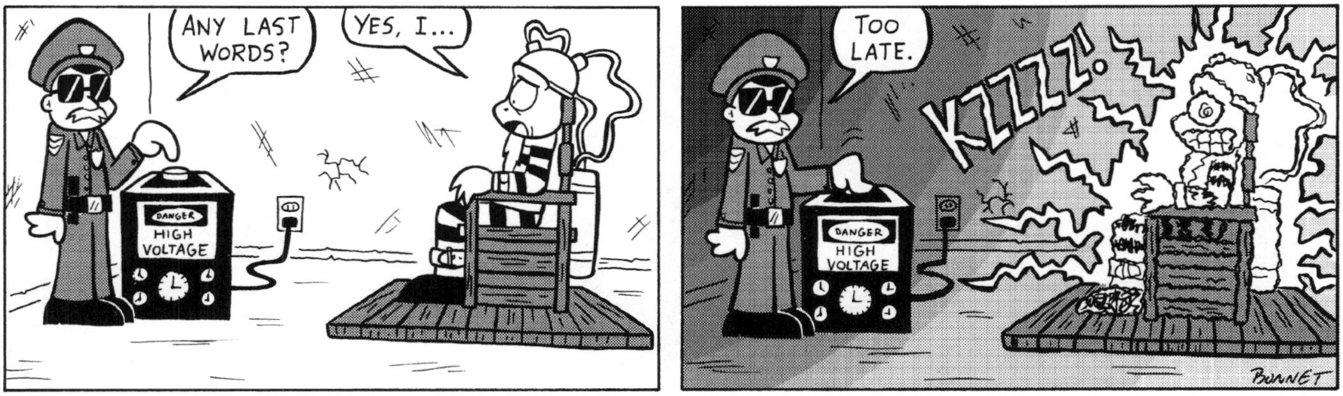
ANY LAST WORDS?
YES, I...
DANGER
HIGH VOLTAGE
TOO LATE.
KZZZZ!
DANGER
HIGH VOLTAGE
BONNET

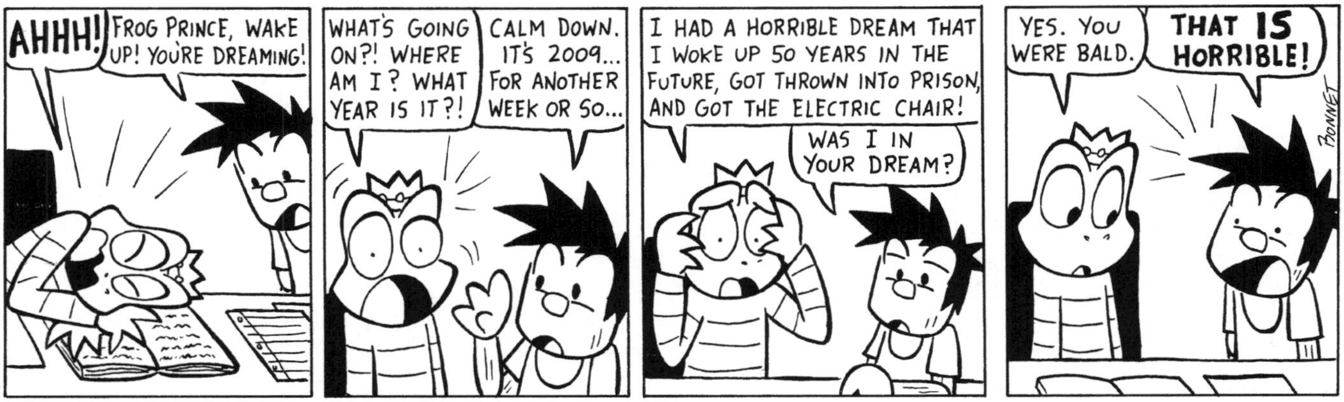
AHHH!
FROG PRINCE, WAKE UP! YOU'RE DREAMING!
WHAT'S GOING ON?! WHERE AM I? WHAT YEAR IS IT?!
CALM DOWN. IT'S 2009... FOR ANOTHER WEEK OR SO...
I HAD A HORRIBLE DREAM THAT I WOKE UP 50 YEARS IN THE FUTURE, GOT THROWN INTO PRISON, AND GOT THE ELECTRIC CHAIR!
WAS I IN YOUR DREAM?
YES. YOU WERE BALD.
THAT IS HORRIBLE!
BONNET

Dec. 18, 21, 23, 2009

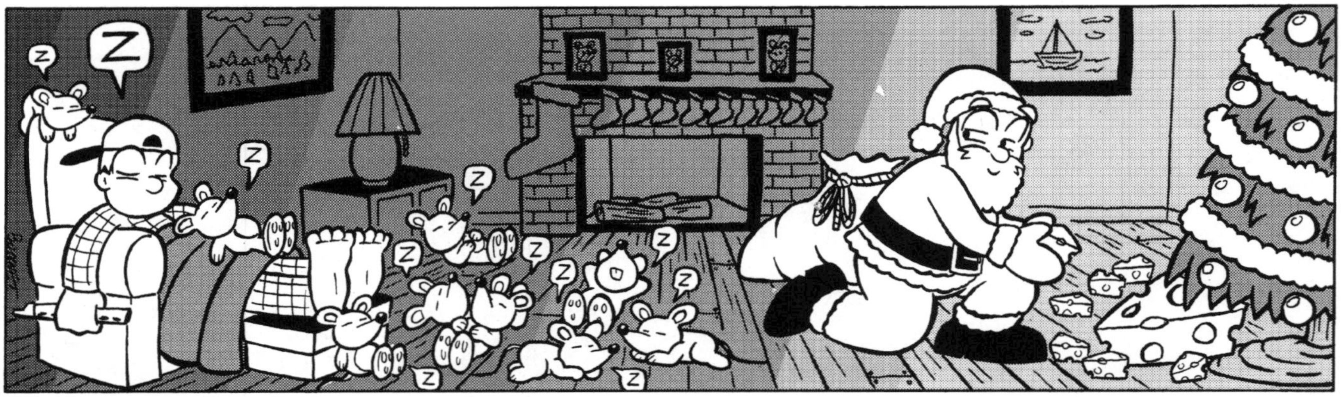
Z
Z
Z
Z
Z
Z
Z
Z
Z
Z
Z
BONNET

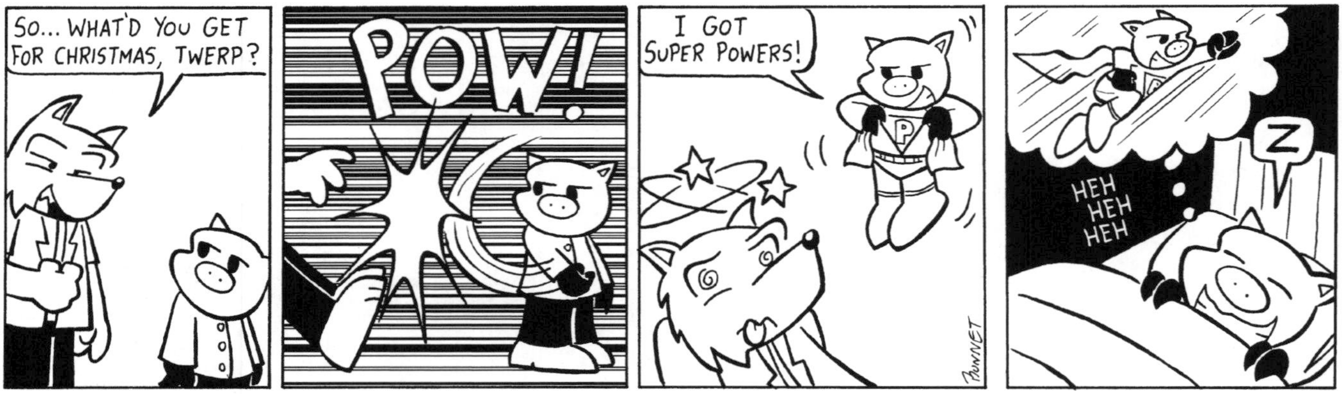
SO... WHAT'D YOU GET FOR CHRISTMAS, TWERP?
POW!
I GOT SUPER POWERS!
BONNET
HEH HEH HEH
Z

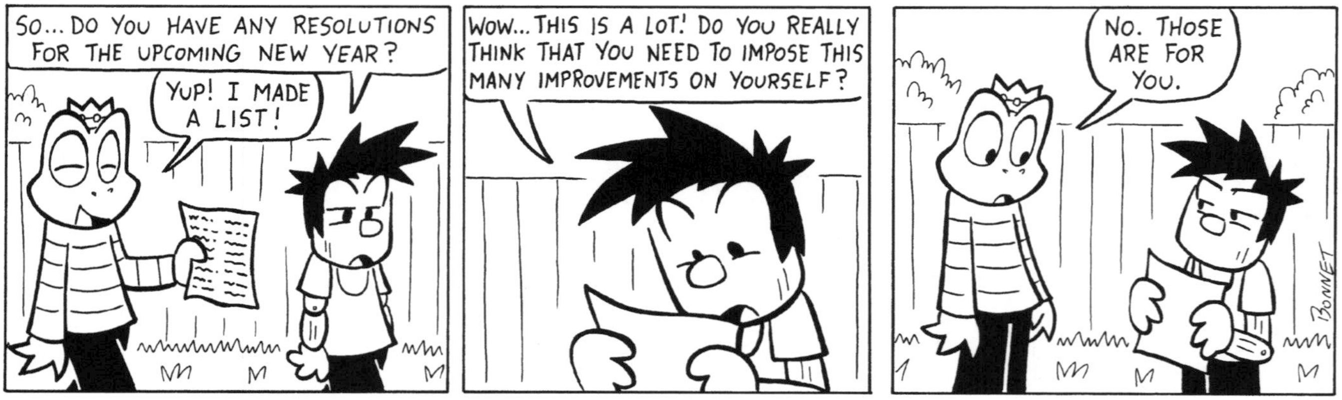
SO... DO YOU HAVE ANY RESOLUTIONS FOR THE UPCOMING NEW YEAR?
YUP! I MADE A LIST!
WOW... THIS IS A LOT! DO YOU REALLY THINK THAT YOU NEED TO IMPOSE THIS MANY IMPROVEMENTS ON YOURSELF?
NO. THOSE ARE FOR YOU.
BONNET

Dec. 25, 28, 30, 2009

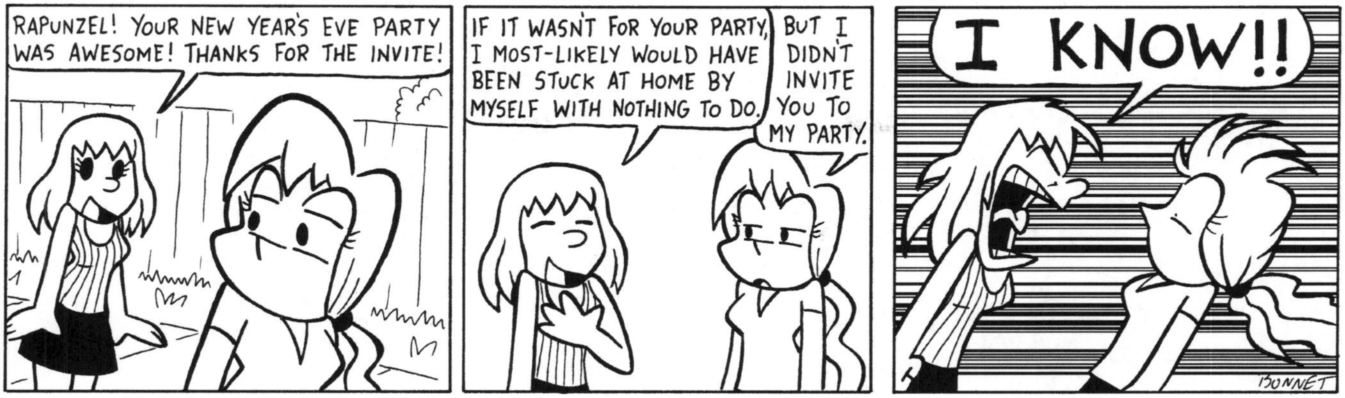
RAPUNZEL! YOUR NEW YEAR'S EVE PARTY WAS AWESOME! THANKS FOR THE INVITE!
IF IT WASN'T FOR YOUR PARTY, I MOST-LIKELY WOULD HAVE BEEN STUCK AT HOME BY MYSELF WITH NOTHING TO DO.
BUT I DIDN'T INVITE YOU TO MY PARTY.
I KNOW!!
BONNET

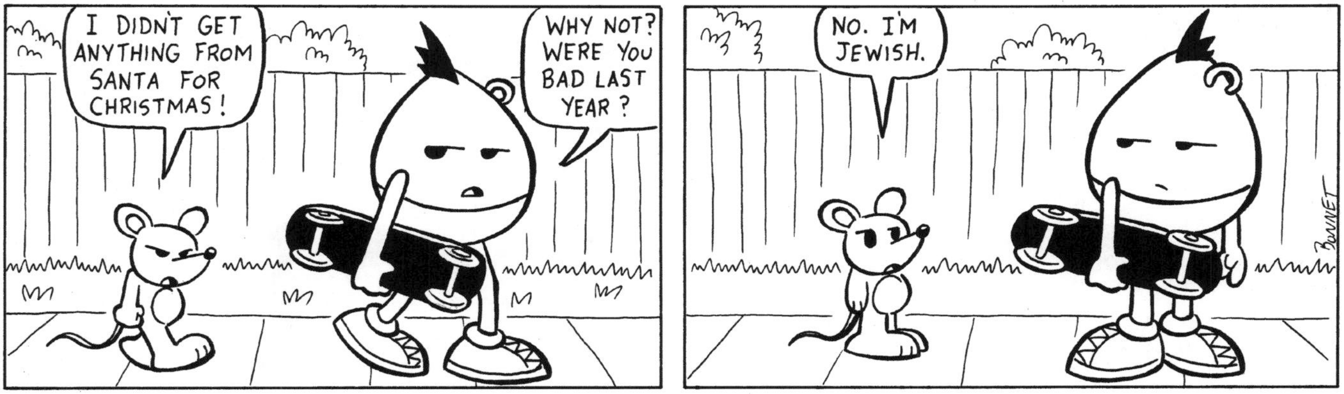
I DIDN'T GET ANYTHING FROM SANTA FOR CHRISTMAS!
WHY NOT? WERE YOU BAD LAST YEAR?
NO. I'M JEWISH.
BONNET

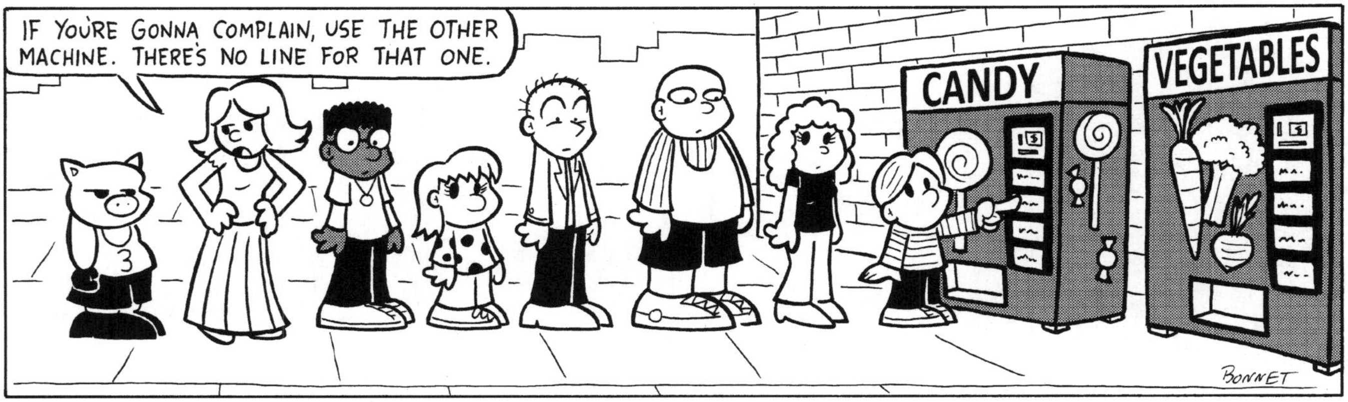
IF YOU'RE GONNA COMPLAIN, USE THE OTHER MACHINE. THERE'S NO LINE FOR THAT ONE.
CANDY
VEGETABLES
BONNET

Jan. 1, 4, 6, 2010

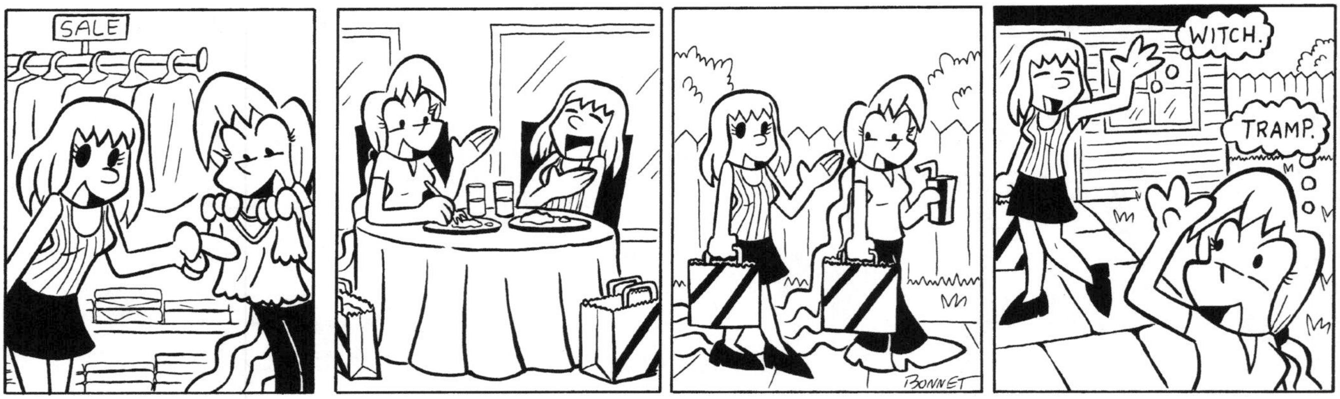
SALE
WITCH.
TRAMP.
BONNET

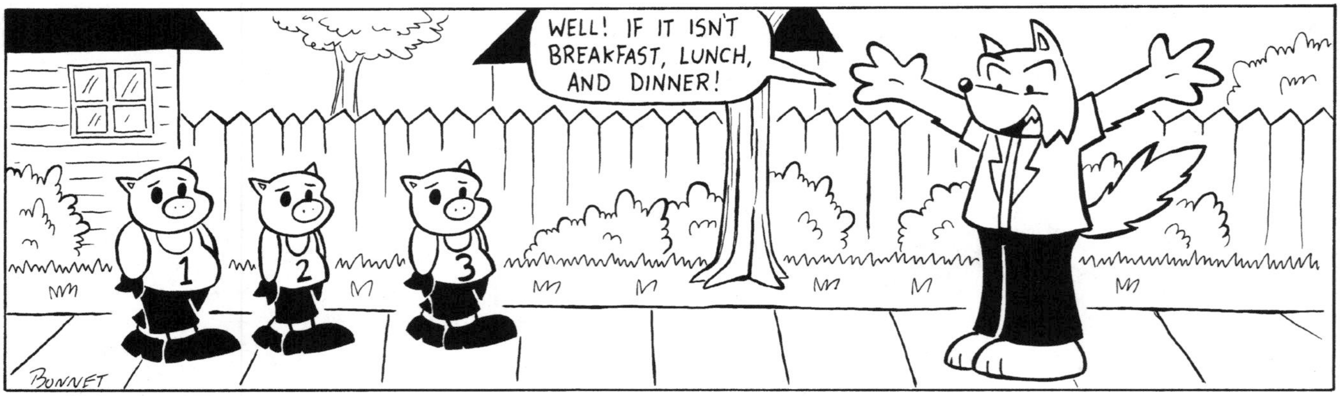
WELL! IF IT ISN'T BREAKFAST, LUNCH, AND DINNER!
1
2
3
BONNET

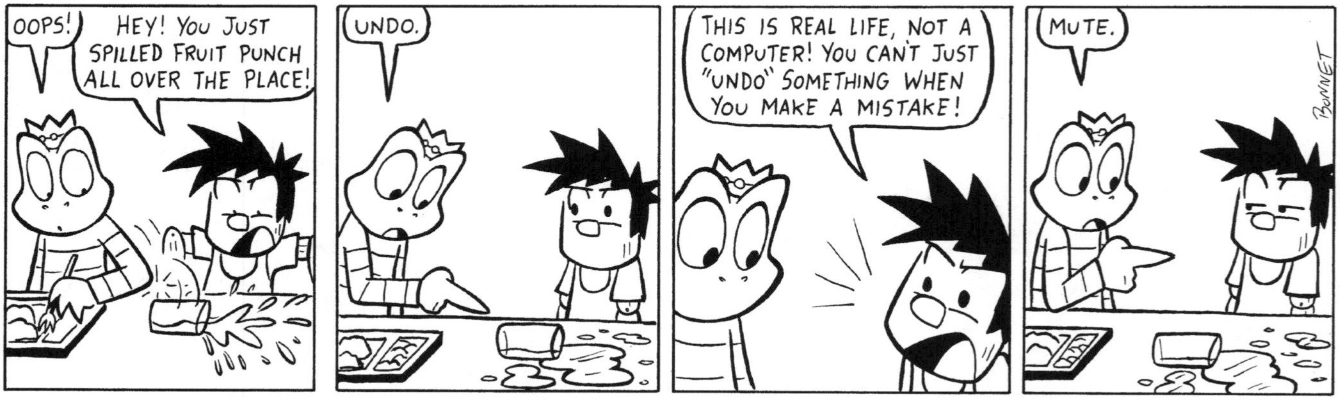
OOPS!
HEY! YOU JUST SPILLED FRUIT PUNCH ALL OVER THE PLACE!
UNDO.
THIS IS REAL LIFE, NOT A COMPUTER! YOU CAN'T JUST "UNDO" SOMETHING WHEN YOU MAKE A MISTAKE!
MUTE.
BONNET

Jan. 8, 11, 13, 2010

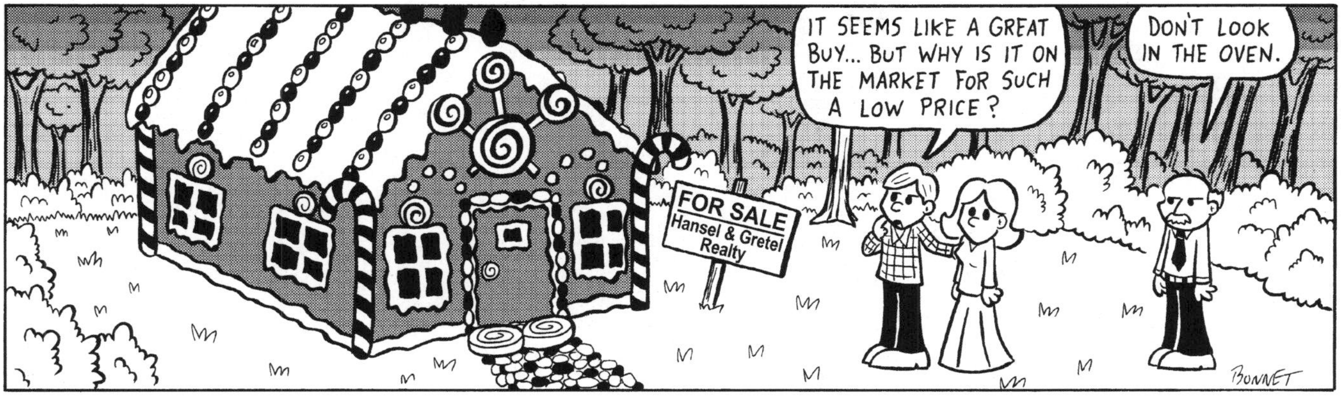
IT SEEMS LIKE A GREAT BUY... BUT WHY IS IT ON THE MARKET FOR SUCH A LOW PRICE?
DON'T LOOK IN THE OVEN.
FOR SALE
Hansel & Gretel Realty
BONNET

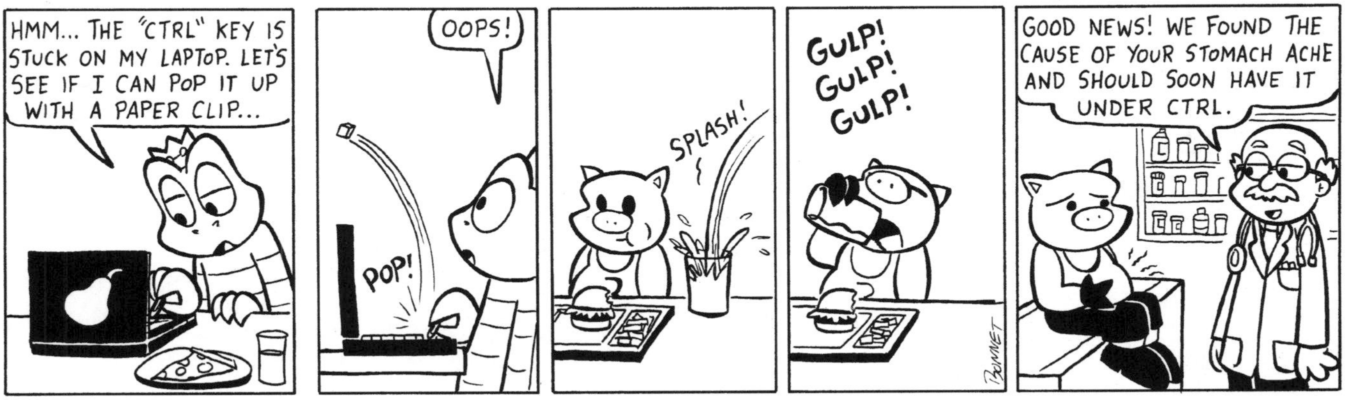
HMM... THE "CTRL" KEY IS STUCK ON MY LAPTOP. LET'S SEE IF I CAN POP IT UP WITH A PAPER CLIP...
OOPS!
POP!
SPLASH!
GULP! GULP! GULP!
BONNET
GOOD NEWS! WE FOUND THE CAUSE OF YOUR STOMACH ACHE AND SHOULD SOON HAVE IT UNDER CTRL.

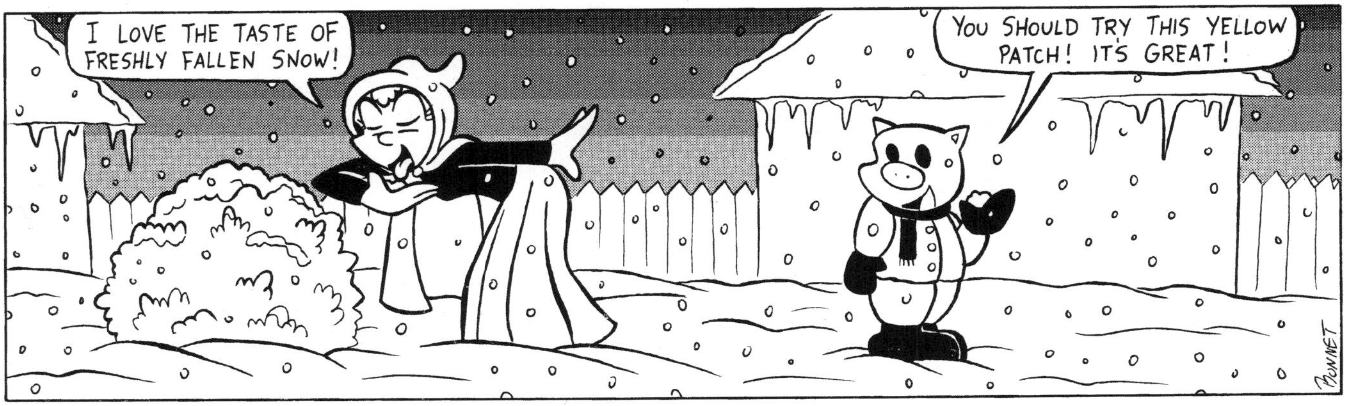
I LOVE THE TASTE OF FRESHLY FALLEN SNOW!
YOU SHOULD TRY THIS YELLOW PATCH! IT'S GREAT!
BONNET

Jan. 15, 18, 20, 2010

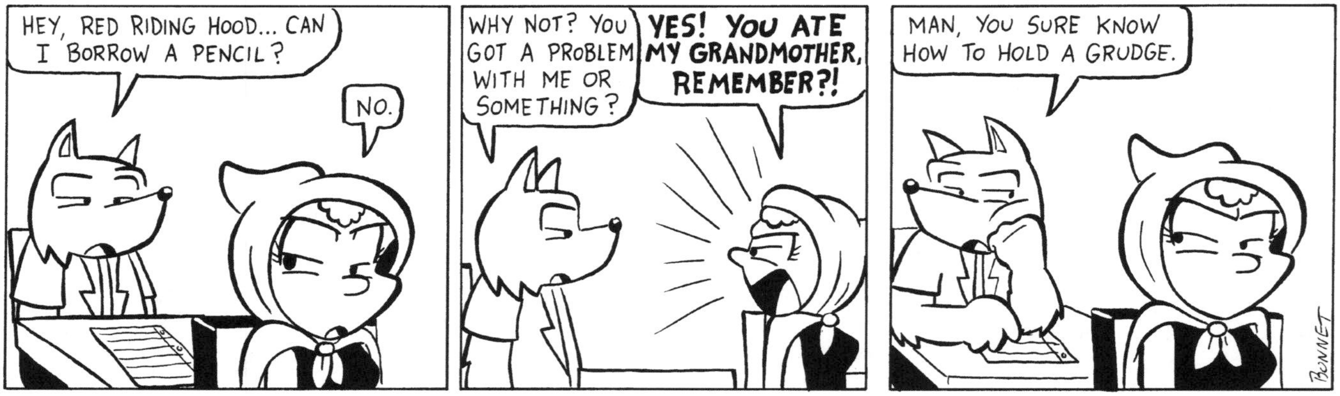
HEY, RED RIDING HOOD... CAN I BORROW A PENCIL?
NO.
WHY NOT? YOU GOT A PROBLEM WITH ME OR SOMETHING?
YES! YOU ATE MY GRANDMOTHER, REMEMBER?!
MAN, YOU SURE KNOW HOW TO HOLD A GRUDGE.
BONNET

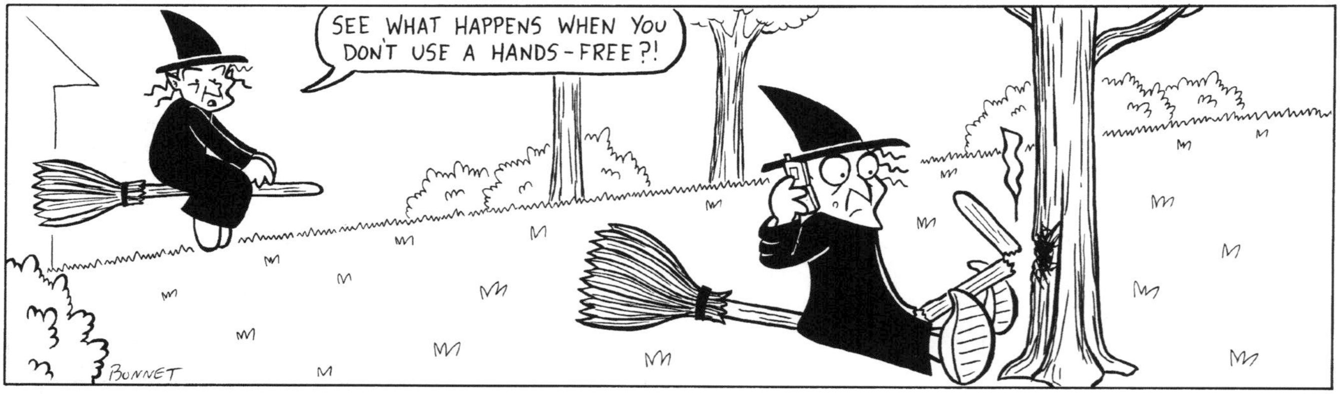
SEE WHAT HAPPENS WHEN YOU DON'T USE A HANDS-FREE?!
BONNET

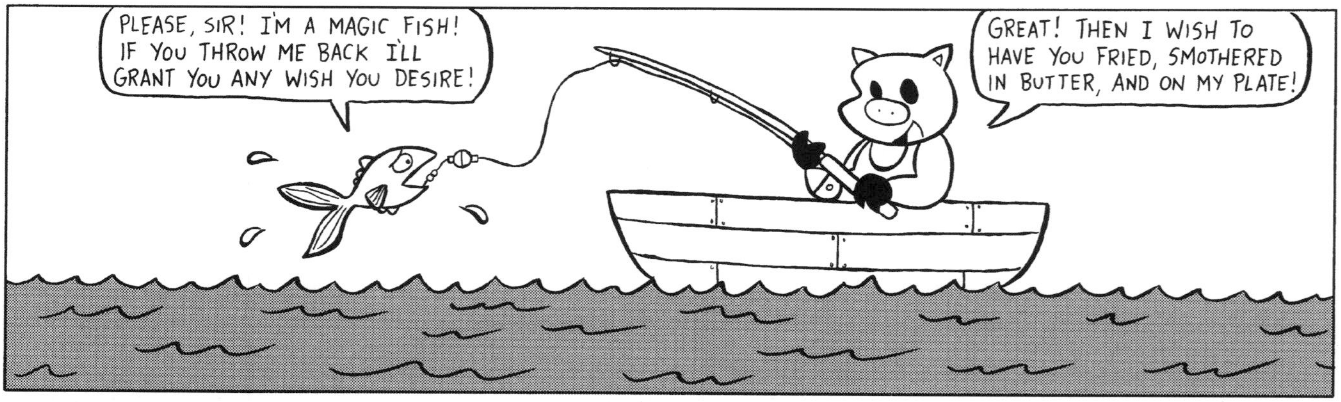
PLEASE, SIR! I'M A MAGIC FISH! IF YOU THROW ME BACK I'LL GRANT YOU ANY WISH YOU DESIRE!
GREAT! THEN I WISH TO HAVE YOU FRIED, SMOTHERED IN BUTTER, AND ON MY PLATE!

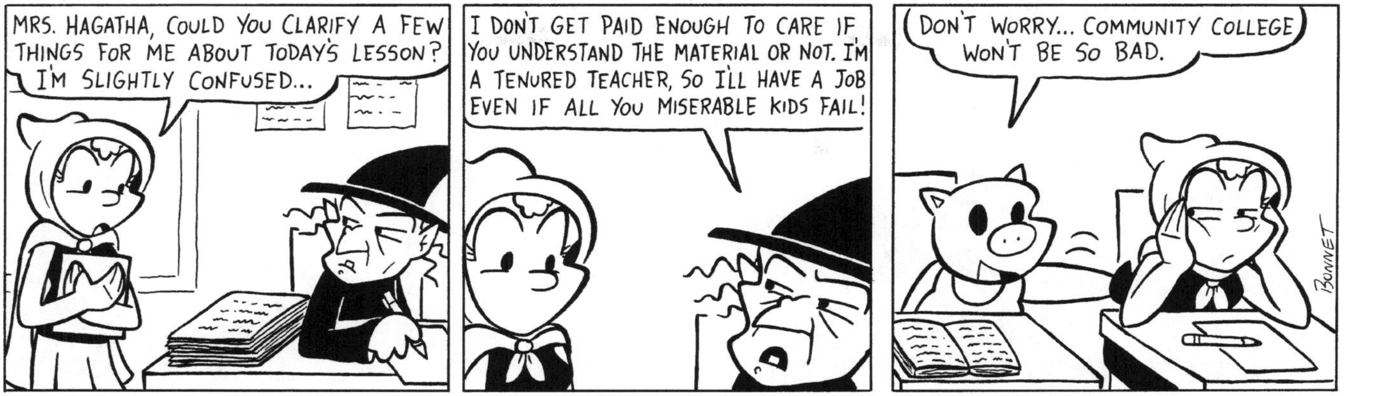
MRS. HAGATHA, COULD YOU CLARIFY A FEW THINGS FOR ME ABOUT TODAY'S LESSON? I'M SLIGHTLY CONFUSED...
I DON'T GET PAID ENOUGH TO CARE IF YOU UNDERSTAND THE MATERIAL OR NOT. I'M A TENURED TEACHER, SO I'LL HAVE A JOB EVEN IF ALL YOU MISERABLE KIDS FAIL!
DON'T WORRY... COMMUNITY COLLEGE WON'T BE SO BAD.
BONNET

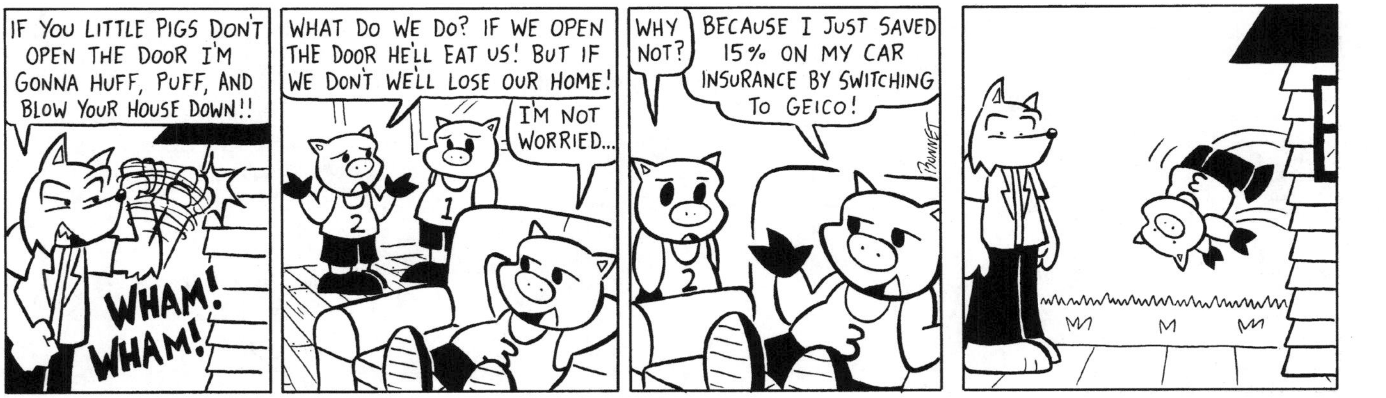
IF YOU LITTLE PIGS DON'T OPEN THE DOOR I'M GONNA HUFF, PUFF, AND BLOW YOUR HOUSE DOWN!!
WHAM! WHAM!
WHAT DO WE DO? IF WE OPEN THE DOOR HE'LL EAT US! BUT IF WE DON'T WE'LL LOSE OUR HOME!
I'M NOT WORRIED...
WHY NOT?
BECAUSE I JUST SAVED 15% ON MY CAR INSURANCE BY SWITCHING TO GEICO!
BONNET

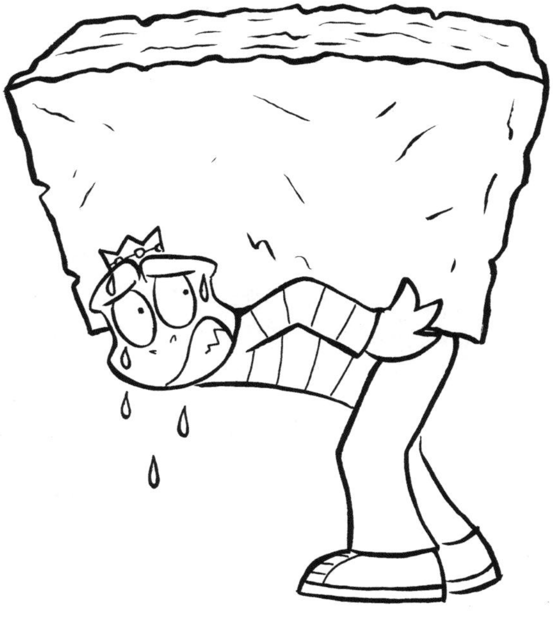

Jan. 29, Feb. 1, 2010

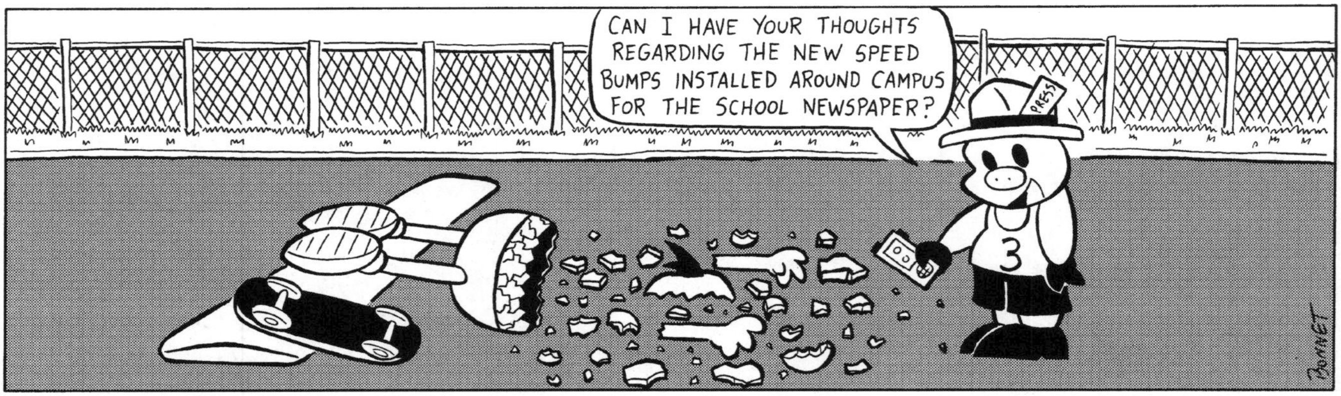
CAN I HAVE YOUR THOUGHTS REGARDING THE NEW SPEED BUMPS INSTALLED AROUND CAMPUS FOR THE SCHOOL NEWSPAPER?
PRESS
BONNET

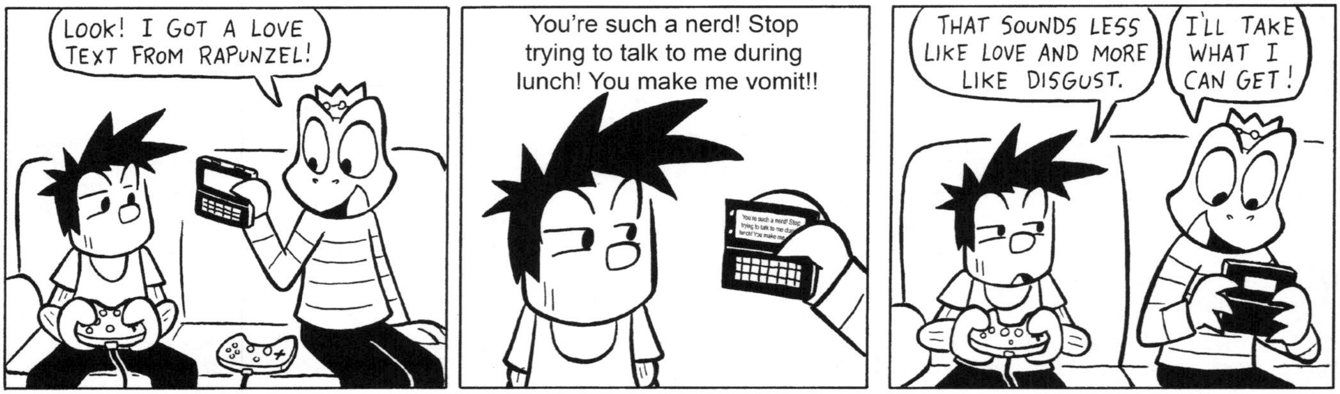
LOOK! I GOT A LOVE TEXT FROM RAPUNZEL!
You're such a nerd! Stop trying to talk to me during lunch! You make me vomit!!
THAT SOUNDS LESS LIKE LOVE AND MORE LIKE DISGUST.
I'LL TAKE WHAT I CAN GET!

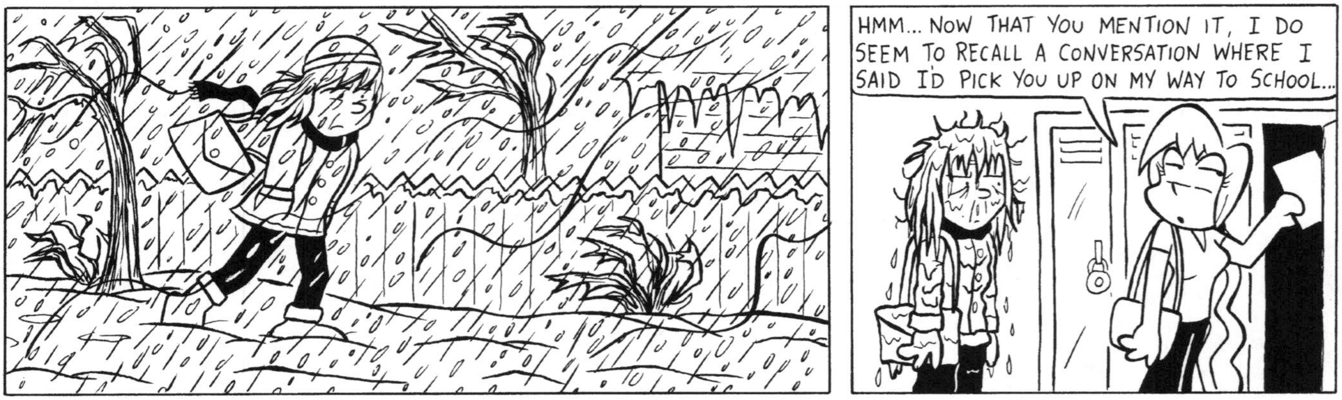
HMM... NOW THAT YOU MENTION IT, I DO SEEM TO RECALL A CONVERSATION WHERE I SAID I'D PICK YOU UP ON MY WAY TO SCHOOL...

Feb. 3, 5, 8, 2010

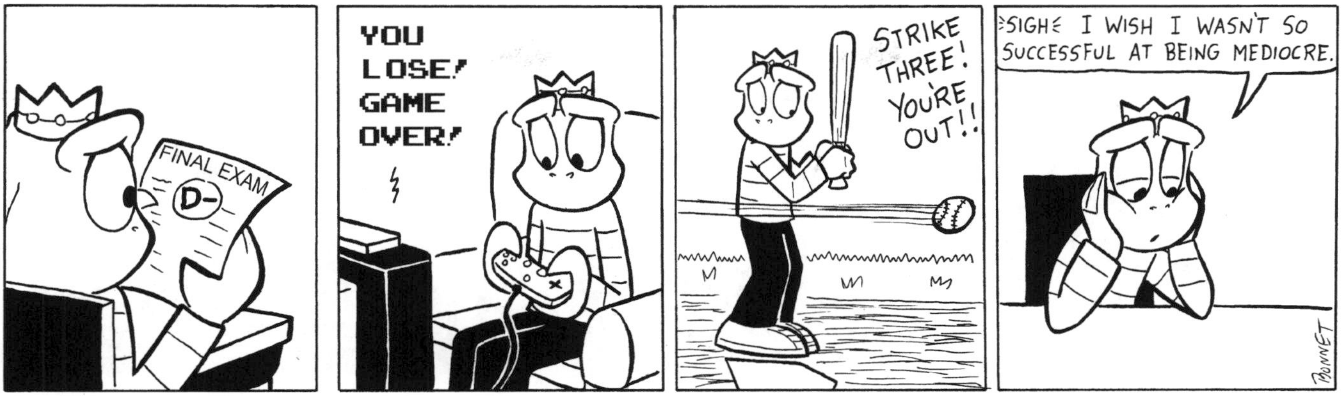
FINAL EXAM
D-
YOU LOSE! GAME OVER!
STRIKE THREE! YOU'RE OUT!!
ᵋSIGHᵋ I WISH I WASN'T SO SUCCESSFUL AT BEING MEDIOCRE.
BONNET

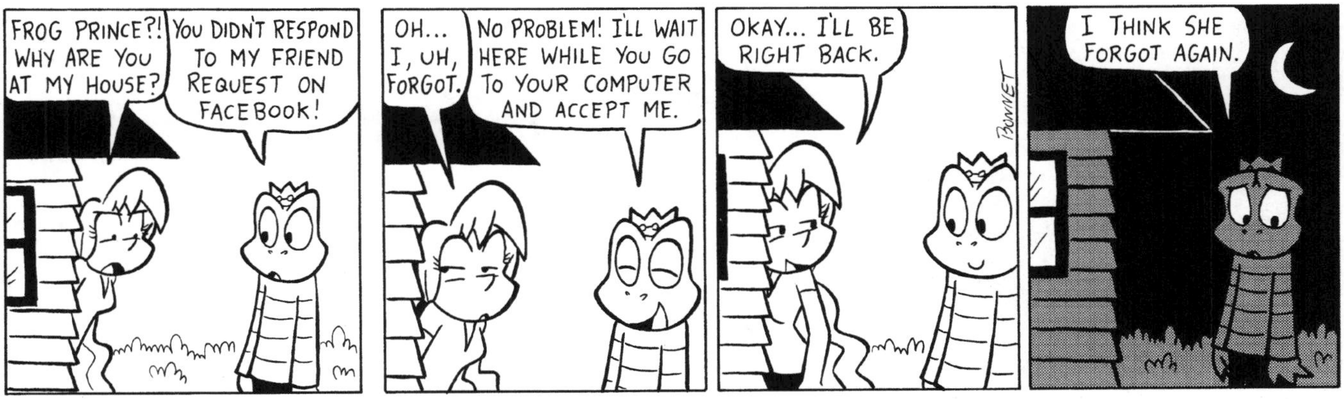
FROG PRINCE?! WHY ARE YOU AT MY HOUSE?
YOU DIDN'T RESPOND TO MY FRIEND REQUEST ON FACEBOOK!
OH... I, UH, FORGOT.
NO PROBLEM! I'LL WAIT HERE WHILE YOU GO TO YOUR COMPUTER AND ACCEPT ME.
OKAY... I'LL BE RIGHT BACK.
BONNET
I THINK SHE FORGOT AGAIN.

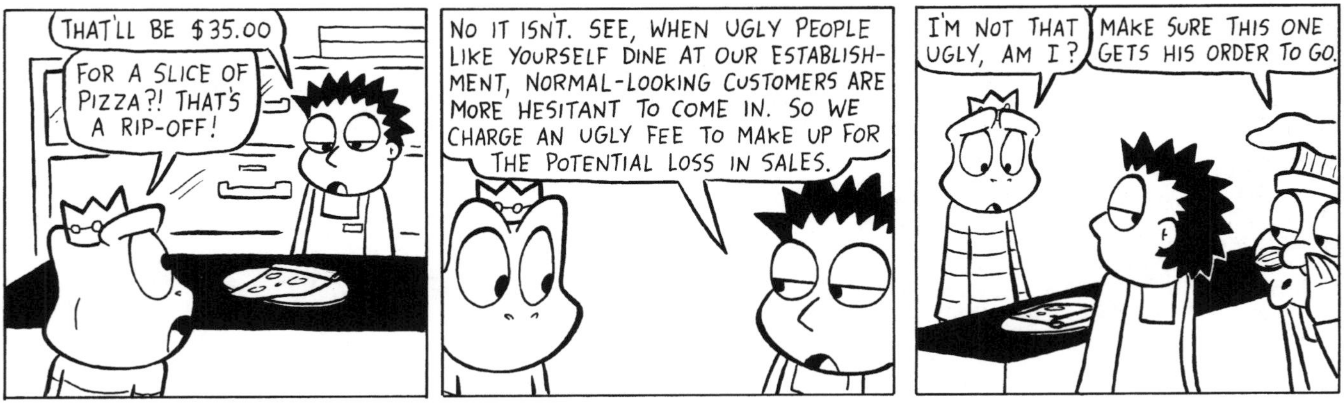
THAT'LL BE $35.00
FOR A SLICE OF PIZZA?! THAT'S A RIP-OFF!
NO IT ISN'T. SEE, WHEN UGLY PEOPLE LIKE YOURSELF DINE AT OUR ESTABLISHMENT, NORMAL-LOOKING CUSTOMERS ARE MORE HESITANT TO COME IN. SO WE CHARGE AN UGLY FEE TO MAKE UP FOR THE POTENTIAL LOSS IN SALES.
I'M NOT THAT UGLY, AM I?
MAKE SURE THIS ONE GETS HIS ORDER TO GO.

Feb. 10, 12, 15, 2010

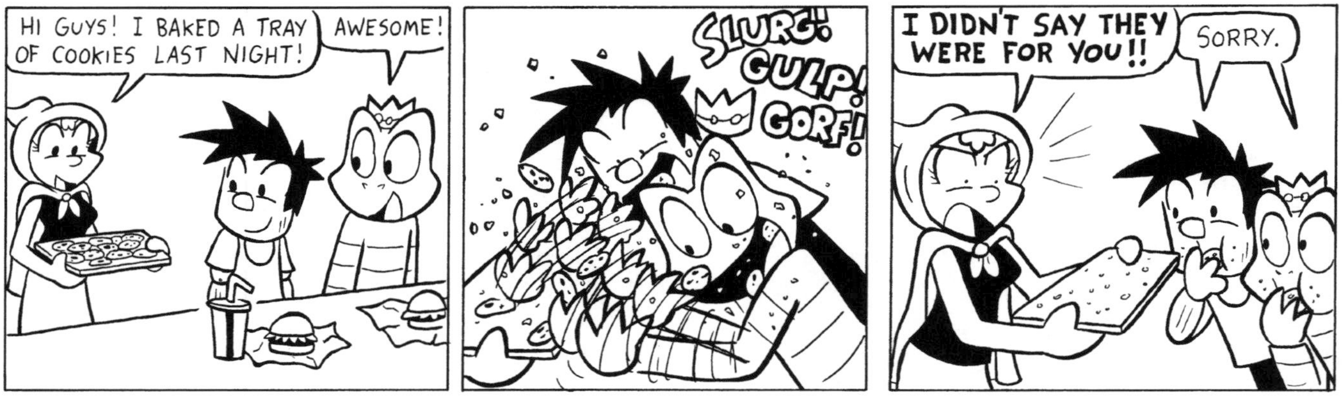
HI GUYS! I BAKED A TRAY OF COOKIES LAST NIGHT!
AWESOME!
SLURG! GULP! GORF!
I DIDN'T SAY THEY WERE FOR YOU!!
SORRY.

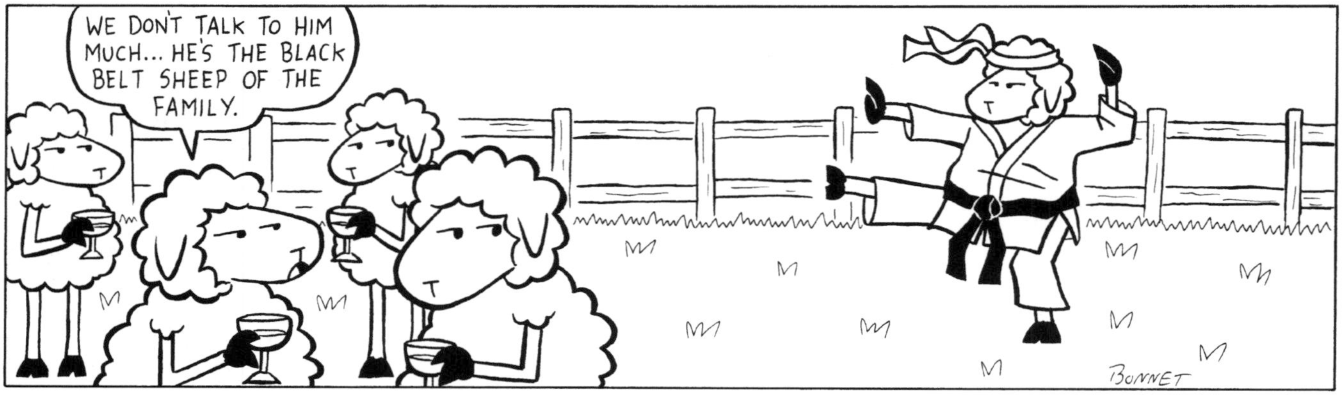
WE DON'T TALK TO HIM MUCH... HE'S THE BLACK BELT SHEEP OF THE FAMILY.
BONNET

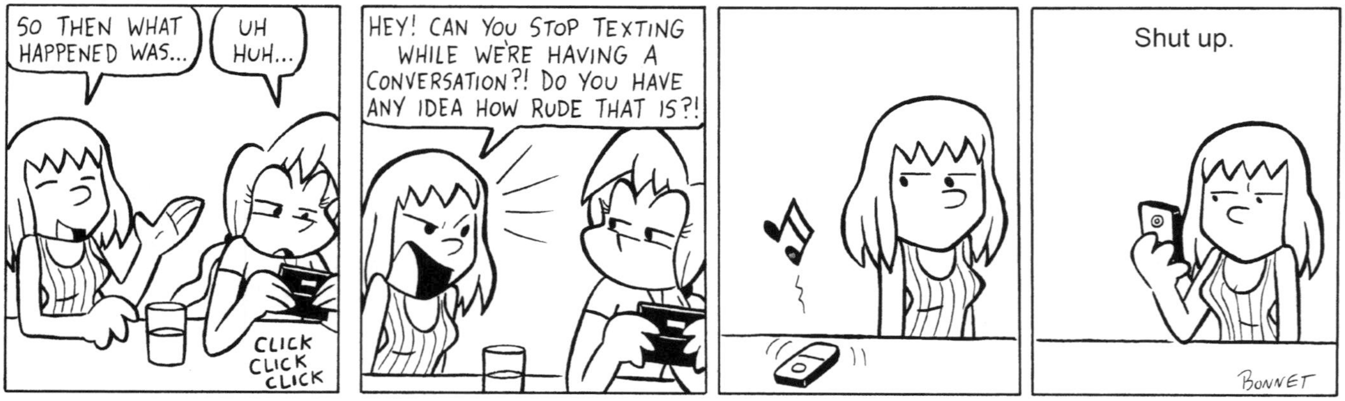
SO THEN WHAT HAPPENED WAS...
UH HUH...
CLICK CLICK CLICK
HEY! CAN YOU STOP TEXTING WHILE WE'RE HAVING A CONVERSATION?! DO YOU HAVE ANY IDEA HOW RUDE THAT IS?!
Shut up.
BONNET

Feb. 17, 19, 22, 2010

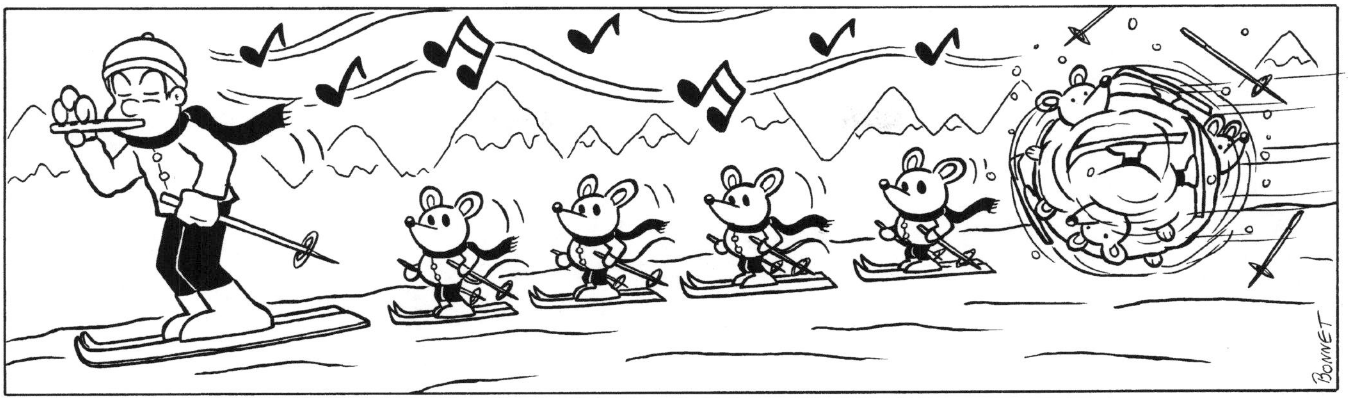
BONNET

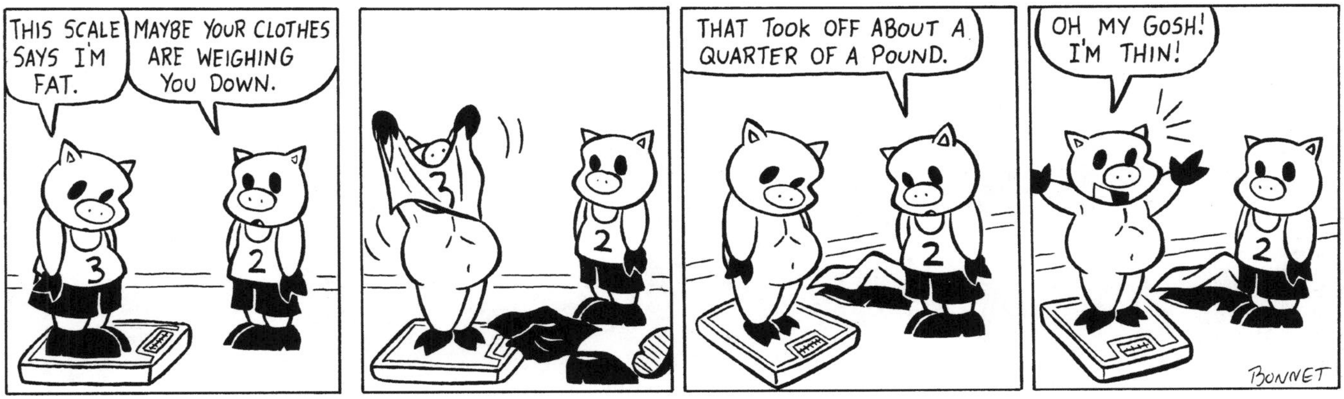
THIS SCALE SAYS I'M FAT.
MAYBE YOUR CLOTHES ARE WEIGHING YOU DOWN.
THAT TOOK OFF ABOUT A QUARTER OF A POUND.
OH MY GOSH! I'M THIN!
BONNET

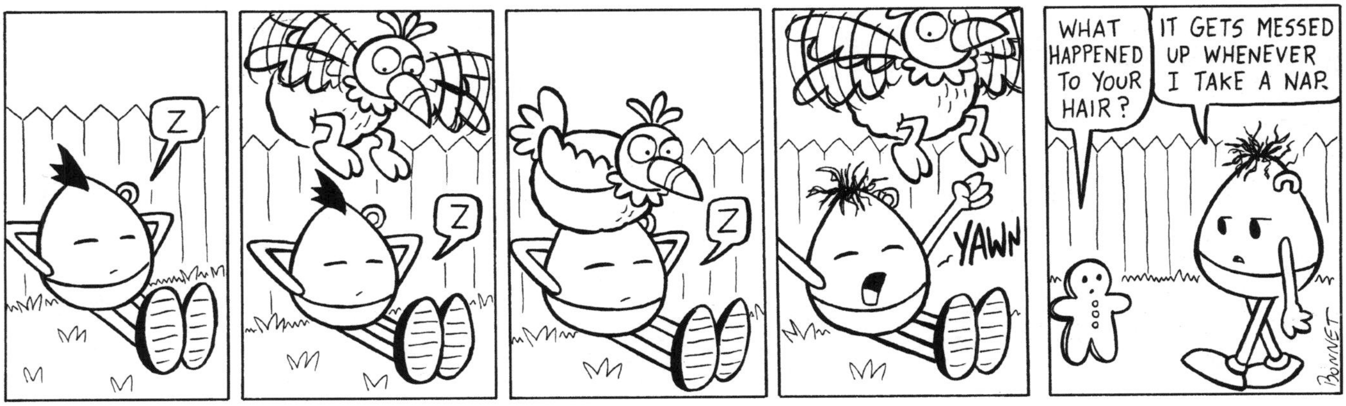
Z
Z
Z
YAWN
WHAT HAPPENED TO YOUR HAIR?
IT GETS MESSED UP WHENEVER I TAKE A NAP.
BONNET

Feb. 24, 26, March 1, 2010

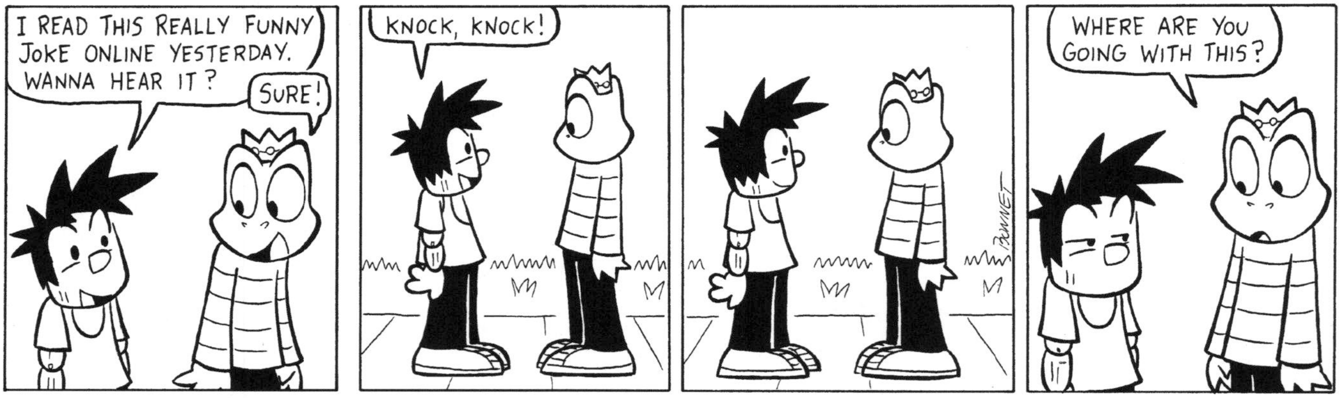
I READ THIS REALLY FUNNY JOKE ONLINE YESTERDAY. WANNA HEAR IT?
SURE!
KNOCK, KNOCK!
WHERE ARE YOU GOING WITH THIS?

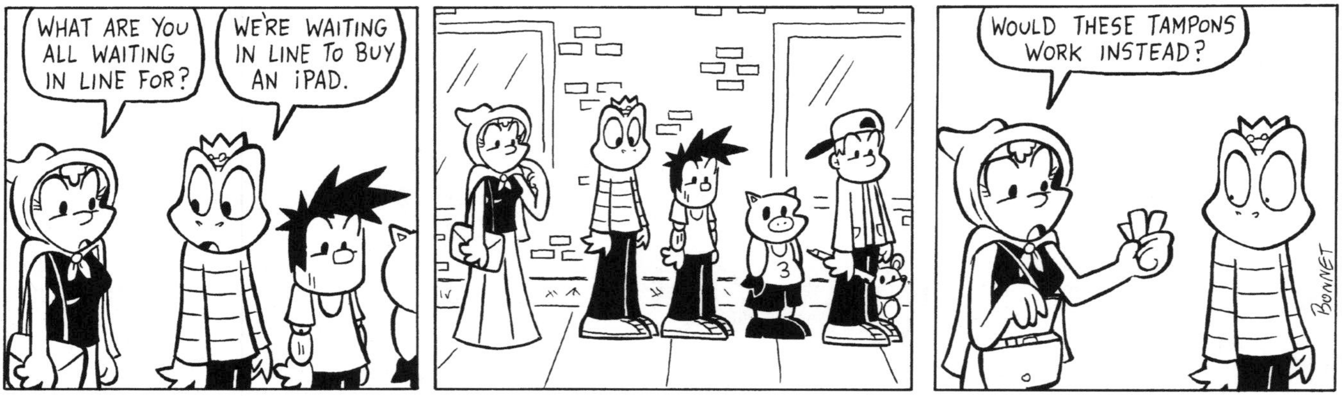
WHAT ARE YOU ALL WAITING IN LINE FOR?
WE'RE WAITING IN LINE TO BUY AN iPAD.
WOULD THESE TAMPONS WORK INSTEAD?

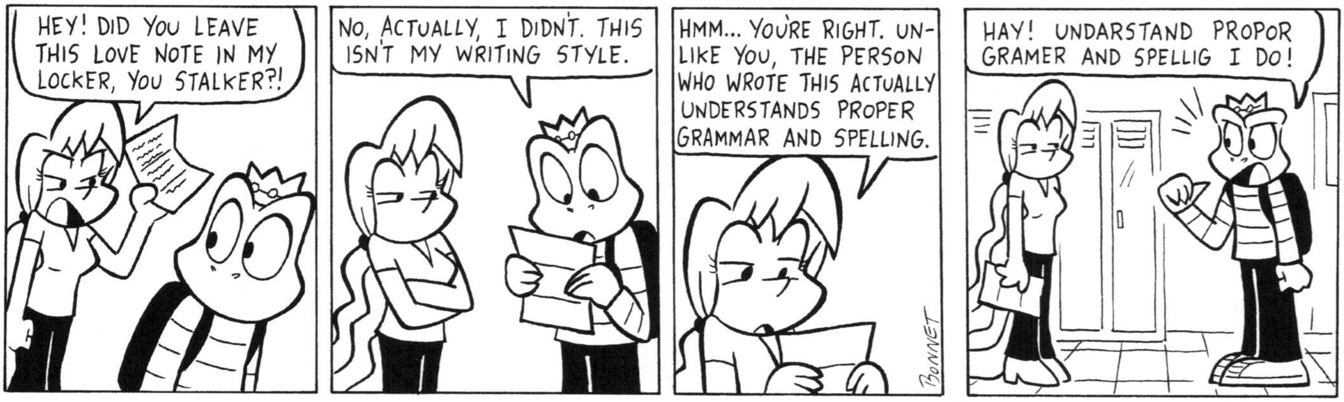
HEY! DID YOU LEAVE THIS LOVE NOTE IN MY LOCKER, YOU STALKER?!
NO, ACTUALLY, I DIDN'T. THIS ISN'T MY WRITING STYLE.
HMM... YOU'RE RIGHT. UN-LIKE YOU, THE PERSON WHO WROTE THIS ACTUALLY UNDERSTANDS PROPER GRAMMAR AND SPELLING.
HAY! UNDARSTAND PROPOR GRAMER AND SPELLIG I DO!

March 3, 5, 8, 2010

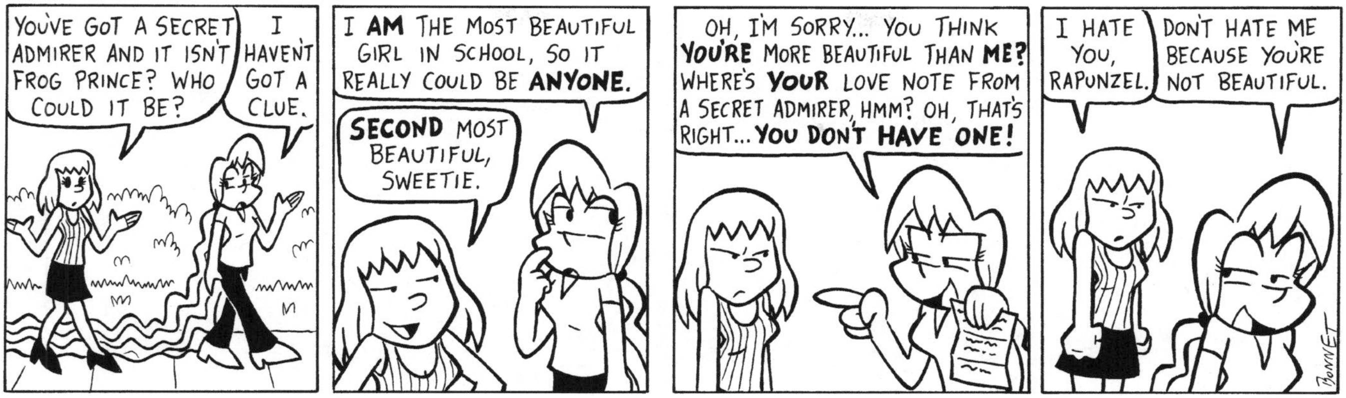
YOU'VE GOT A SECRET ADMIRER AND IT ISN'T FROG PRINCE? WHO COULD IT BE?
I HAVEN'T GOT A CLUE.
I AM THE MOST BEAUTIFUL GIRL IN SCHOOL, SO IT REALLY COULD BE ANYONE.
SECOND MOST BEAUTIFUL, SWEETIE.
OH, I'M SORRY... YOU THINK YOU'RE MORE BEAUTIFUL THAN ME? WHERE'S YOUR LOVE NOTE FROM A SECRET ADMIRER, HMM? OH, THAT'S RIGHT... YOU DON'T HAVE ONE!
I HATE YOU, RAPUNZEL.
DON'T HATE ME BECAUSE YOU'RE NOT BEAUTIFUL.
BONNET

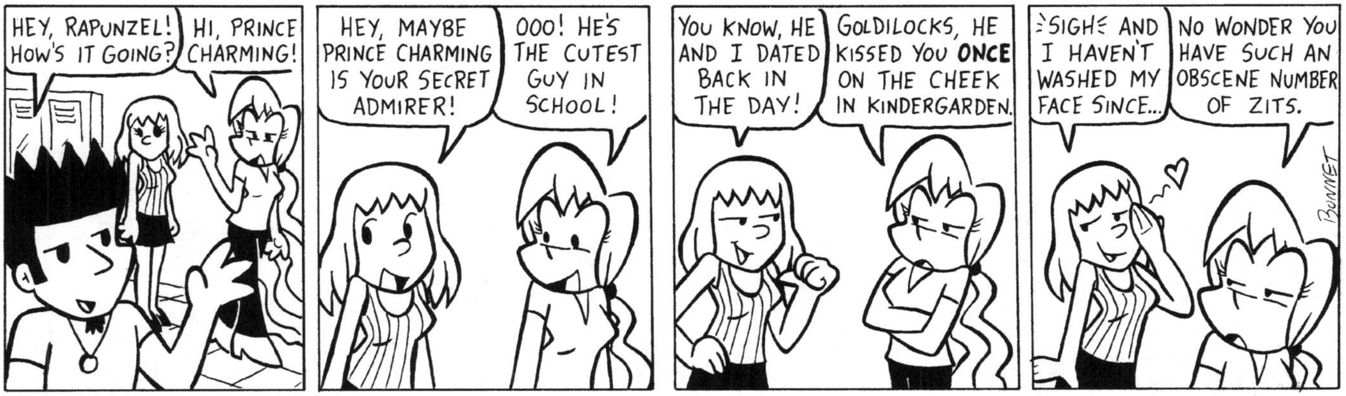
HEY, RAPUNZEL! HOW'S IT GOING?
HI, PRINCE CHARMING!
HEY, MAYBE PRINCE CHARMING IS YOUR SECRET ADMIRER!
OOO! HE'S THE CUTEST GUY IN SCHOOL!
YOU KNOW, HE AND I DATED BACK IN THE DAY!
GOLDILOCKS, HE KISSED YOU ONCE ON THE CHEEK IN KINDERGARDEN.
SIGH AND I HAVEN'T WASHED MY FACE SINCE...
NO WONDER YOU HAVE SUCH AN OBSCENE NUMBER OF ZITS.
BONNET

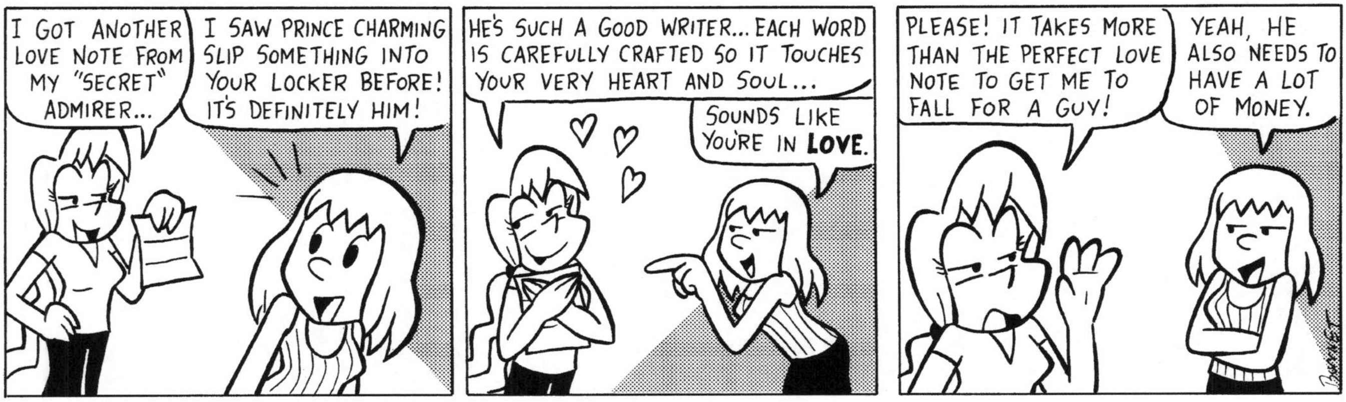
I GOT ANOTHER LOVE NOTE FROM MY "SECRET" ADMIRER...
I SAW PRINCE CHARMING SLIP SOMETHING INTO YOUR LOCKER BEFORE! IT'S DEFINITELY HIM!
HE'S SUCH A GOOD WRITER... EACH WORD IS CAREFULLY CRAFTED SO IT TOUCHES YOUR VERY HEART AND SOUL...
SOUNDS LIKE YOU'RE IN LOVE.
PLEASE! IT TAKES MORE THAN THE PERFECT LOVE NOTE TO GET ME TO FALL FOR A GUY!
YEAH, HE ALSO NEEDS TO HAVE A LOT OF MONEY.
BONNET

March 10, 12, 15, 2010

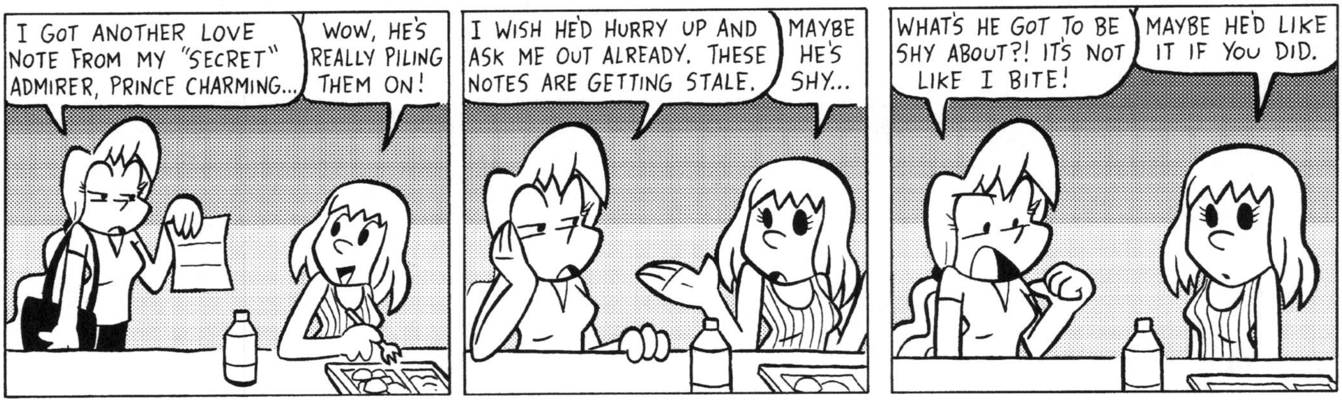
I GOT ANOTHER LOVE NOTE FROM MY "SECRET" ADMIRER, PRINCE CHARMING...
WOW, HE'S REALLY PILING THEM ON!
I WISH HE'D HURRY UP AND ASK ME OUT ALREADY. THESE NOTES ARE GETTING STALE.
MAYBE HE'S SHY...
WHAT'S HE GOT TO BE SHY ABOUT?! IT'S NOT LIKE I BITE!
MAYBE HE'D LIKE IT IF YOU DID.

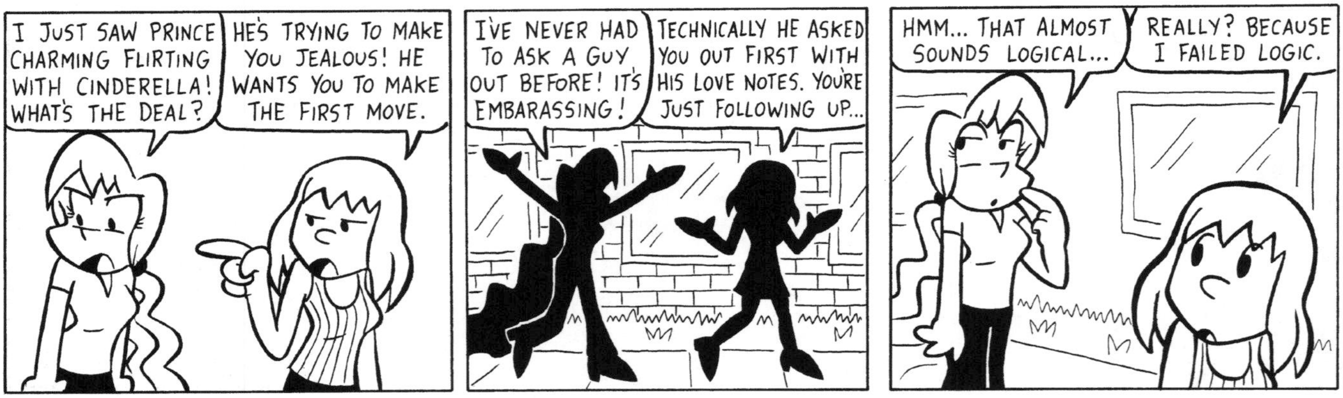
I JUST SAW PRINCE CHARMING FLIRTING WITH CINDERELLA! WHAT'S THE DEAL?
HE'S TRYING TO MAKE YOU JEALOUS! HE WANTS YOU TO MAKE THE FIRST MOVE.
I'VE NEVER HAD TO ASK A GUY OUT BEFORE! IT'S EMBARASSING!
TECHNICALLY HE ASKED YOU OUT FIRST WITH HIS LOVE NOTES. YOU'RE JUST FOLLOWING UP...
HMM... THAT ALMOST SOUNDS LOGICAL...
REALLY? BECAUSE I FAILED LOGIC.

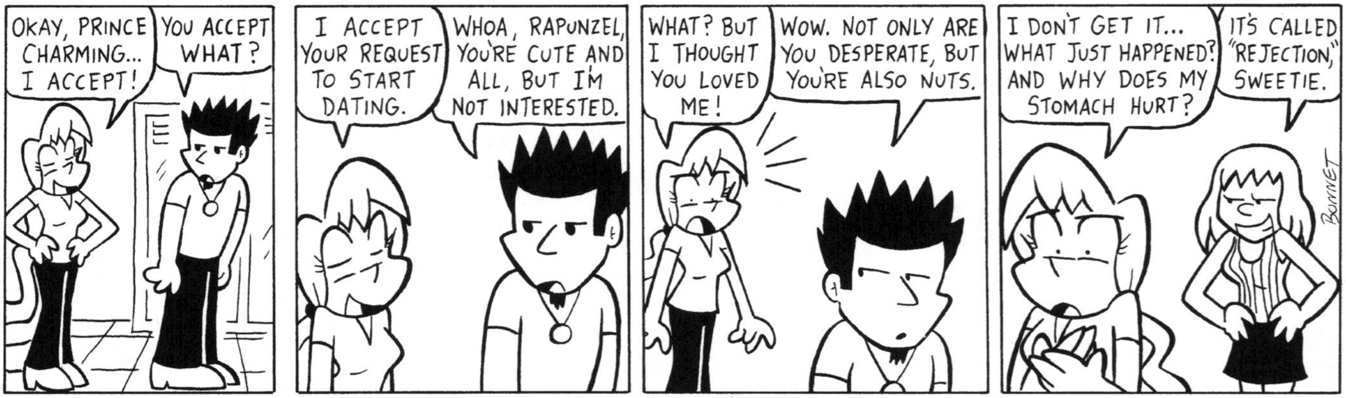
OKAY, PRINCE CHARMING... I ACCEPT!
YOU ACCEPT WHAT?
I ACCEPT YOUR REQUEST TO START DATING.
WHOA, RAPUNZEL, YOU'RE CUTE AND ALL, BUT I'M NOT INTERESTED.
WHAT? BUT I THOUGHT YOU LOVED ME!
WOW. NOT ONLY ARE YOU DESPERATE, BUT YOU'RE ALSO NUTS.
I DON'T GET IT... WHAT JUST HAPPENED? AND WHY DOES MY STOMACH HURT?
IT'S CALLED "REJECTION," SWEETIE.
BONNET

March 17, 19, 22, 2010

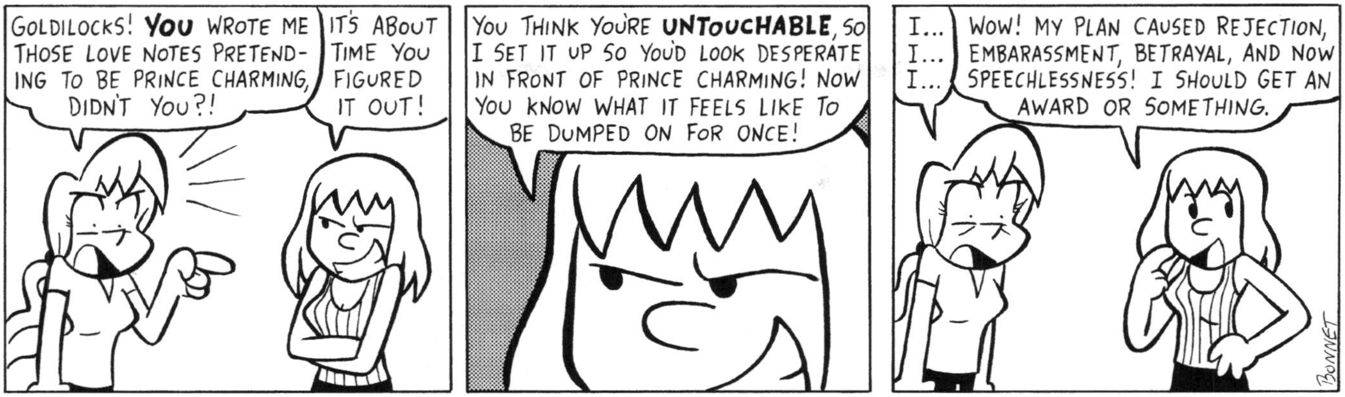
GOLDILOCKS! **YOU** WROTE ME THOSE LOVE NOTES PRETENDING TO BE PRINCE CHARMING, DIDN'T YOU?!
IT'S ABOUT TIME YOU FIGURED IT OUT!
YOU THINK YOU'RE **UNTOUCHABLE**, SO I SET IT UP SO YOU'D LOOK DESPERATE IN FRONT OF PRINCE CHARMING! NOW YOU KNOW WHAT IT FEELS LIKE TO BE DUMPED ON FOR ONCE!
I... I... I...
WOW! MY PLAN CAUSED REJECTION, EMBARASSMENT, BETRAYAL, AND NOW SPEECHLESSNESS! I SHOULD GET AN AWARD OR SOMETHING.

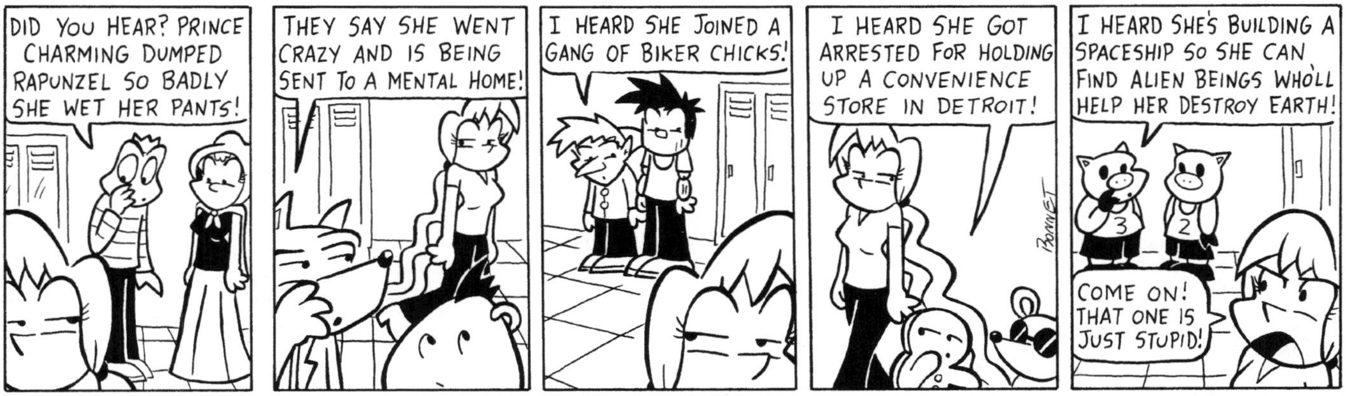
DID YOU HEAR? PRINCE CHARMING DUMPED RAPUNZEL SO BADLY SHE WET HER PANTS!
THEY SAY SHE WENT CRAZY AND IS BEING SENT TO A MENTAL HOME!
I HEARD SHE JOINED A GANG OF BIKER CHICKS!
I HEARD SHE GOT ARRESTED FOR HOLDING UP A CONVENIENCE STORE IN DETROIT!
I HEARD SHE'S BUILDING A SPACESHIP SO SHE CAN FIND ALIEN BEINGS WHO'LL HELP HER DESTROY EARTH!
COME ON! THAT ONE IS JUST STUPID!

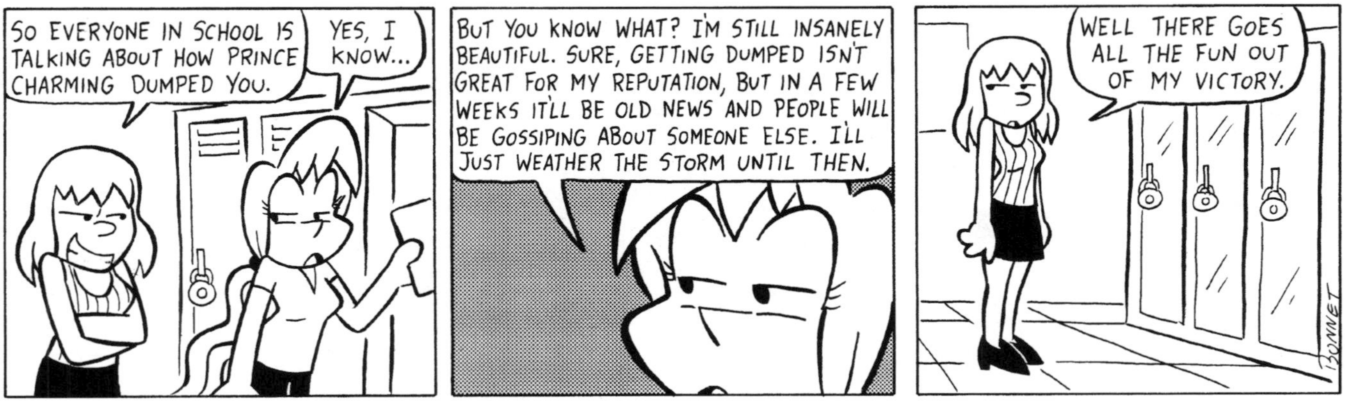
SO EVERYONE IN SCHOOL IS TALKING ABOUT HOW PRINCE CHARMING DUMPED YOU.
YES, I KNOW...
BUT YOU KNOW WHAT? I'M STILL INSANELY BEAUTIFUL. SURE, GETTING DUMPED ISN'T GREAT FOR MY REPUTATION, BUT IN A FEW WEEKS IT'LL BE OLD NEWS AND PEOPLE WILL BE GOSSIPING ABOUT SOMEONE ELSE. I'LL JUST WEATHER THE STORM UNTIL THEN.
WELL THERE GOES ALL THE FUN OUT OF MY VICTORY.

March 24, 26, 29, 2010

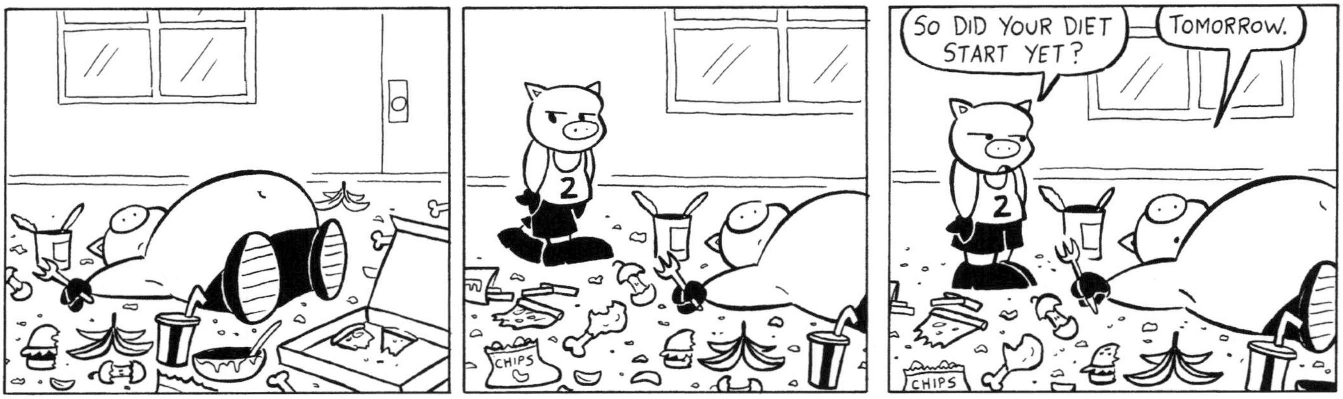
SO DID YOUR DIET START YET?
TOMORROW.
CHIPS
CHIPS

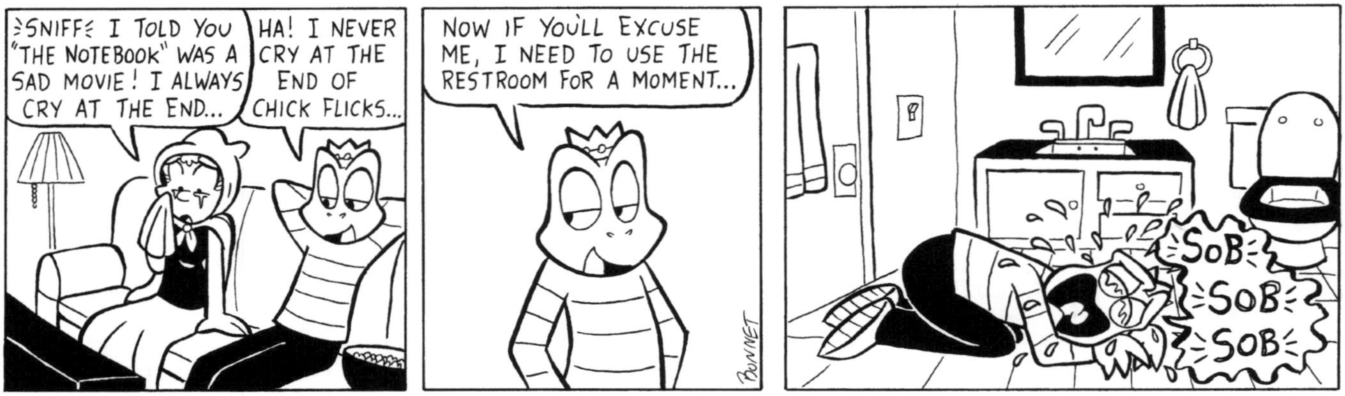
≷SNIFF≶ I TOLD YOU "THE NOTEBOOK" WAS A SAD MOVIE! I ALWAYS CRY AT THE END...
HA! I NEVER CRY AT THE END OF CHICK FLICKS...
NOW IF YOU'LL EXCUSE ME, I NEED TO USE THE RESTROOM FOR A MOMENT...
BONNET
SOB
SOB
SOB

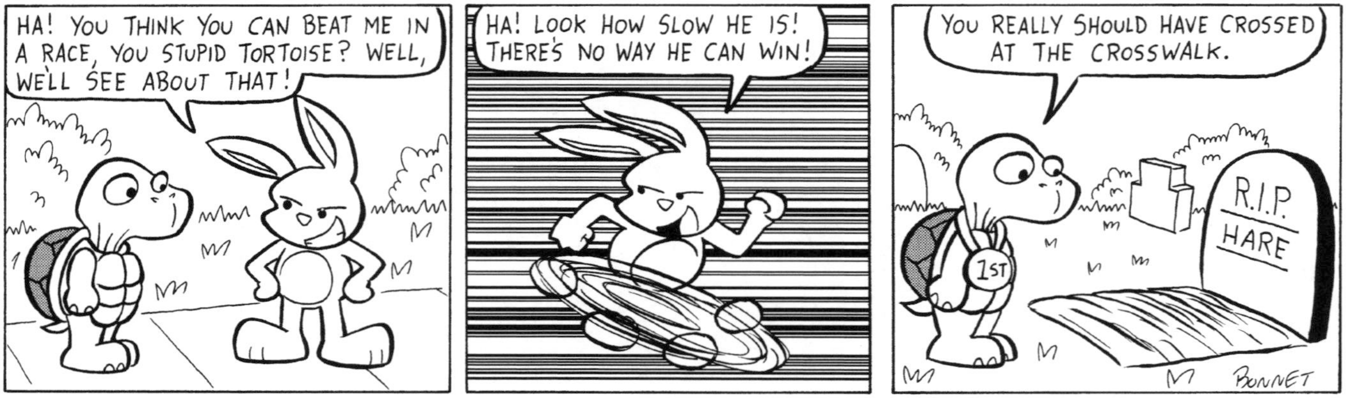
HA! YOU THINK YOU CAN BEAT ME IN A RACE, YOU STUPID TORTOISE? WELL, WE'LL SEE ABOUT THAT!
HA! LOOK HOW SLOW HE IS! THERE'S NO WAY HE CAN WIN!
YOU REALLY SHOULD HAVE CROSSED AT THE CROSSWALK.
R.I.P. HARE
1ST
BONNET

March 31, April 2, 5, 2010

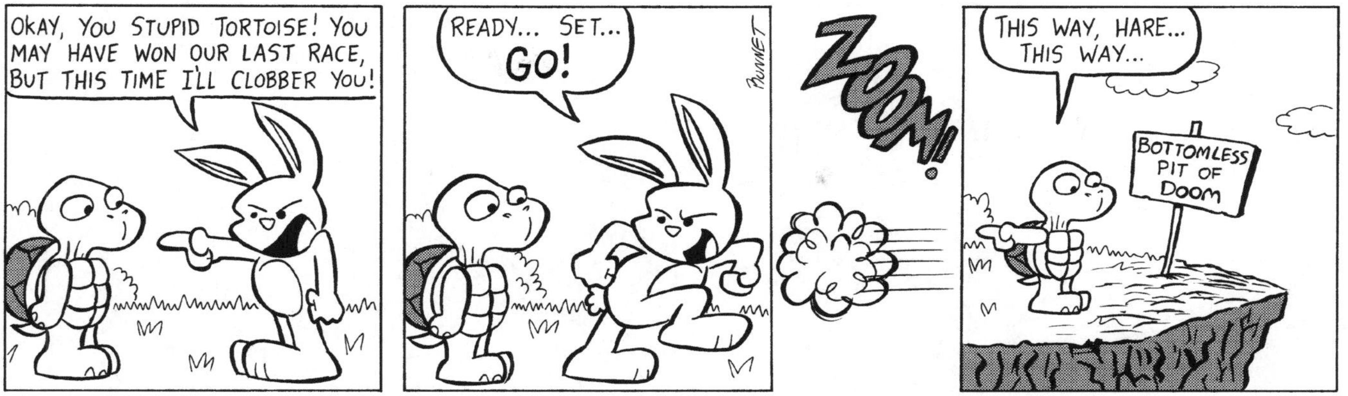
OKAY, YOU STUPID TORTOISE! YOU MAY HAVE WON OUR LAST RACE, BUT THIS TIME I'LL CLOBBER YOU!
READY... SET... GO!
BONNET
ZOOM!
THIS WAY, HARE... THIS WAY...
BOTTOMLESS PIT OF DOOM

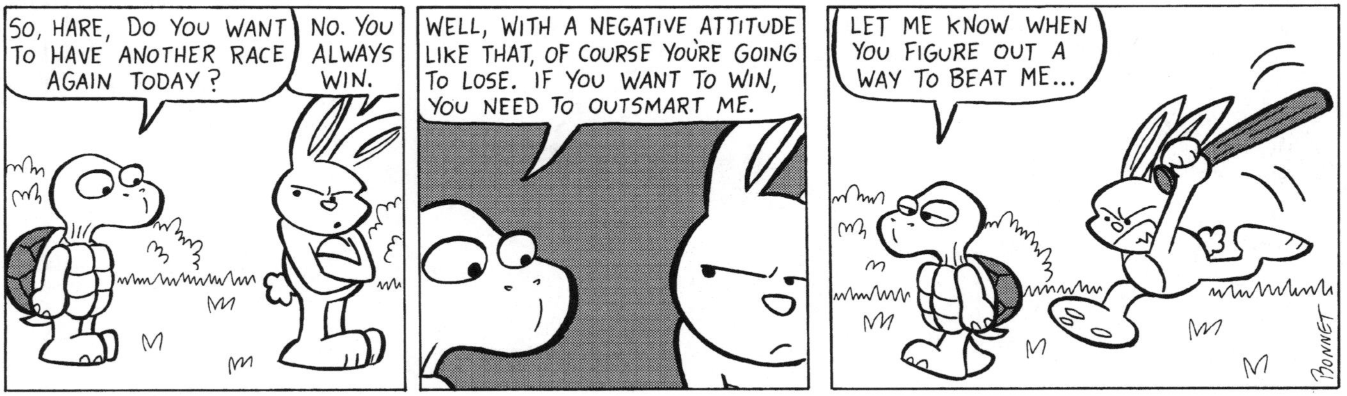
SO, HARE, DO YOU WANT TO HAVE ANOTHER RACE AGAIN TODAY?
NO. YOU ALWAYS WIN.
WELL, WITH A NEGATIVE ATTITUDE LIKE THAT, OF COURSE YOU'RE GOING TO LOSE. IF YOU WANT TO WIN, YOU NEED TO OUTSMART ME.
LET ME KNOW WHEN YOU FIGURE OUT A WAY TO BEAT ME...
BONNET

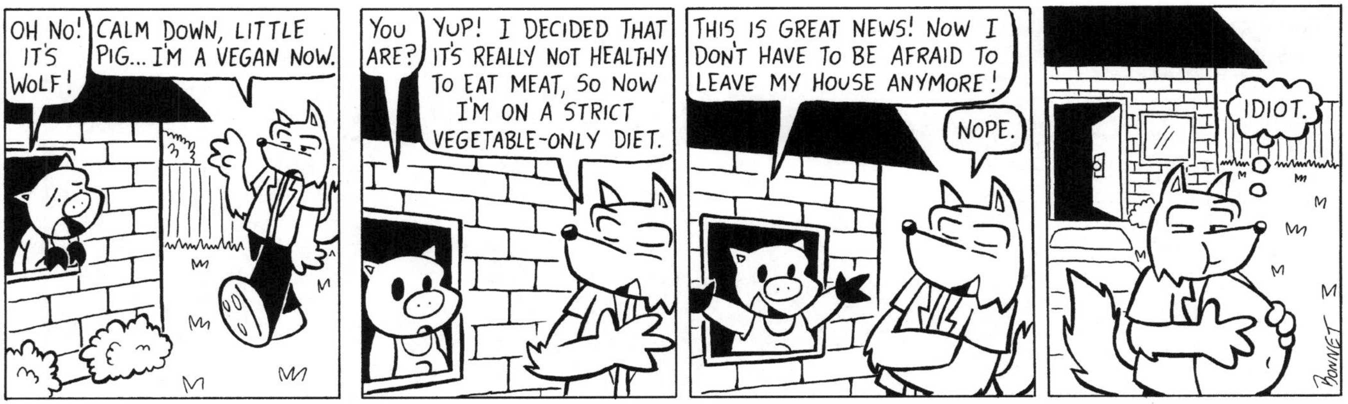
OH NO! IT'S WOLF!
CALM DOWN, LITTLE PIG... I'M A VEGAN NOW.
YOU ARE?
YUP! I DECIDED THAT IT'S REALLY NOT HEALTHY TO EAT MEAT, SO NOW I'M ON A STRICT VEGETABLE-ONLY DIET.
THIS IS GREAT NEWS! NOW I DON'T HAVE TO BE AFRAID TO LEAVE MY HOUSE ANYMORE!
NOPE.
IDIOT.
BONNET

April 7, 9, 12, 2010

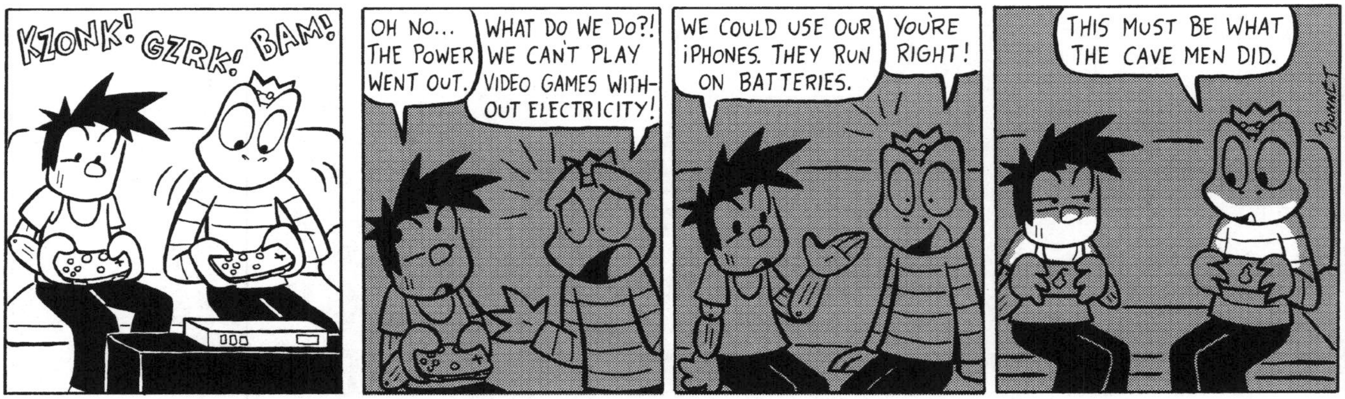
KZONK! GZRK! BAM!
OH NO... THE POWER WENT OUT.
WHAT DO WE DO?! WE CAN'T PLAY VIDEO GAMES WITH-OUT ELECTRICITY!
WE COULD USE OUR iPHONES. THEY RUN ON BATTERIES.
YOU'RE RIGHT!
THIS MUST BE WHAT THE CAVE MEN DID.

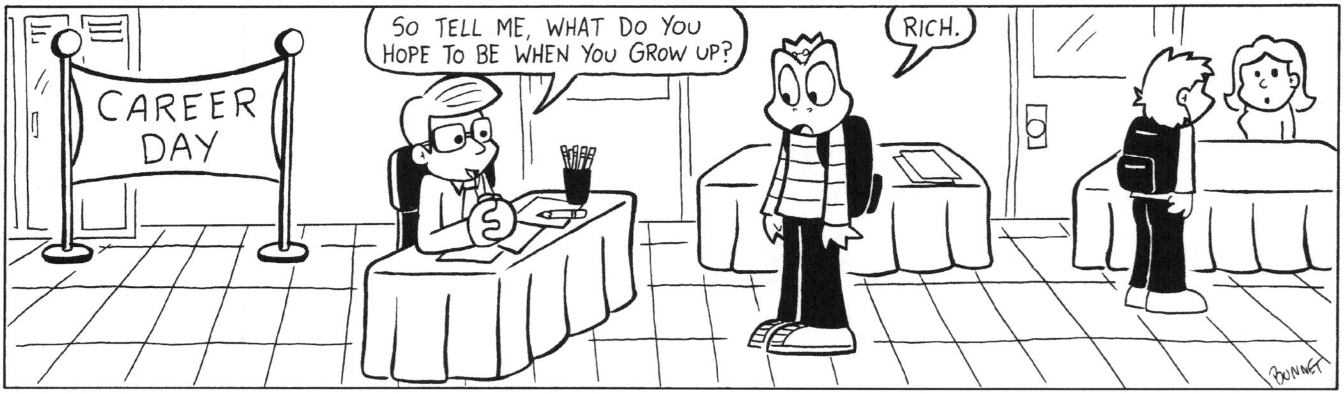
CAREER DAY
SO TELL ME, WHAT DO YOU HOPE TO BE WHEN YOU GROW UP?
RICH.

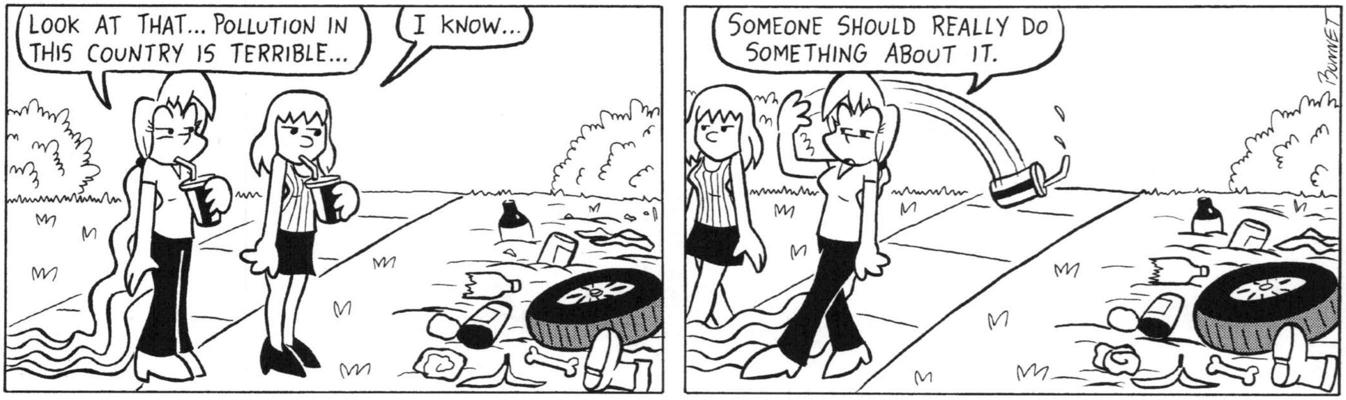
LOOK AT THAT... POLLUTION IN THIS COUNTRY IS TERRIBLE...
I KNOW...
SOMEONE SHOULD REALLY DO SOMETHING ABOUT IT.

April 14, 16, 19, 2010

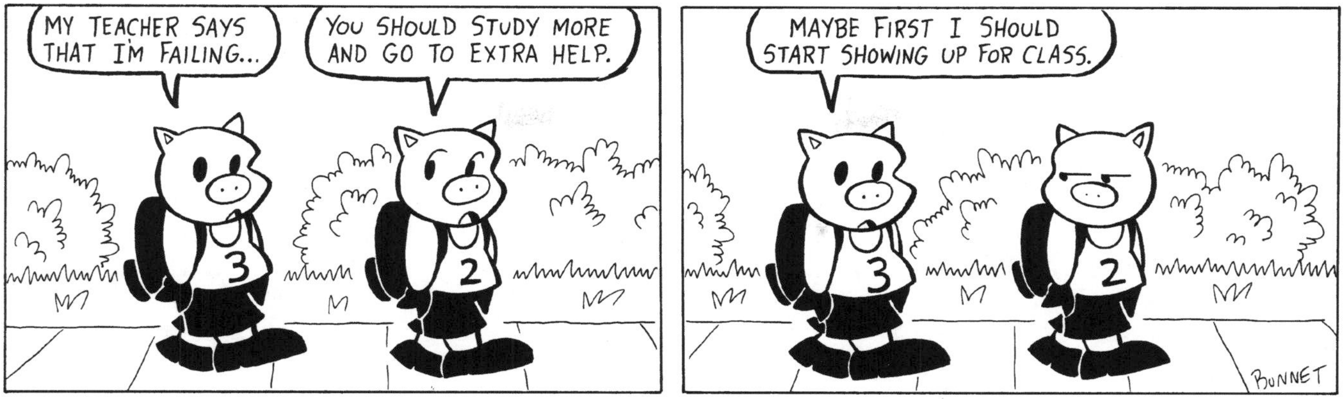
MY TEACHER SAYS THAT I'M FAILING...
YOU SHOULD STUDY MORE AND GO TO EXTRA HELP.
MAYBE FIRST I SHOULD START SHOWING UP FOR CLASS.
BONNET

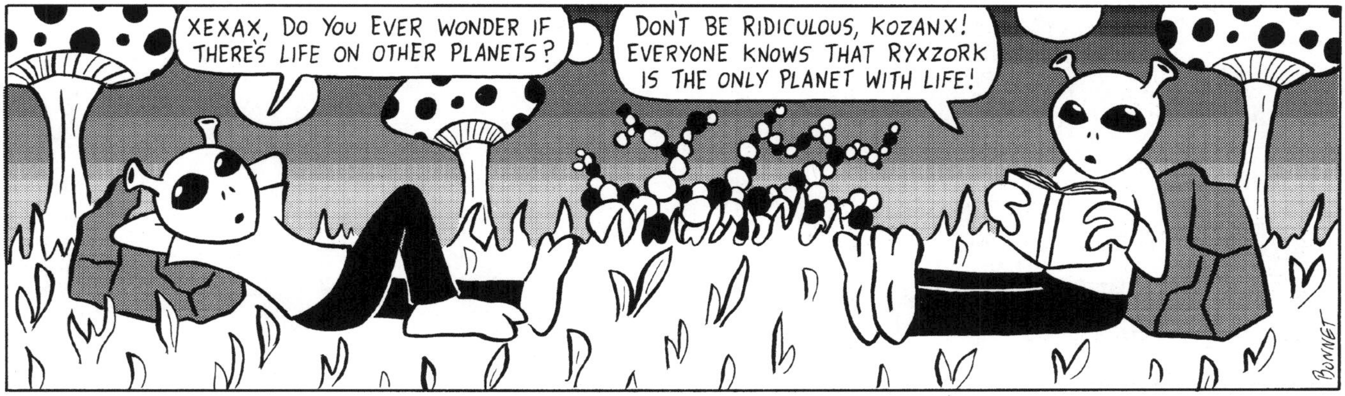
XEXAX, DO YOU EVER WONDER IF THERE'S LIFE ON OTHER PLANETS?
DON'T BE RIDICULOUS, KOZANX! EVERYONE KNOWS THAT RYXZORK IS THE ONLY PLANET WITH LIFE!
BONNET

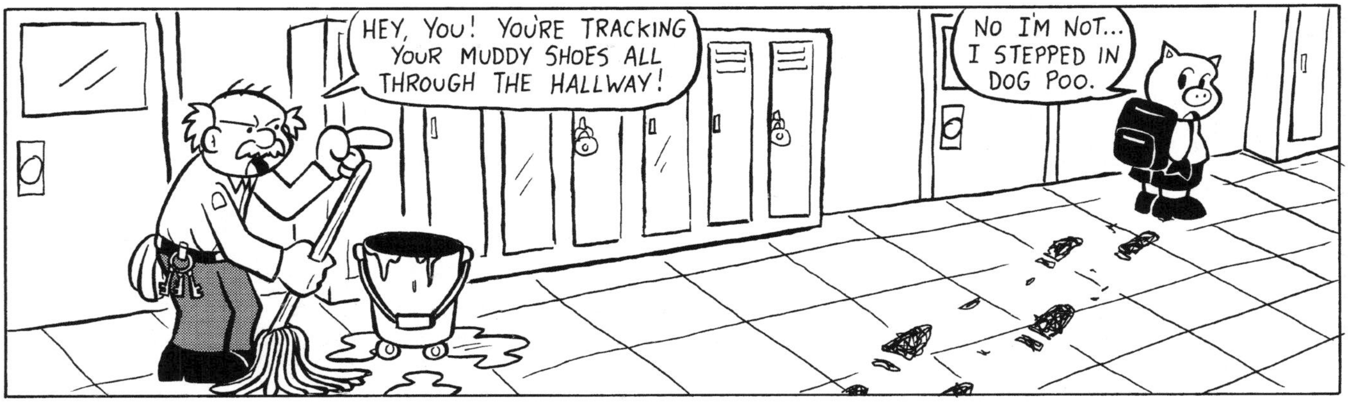
HEY, YOU! YOU'RE TRACKING YOUR MUDDY SHOES ALL THROUGH THE HALLWAY!
NO I'M NOT... I STEPPED IN DOG POO.

April 21, 23, 26, 2010

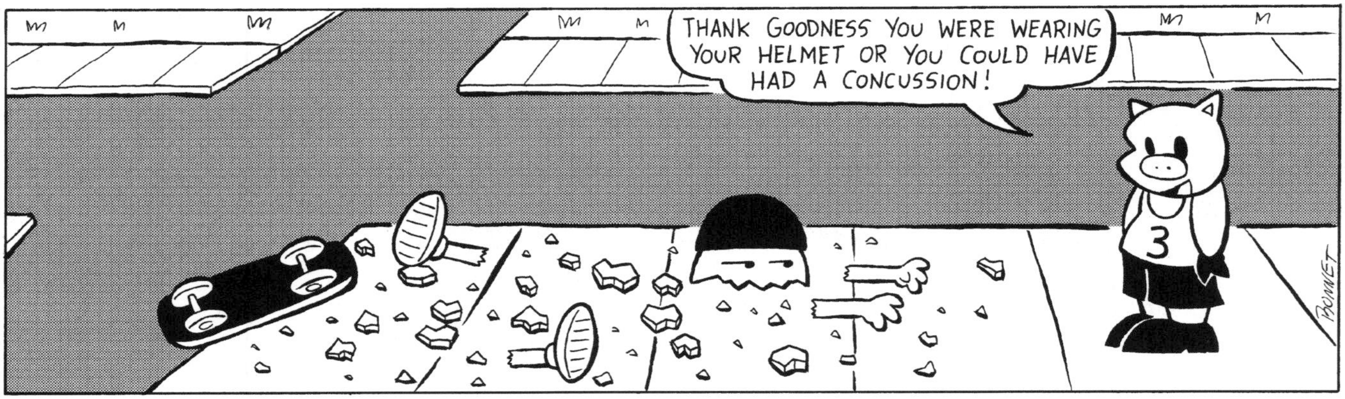
THANK GOODNESS YOU WERE WEARING YOUR HELMET OR YOU COULD HAVE HAD A CONCUSSION!
3
BONNET

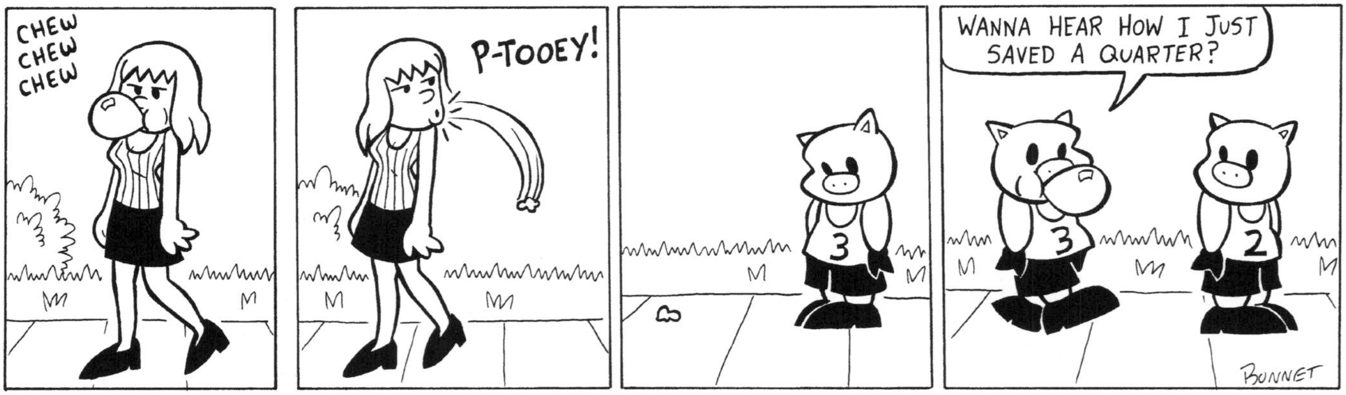
CHEW CHEW CHEW
P-TOOEY!
3
WANNA HEAR HOW I JUST SAVED A QUARTER?
3
2
BONNET

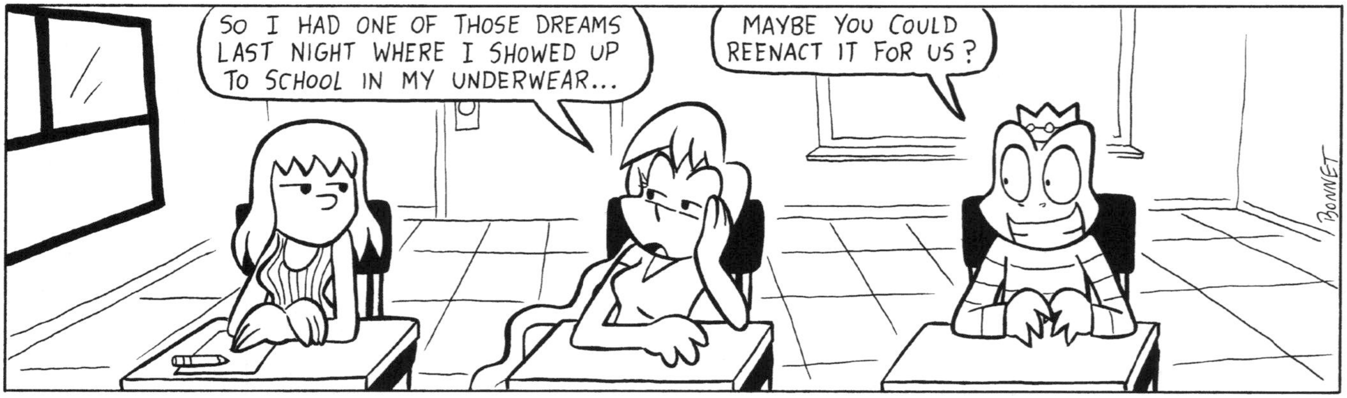
SO I HAD ONE OF THOSE DREAMS LAST NIGHT WHERE I SHOWED UP TO SCHOOL IN MY UNDERWEAR...
MAYBE YOU COULD REENACT IT FOR US?
BONNET

April 28, 30, May 3, 2010

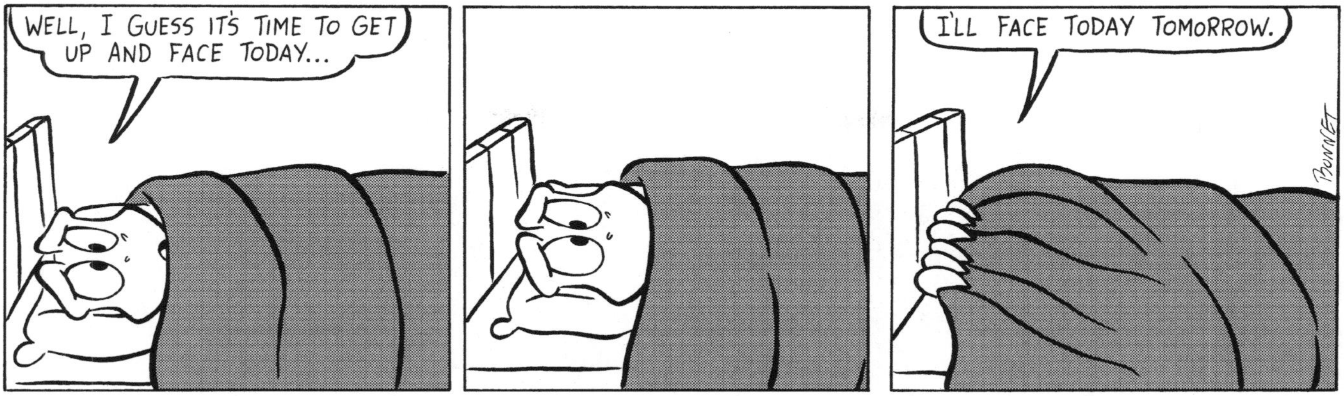
WELL, I GUESS IT'S TIME TO GET UP AND FACE TODAY...
I'LL FACE TODAY TOMORROW.
BONNET

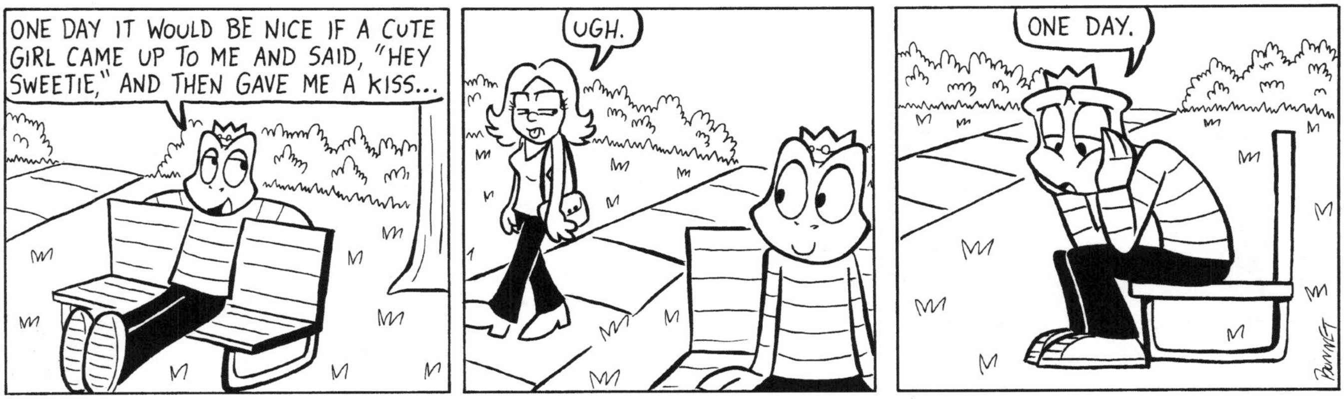
ONE DAY IT WOULD BE NICE IF A CUTE GIRL CAME UP TO ME AND SAID, "HEY SWEETIE," AND THEN GAVE ME A KISS...
UGH.
ONE DAY.
BONNET

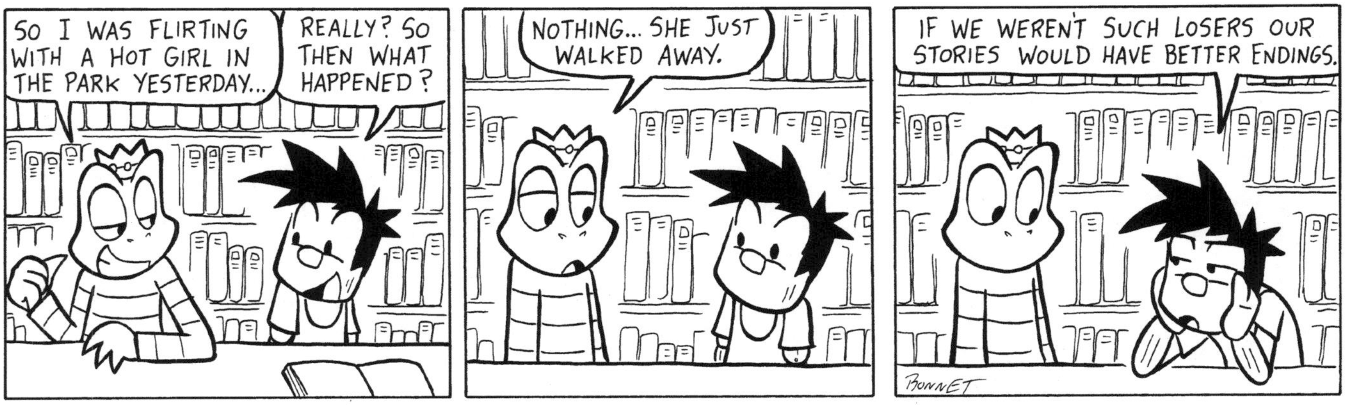
SO I WAS FLIRTING WITH A HOT GIRL IN THE PARK YESTERDAY...
REALLY? SO THEN WHAT HAPPENED?
NOTHING... SHE JUST WALKED AWAY.
IF WE WEREN'T SUCH LOSERS OUR STORIES WOULD HAVE BETTER ENDINGS.
BONNET

May 5, 7, 10, 2010

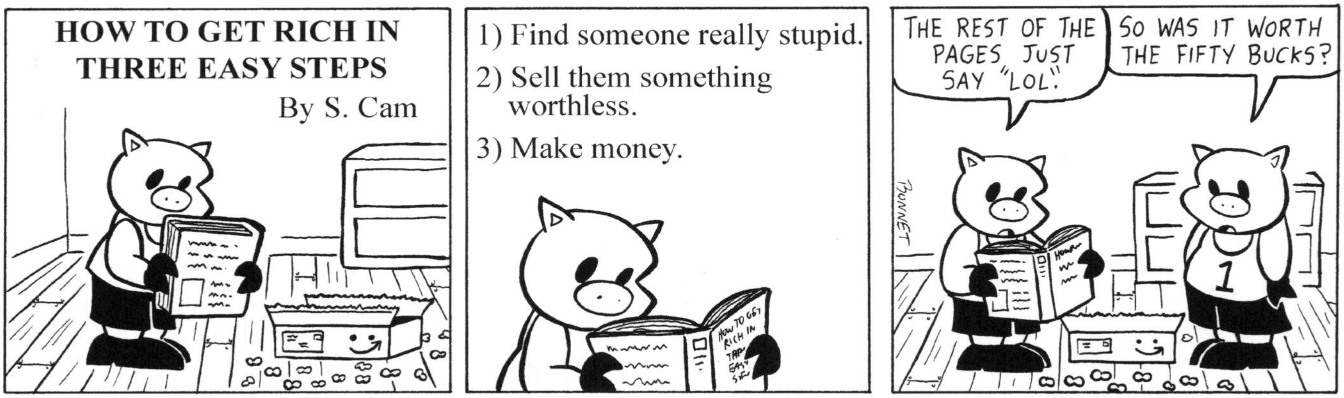
HOW TO GET RICH IN THREE EASY STEPS
By S. Cam
1) Find someone really stupid.
2) Sell them something worthless.
3) Make money.
THE REST OF THE PAGES JUST SAY "LOL".
SO WAS IT WORTH THE FIFTY BUCKS?
BONNET

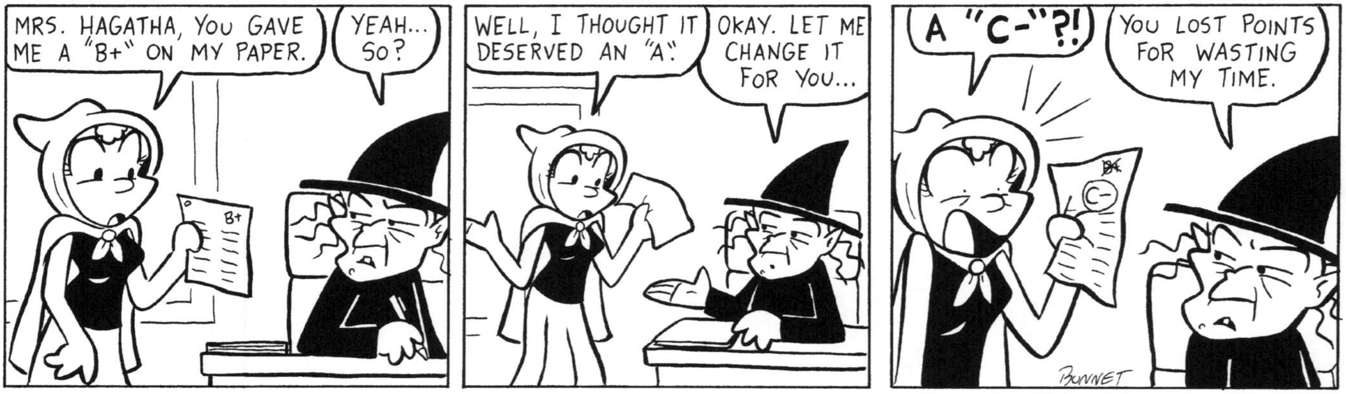
MRS. HAGATHA, YOU GAVE ME A "B+" ON MY PAPER.
YEAH... SO?
WELL, I THOUGHT IT DESERVED AN "A".
OKAY. LET ME CHANGE IT FOR YOU...
A "C-"?!
YOU LOST POINTS FOR WASTING MY TIME.
BONNET

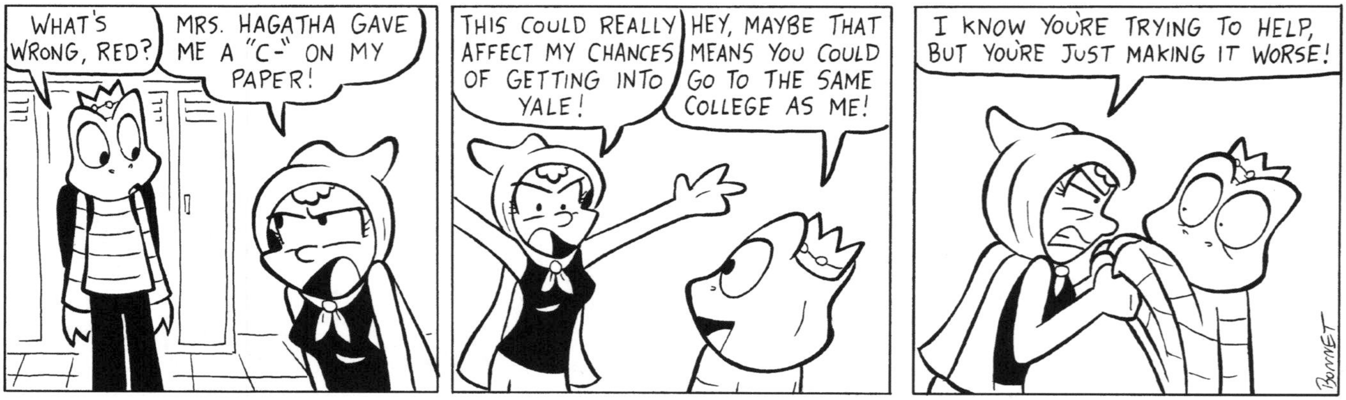
WHAT'S WRONG, RED?
MRS. HAGATHA GAVE ME A "C-" ON MY PAPER!
THIS COULD REALLY AFFECT MY CHANCES OF GETTING INTO YALE!
HEY, MAYBE THAT MEANS YOU COULD GO TO THE SAME COLLEGE AS ME!
I KNOW YOU'RE TRYING TO HELP, BUT YOU'RE JUST MAKING IT WORSE!
BONNET

May 12, 14, 17, 2010

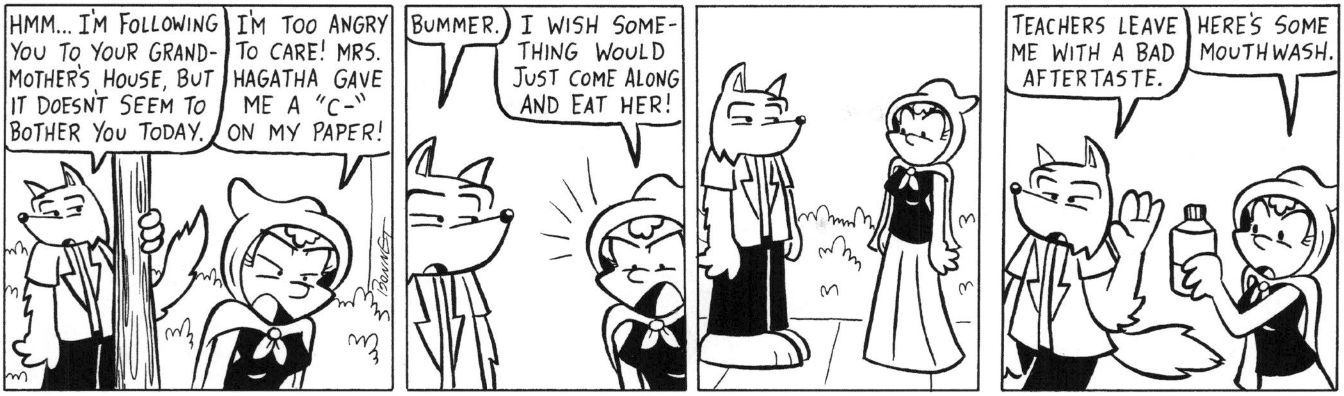
HMM... I'M FOLLOWING YOU TO YOUR GRAND-MOTHER'S HOUSE, BUT IT DOESN'T SEEM TO BOTHER YOU TODAY.
I'M TOO ANGRY TO CARE! MRS. HAGATHA GAVE ME A "C-" ON MY PAPER!
BONNET
BUMMER.
I WISH SOME-THING WOULD JUST COME ALONG AND EAT HER!
TEACHERS LEAVE ME WITH A BAD AFTERTASTE.
HERE'S SOME MOUTHWASH.

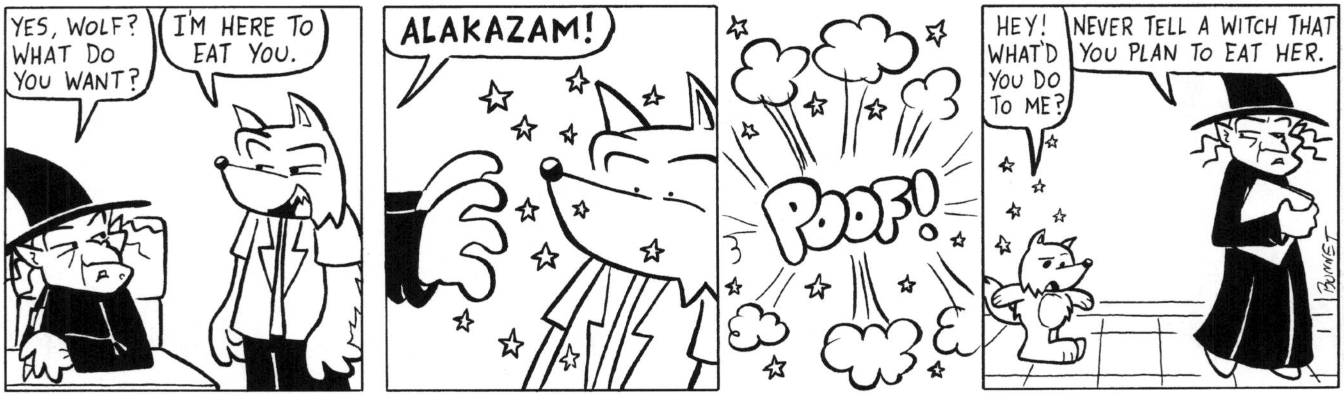
YES, WOLF? WHAT DO YOU WANT?
I'M HERE TO EAT YOU.
ALAKAZAM!
POOF!
HEY! WHAT'D YOU DO TO ME?
NEVER TELL A WITCH THAT YOU PLAN TO EAT HER.
BONNET

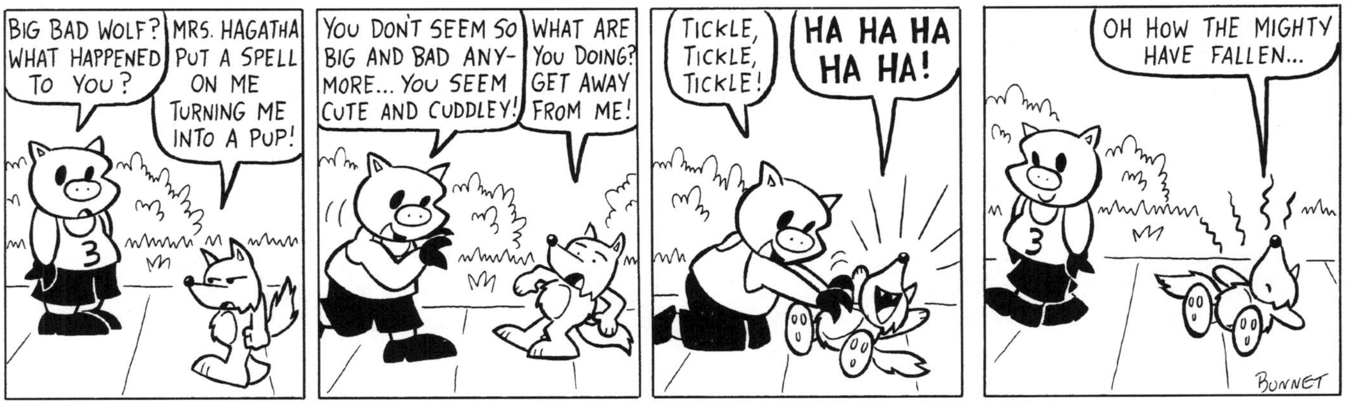
BIG BAD WOLF? WHAT HAPPENED TO YOU?
MRS. HAGATHA PUT A SPELL ON ME TURNING ME INTO A PUP!
YOU DON'T SEEM SO BIG AND BAD ANY-MORE... YOU SEEM CUTE AND CUDDLEY!
WHAT ARE YOU DOING? GET AWAY FROM ME!
TICKLE, TICKLE, TICKLE!
HA HA HA HA HA!
OH HOW THE MIGHTY HAVE FALLEN...
BONNET

May 19, 21, 24, 2010

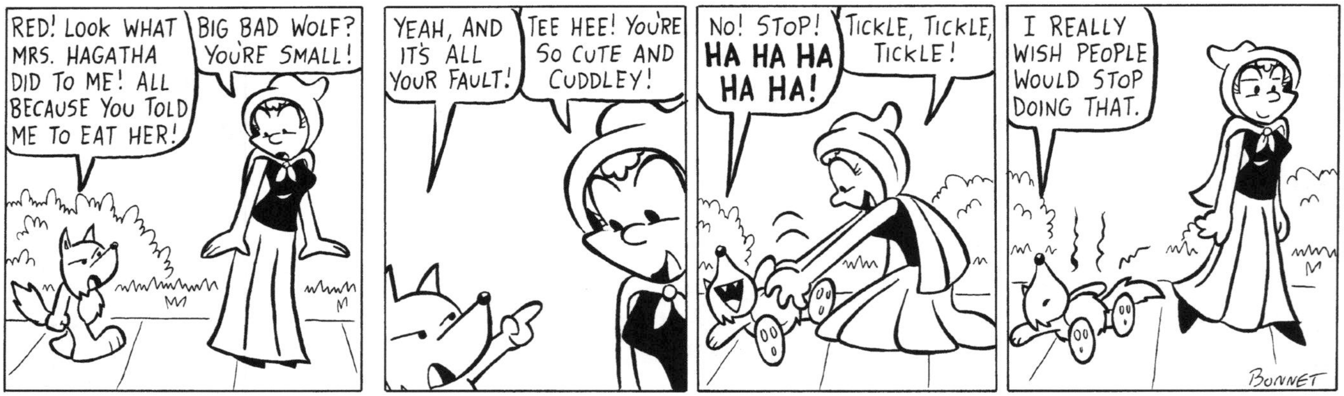
RED! LOOK WHAT MRS. HAGATHA DID TO ME! ALL BECAUSE YOU TOLD ME TO EAT HER!
BIG BAD WOLF? YOU'RE SMALL!
YEAH, AND IT'S ALL YOUR FAULT!
TEE HEE! YOU'RE SO CUTE AND CUDDLEY!
NO! STOP! **HA HA HA HA HA!**
TICKLE, TICKLE, TICKLE!
I REALLY WISH PEOPLE WOULD STOP DOING THAT.
BONNET

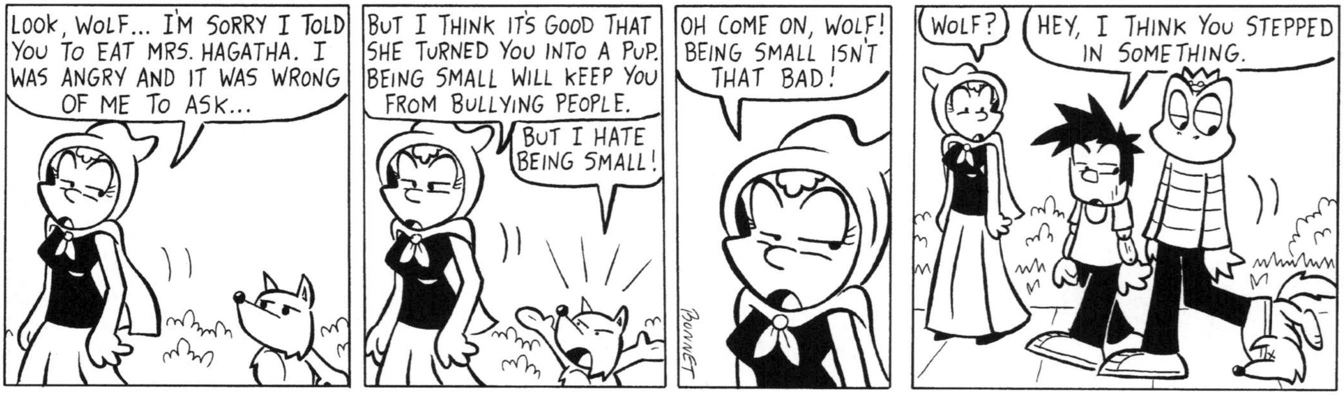
LOOK, WOLF... I'M SORRY I TOLD YOU TO EAT MRS. HAGATHA. I WAS ANGRY AND IT WAS WRONG OF ME TO ASK...
BUT I THINK IT'S GOOD THAT SHE TURNED YOU INTO A PUP. BEING SMALL WILL KEEP YOU FROM BULLYING PEOPLE.
BUT I HATE BEING SMALL!
BONNET
OH COME ON, WOLF! BEING SMALL ISN'T THAT BAD!
WOLF?
HEY, I THINK YOU STEPPED IN SOMETHING.

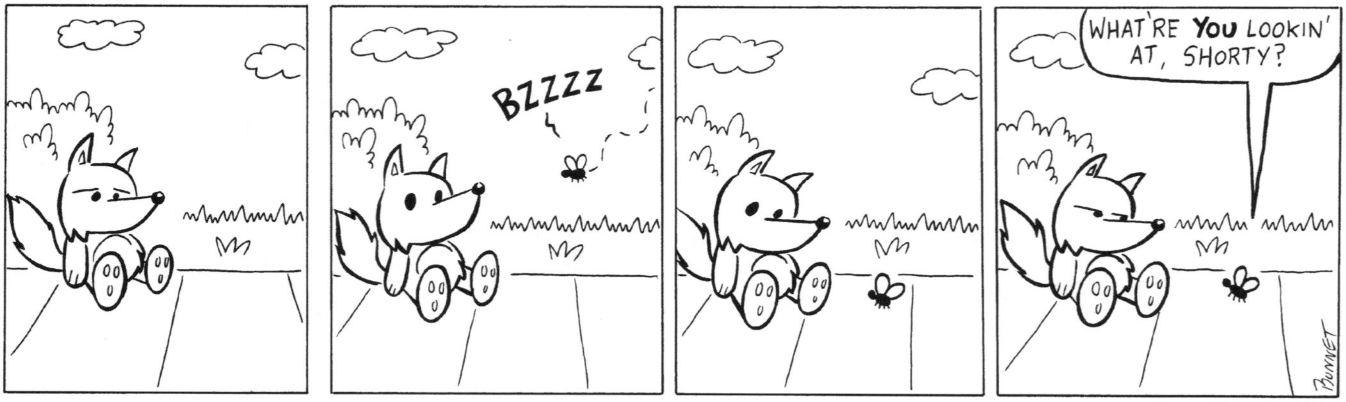
BZZZZ
WHAT'RE **YOU** LOOKIN' AT, SHORTY?
BONNET

May 26, 28, 31, 2010

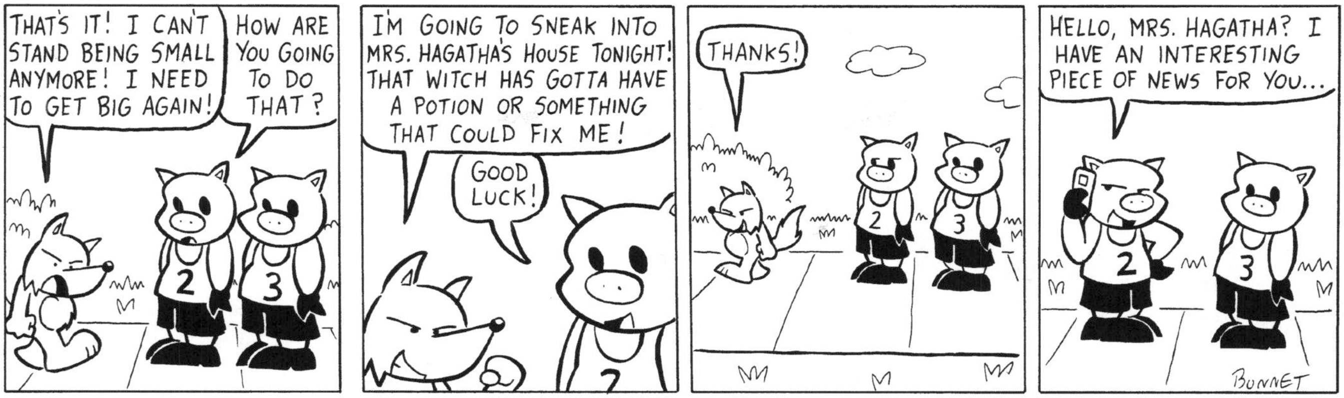
THAT'S IT! I CAN'T STAND BEING SMALL ANYMORE! I NEED TO GET BIG AGAIN!
HOW ARE YOU GOING TO DO THAT?
I'M GOING TO SNEAK INTO MRS. HAGATHA'S HOUSE TONIGHT! THAT WITCH HAS GOTTA HAVE A POTION OR SOMETHING THAT COULD FIX ME!
GOOD LUCK!
THANKS!
HELLO, MRS. HAGATHA? I HAVE AN INTERESTING PIECE OF NEWS FOR YOU...
BONNET

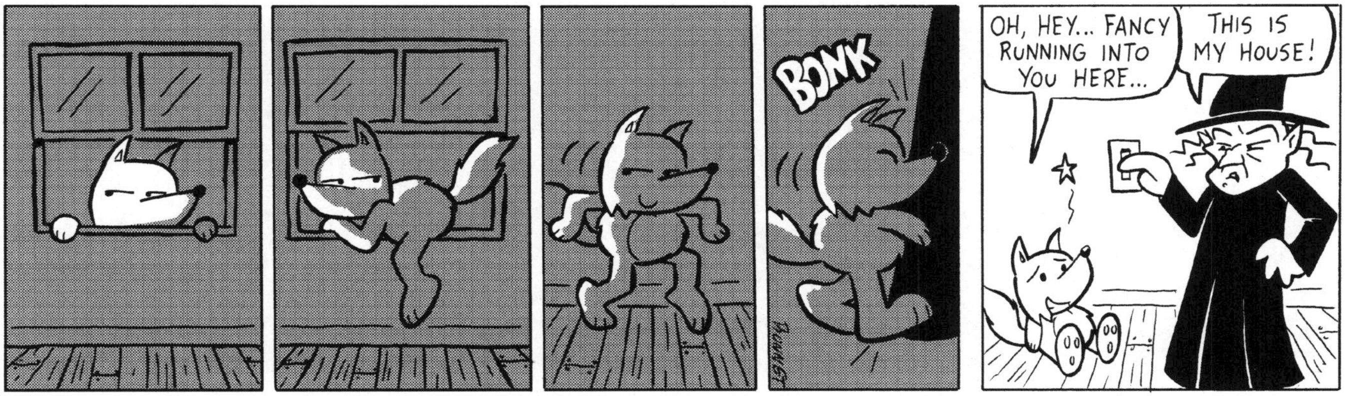
BONK
BONNET
OH, HEY... FANCY RUNNING INTO YOU HERE...
THIS IS MY HOUSE!

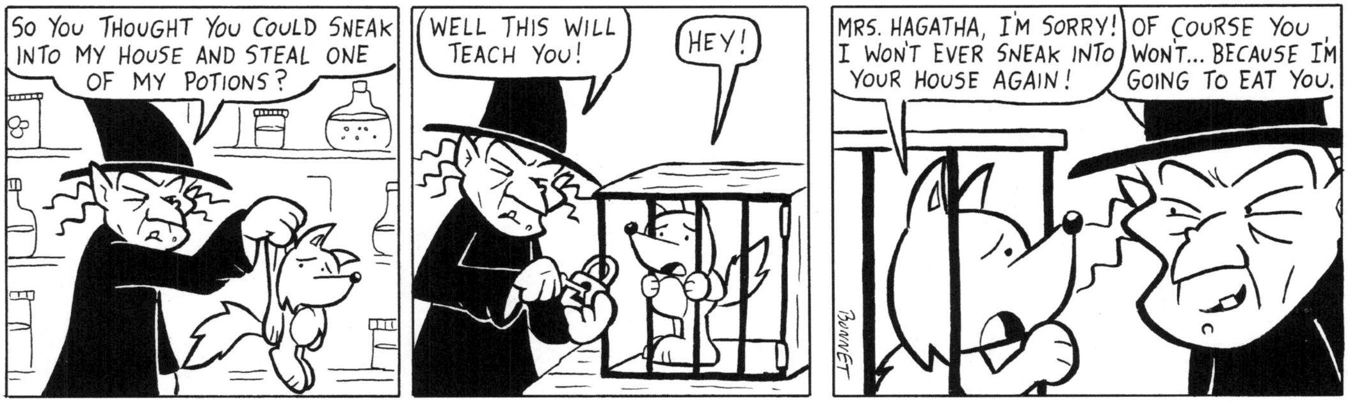
SO YOU THOUGHT YOU COULD SNEAK INTO MY HOUSE AND STEAL ONE OF MY POTIONS?
WELL THIS WILL TEACH YOU!
HEY!
BONNET
MRS. HAGATHA, I'M SORRY! I WON'T EVER SNEAK INTO YOUR HOUSE AGAIN!
OF COURSE YOU WON'T... BECAUSE I'M GOING TO EAT YOU.

June 2, 4, 7, 2010

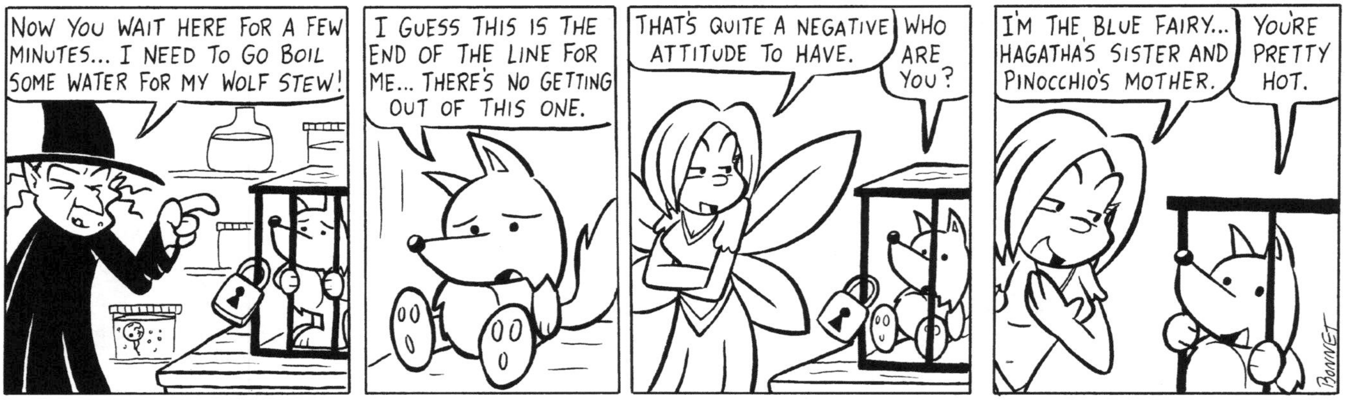
NOW YOU WAIT HERE FOR A FEW MINUTES... I NEED TO GO BOIL SOME WATER FOR MY WOLF STEW!
I GUESS THIS IS THE END OF THE LINE FOR ME... THERE'S NO GETTING OUT OF THIS ONE.
THAT'S QUITE A NEGATIVE ATTITUDE TO HAVE.
WHO ARE YOU?
I'M THE BLUE FAIRY... HAGATHA'S SISTER AND PINOCCHIO'S MOTHER.
YOU'RE PRETTY HOT.
BONNET

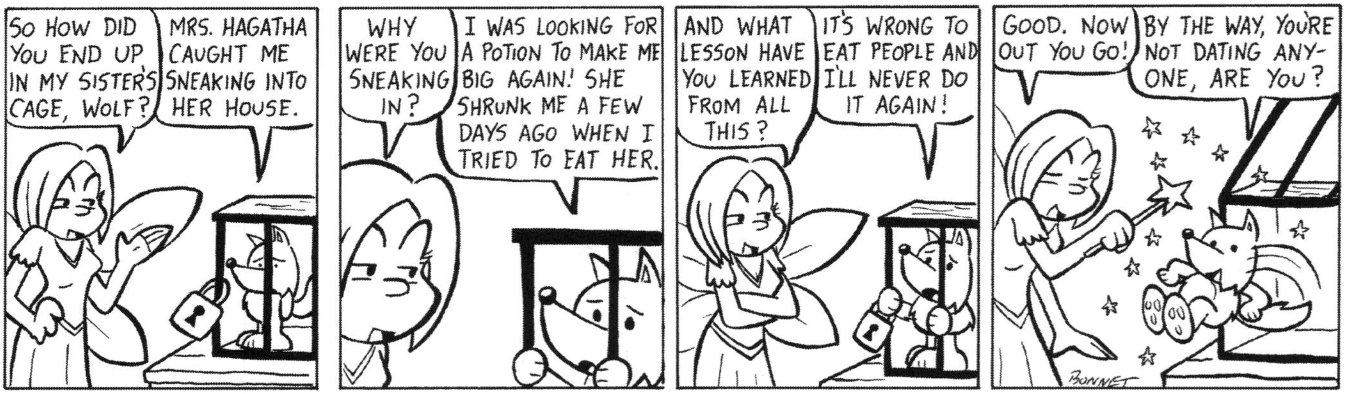
SO HOW DID YOU END UP IN MY SISTER'S CAGE, WOLF?
MRS. HAGATHA CAUGHT ME SNEAKING INTO HER HOUSE.
WHY WERE YOU SNEAKING IN?
I WAS LOOKING FOR A POTION TO MAKE ME BIG AGAIN! SHE SHRUNK ME A FEW DAYS AGO WHEN I TRIED TO EAT HER.
AND WHAT LESSON HAVE YOU LEARNED FROM ALL THIS?
IT'S WRONG TO EAT PEOPLE AND I'LL NEVER DO IT AGAIN!
GOOD. NOW OUT YOU GO!
BY THE WAY, YOU'RE NOT DATING ANYONE, ARE YOU?
BONNET

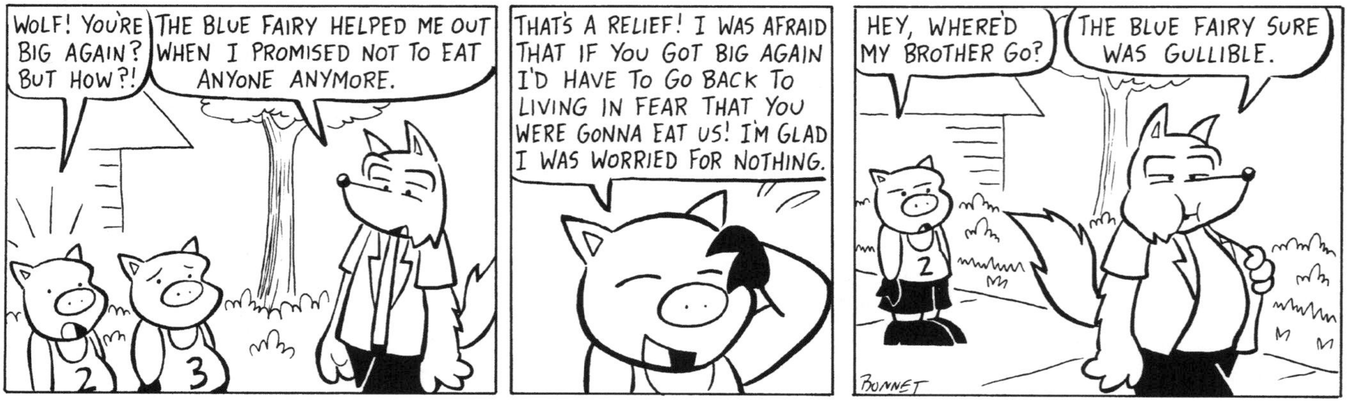
WOLF! YOU'RE BIG AGAIN? BUT HOW?!
THE BLUE FAIRY HELPED ME OUT WHEN I PROMISED NOT TO EAT ANYONE ANYMORE.
THAT'S A RELIEF! I WAS AFRAID THAT IF YOU GOT BIG AGAIN I'D HAVE TO GO BACK TO LIVING IN FEAR THAT YOU WERE GONNA EAT US! I'M GLAD I WAS WORRIED FOR NOTHING.
HEY, WHERE'D MY BROTHER GO?
THE BLUE FAIRY SURE WAS GULLIBLE.
BONNET

June 9, 11, 14, 2010

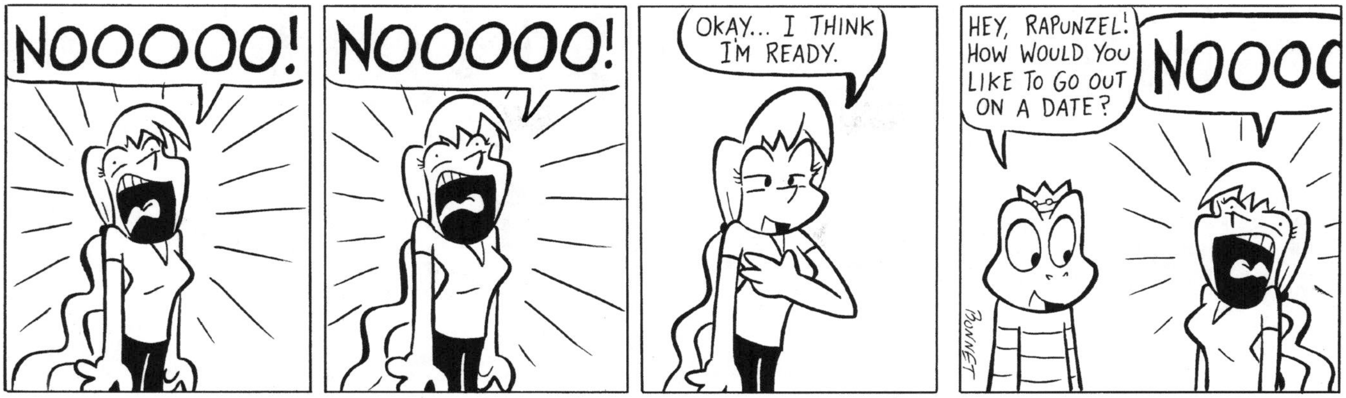
NOOOOO!
NOOOOO!
OKAY... I THINK I'M READY.
HEY, RAPUNZEL! HOW WOULD YOU LIKE TO GO OUT ON A DATE?
NOOOO
BONNET

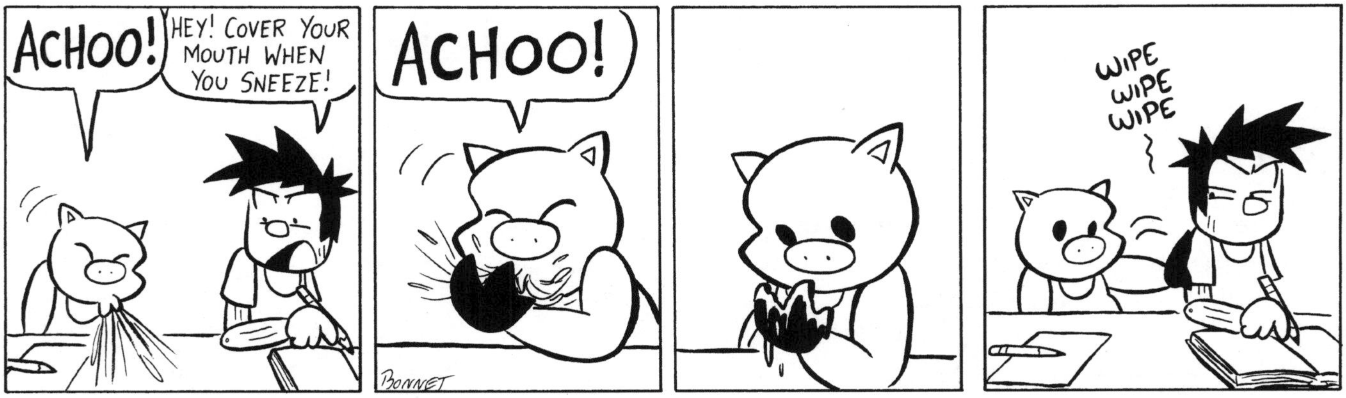
ACHOO!
HEY! COVER YOUR MOUTH WHEN YOU SNEEZE!
ACHOO!
BONNET
WIPE WIPE WIPE

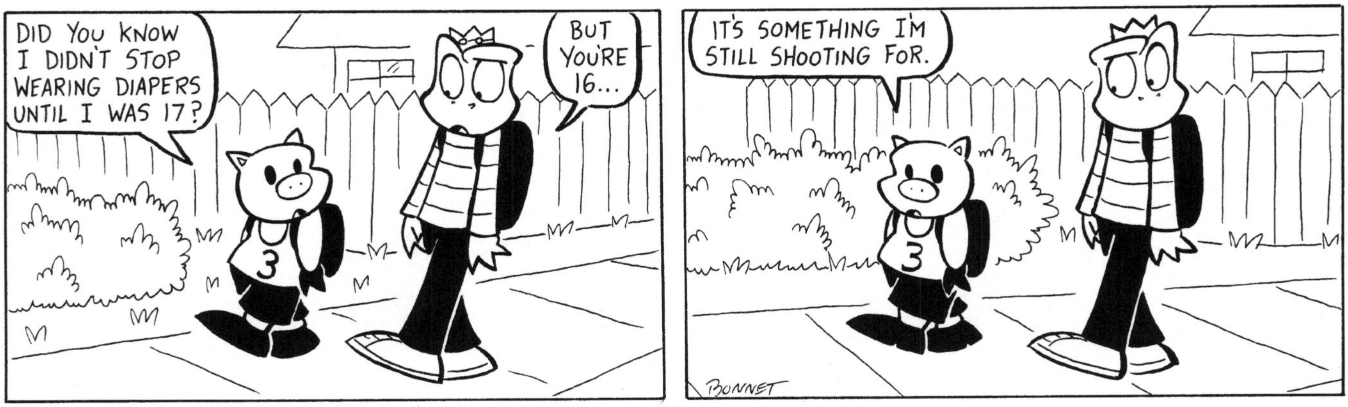
DID YOU KNOW I DIDN'T STOP WEARING DIAPERS UNTIL I WAS 17?
BUT YOU'RE 16...
3
IT'S SOMETHING I'M STILL SHOOTING FOR.
3
BONNET

June 16, 18, 21, 2010

SUBURBAN *Fairy Tales*

EXCLUSIVE BONUS STORY!

Dear Loyal Readers,

The following story was taken directly from my sketchbook. As you can see, the drawings are very rough compared to a finished strip. This is usually how I lay out my ideas before going into the final.

What you are about to read is what I always thought to be one of my weaker stories. It was never completed, nor was it ever officially published online. However, what makes it stand out from my other non-published stories is the fact that the events played out in these strips forever changed the direction of Suburban Fairy Tales.

Early on in the series, it was very apparent that Red Riding Hood had a secret crush on Frog Prince. But somewhere along the way, her crush mysteriously vanished... without any reason as to why! This story fills in those holes.

So without further adieu, I bring you the horrible story that never was!

Sincerely,

Francis Bonnet

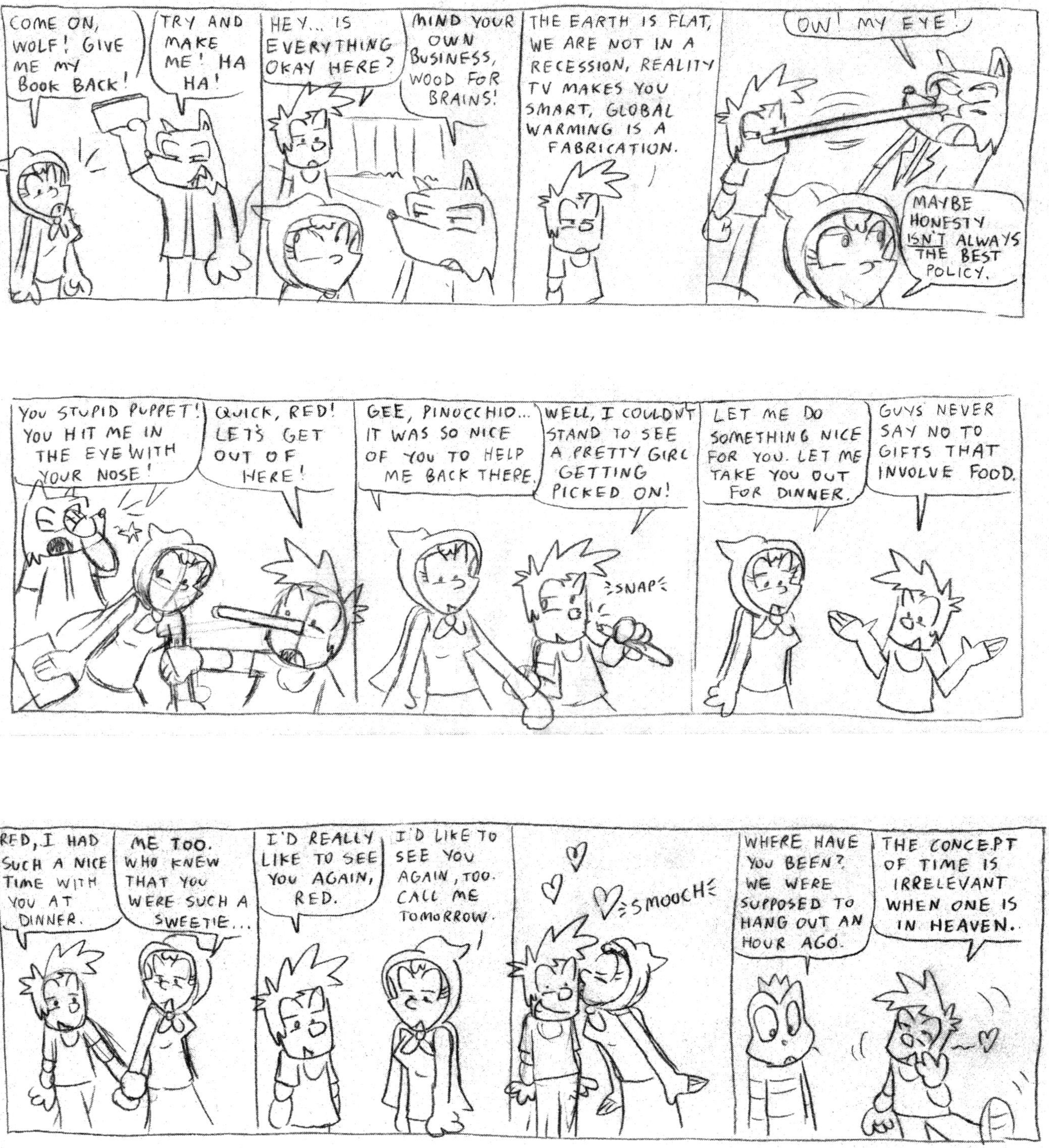
COME ON, WOLF! GIVE ME MY BOOK BACK!
TRY AND MAKE ME! HA HA!
HEY... IS EVERYTHING OKAY HERE?
MIND YOUR OWN BUSINESS, WOOD FOR BRAINS!
THE EARTH IS FLAT, WE ARE NOT IN A RECESSION, REALITY TV MAKES YOU SMART, GLOBAL WARMING IS A FABRICATION.
OW! MY EYE!
MAYBE HONESTY ISN'T ALWAYS THE BEST POLICY.
YOU STUPID PUPPET! YOU HIT ME IN THE EYE WITH YOUR NOSE!
QUICK, RED! LET'S GET OUT OF HERE!
GEE, PINOCCHIO... IT WAS SO NICE OF YOU TO HELP ME BACK THERE.
WELL, I COULDN'T STAND TO SEE A PRETTY GIRL GETTING PICKED ON!
SNAP
LET ME DO SOMETHING NICE FOR YOU. LET ME TAKE YOU OUT FOR DINNER.
GUYS NEVER SAY NO TO GIFTS THAT INVOLVE FOOD.
RED, I HAD SUCH A NICE TIME WITH YOU AT DINNER.
ME TOO. WHO KNEW THAT YOU WERE SUCH A SWEETIE...
I'D REALLY LIKE TO SEE YOU AGAIN, RED.
I'D LIKE TO SEE YOU AGAIN, TOO. CALL ME TOMORROW.
SMOOCH
WHERE HAVE YOU BEEN? WE WERE SUPPOSED TO HANG OUT AN HOUR AGO.
THE CONCEPT OF TIME IS IRRELEVANT WHEN ONE IS IN HEAVEN.

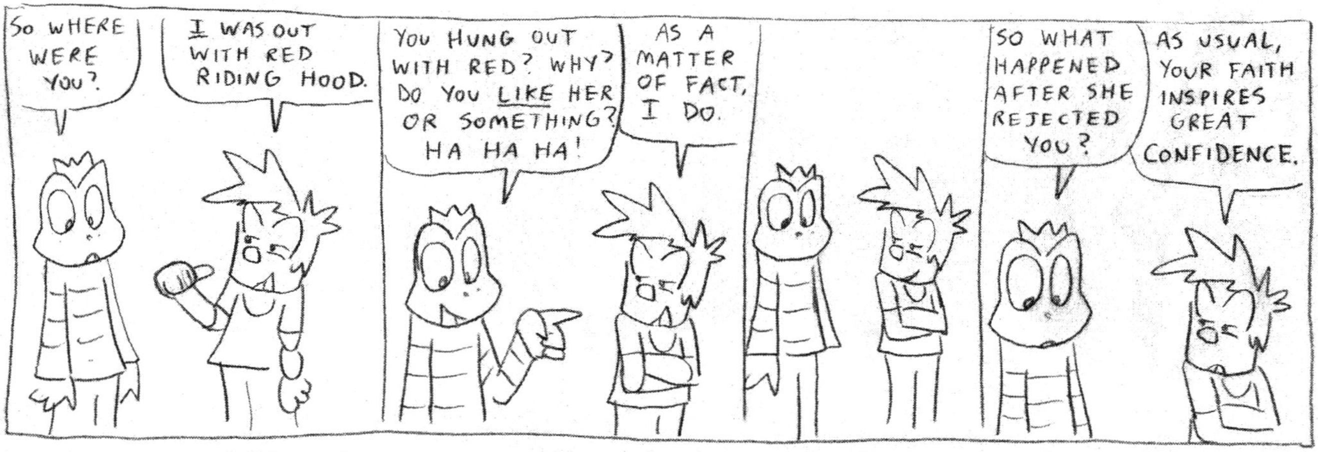
SO WHERE WERE YOU?
I WAS OUT WITH RED RIDING HOOD.
YOU HUNG OUT WITH RED? WHY? DO YOU LIKE HER OR SOMETHING? HA HA HA!
AS A MATTER OF FACT, I DO.
SO WHAT HAPPENED AFTER SHE REJECTED YOU?
AS USUAL, YOUR FAITH INSPIRES GREAT CONFIDENCE.

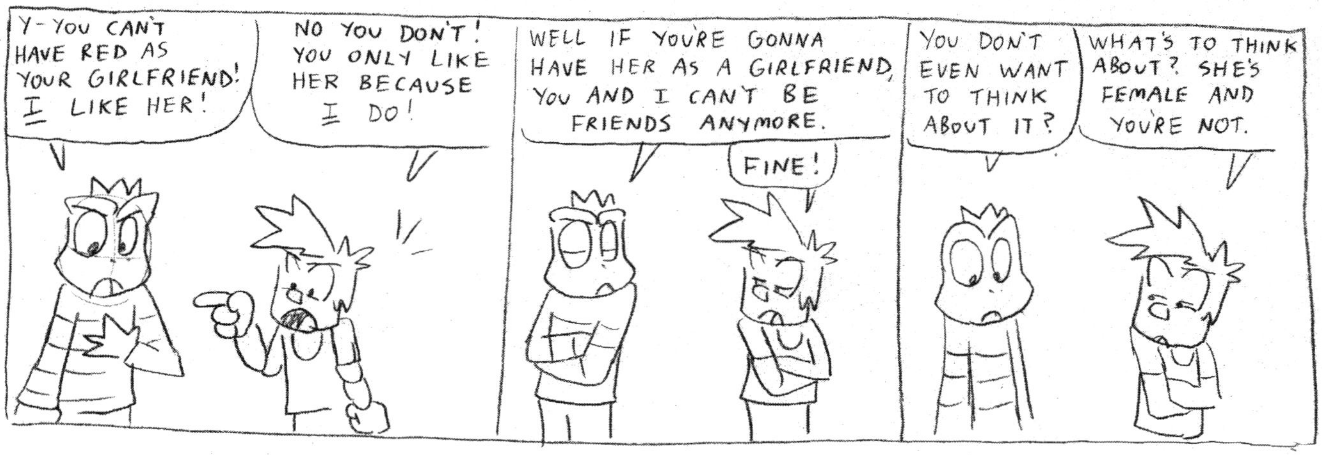
Y-YOU CAN'T HAVE RED AS YOUR GIRLFRIEND! I LIKE HER!
NO YOU DON'T! YOU ONLY LIKE HER BECAUSE I DO!
WELL IF YOU'RE GONNA HAVE HER AS A GIRLFRIEND, YOU AND I CAN'T BE FRIENDS ANYMORE.
FINE!
YOU DON'T EVEN WANT TO THINK ABOUT IT?
WHAT'S TO THINK ABOUT? SHE'S FEMALE AND YOU'RE NOT.

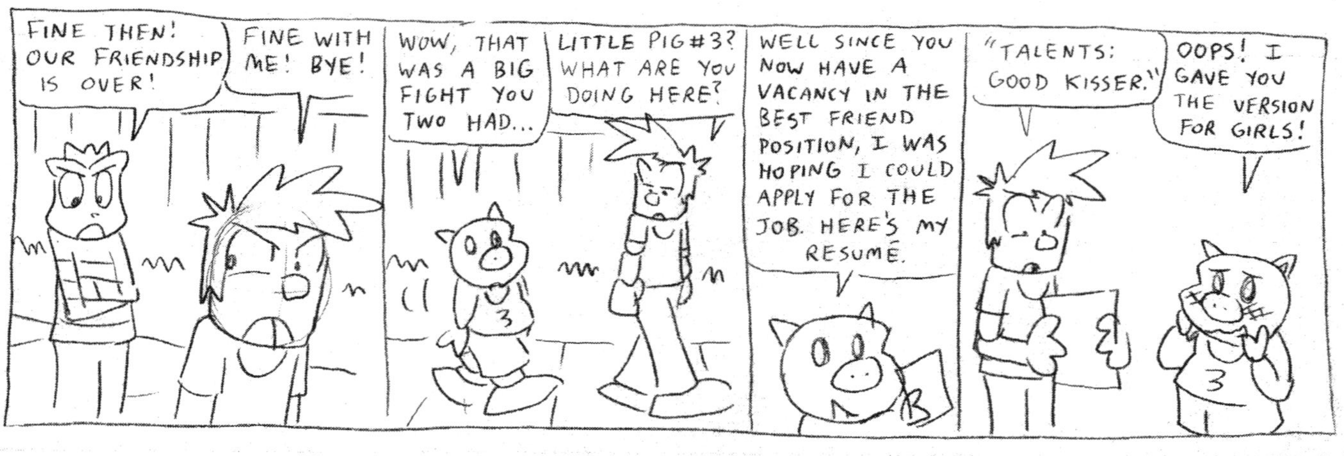
FINE THEN! OUR FRIENDSHIP IS OVER!
FINE WITH ME! BYE!
WOW, THAT WAS A BIG FIGHT YOU TWO HAD...
LITTLE PIG #3? WHAT ARE YOU DOING HERE?
WELL SINCE YOU NOW HAVE A VACANCY IN THE BEST FRIEND POSITION, I WAS HOPING I COULD APPLY FOR THE JOB. HERE'S MY RESUMÉ.
"TALENTS: GOOD KISSER."
OOPS! I GAVE YOU THE VERSION FOR GIRLS!

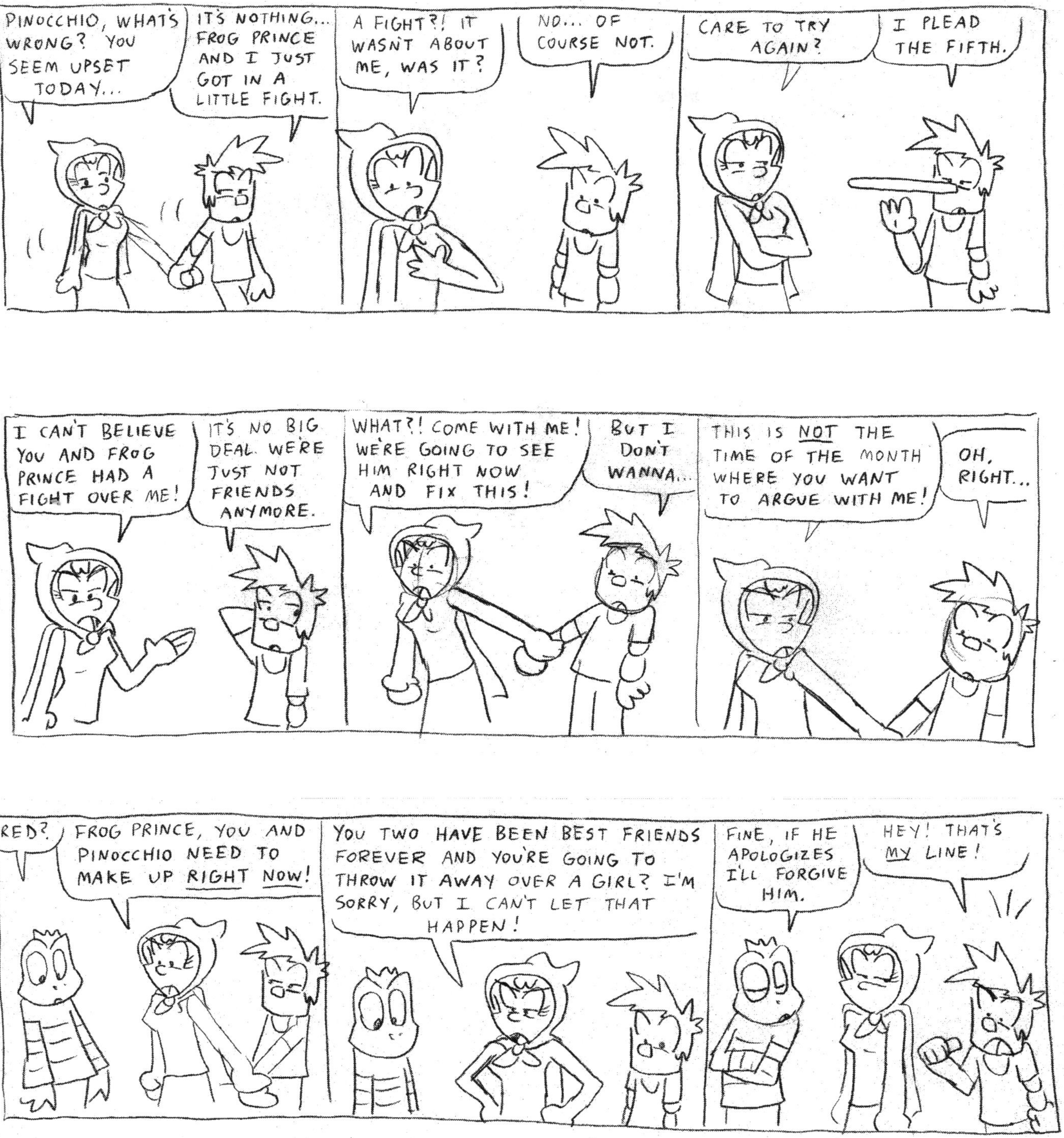
PINOCCHIO, WHAT'S WRONG? YOU SEEM UPSET TODAY...
IT'S NOTHING... FROG PRINCE AND I JUST GOT IN A LITTLE FIGHT.
A FIGHT?! IT WASN'T ABOUT ME, WAS IT?
NO... OF COURSE NOT.
CARE TO TRY AGAIN?
I PLEAD THE FIFTH.
I CAN'T BELIEVE YOU AND FROG PRINCE HAD A FIGHT OVER ME!
IT'S NO BIG DEAL. WE'RE JUST NOT FRIENDS ANYMORE.
WHAT?! COME WITH ME! WE'RE GOING TO SEE HIM RIGHT NOW AND FIX THIS!
BUT I DON'T WANNA...
THIS IS NOT THE TIME OF THE MONTH WHERE YOU WANT TO ARGUE WITH ME!
OH, RIGHT...
RED?
FROG PRINCE, YOU AND PINOCCHIO NEED TO MAKE UP RIGHT NOW!
YOU TWO HAVE BEEN BEST FRIENDS FOREVER AND YOU'RE GOING TO THROW IT AWAY OVER A GIRL? I'M SORRY, BUT I CAN'T LET THAT HAPPEN!
FINE, IF HE APOLOGIZES I'LL FORGIVE HIM.
HEY! THAT'S MY LINE!

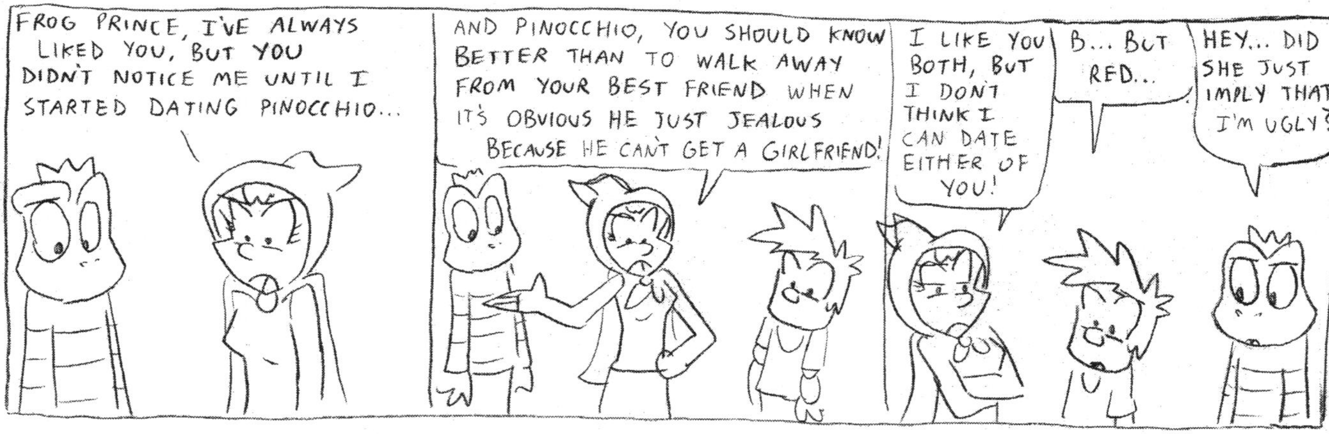
FROG PRINCE, I'VE ALWAYS LIKED YOU, BUT YOU DIDN'T NOTICE ME UNTIL I STARTED DATING PINOCCHIO...
AND PINOCCHIO, YOU SHOULD KNOW BETTER THAN TO WALK AWAY FROM YOUR BEST FRIEND WHEN IT'S OBVIOUS HE JUST JEALOUS BECAUSE HE CAN'T GET A GIRLFRIEND!
I LIKE YOU BOTH, BUT I DON'T THINK I CAN DATE EITHER OF YOU!
B... BUT RED...
HEY... DID SHE JUST IMPLY THAT I'M UGLY?

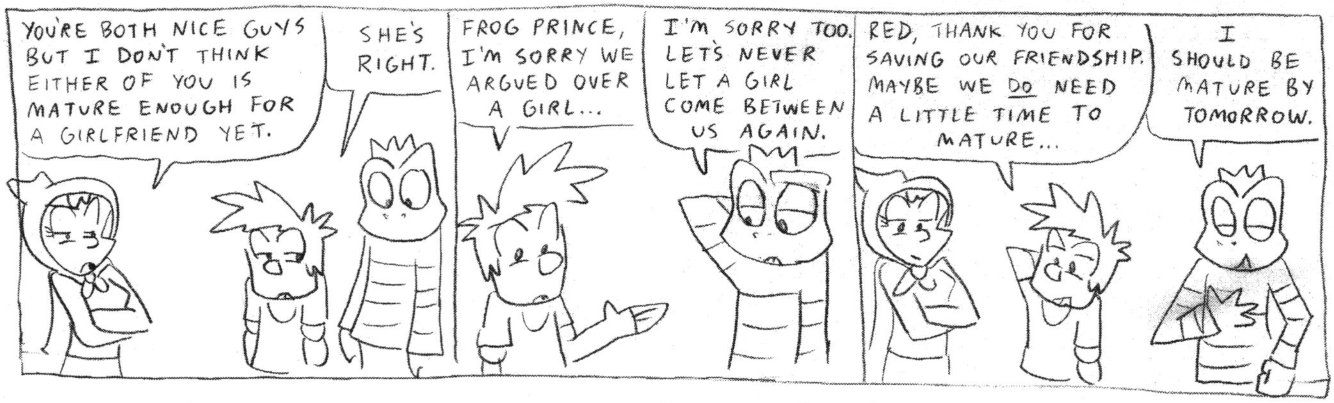
YOU'RE BOTH NICE GUYS BUT I DON'T THINK EITHER OF YOU IS MATURE ENOUGH FOR A GIRLFRIEND YET.
SHE'S RIGHT.
FROG PRINCE, I'M SORRY WE ARGUED OVER A GIRL...
I'M SORRY TOO. LET'S NEVER LET A GIRL COME BETWEEN US AGAIN.
RED, THANK YOU FOR SAVING OUR FRIENDSHIP. MAYBE WE DO NEED A LITTLE TIME TO MATURE...
I SHOULD BE MATURE BY TOMORROW.

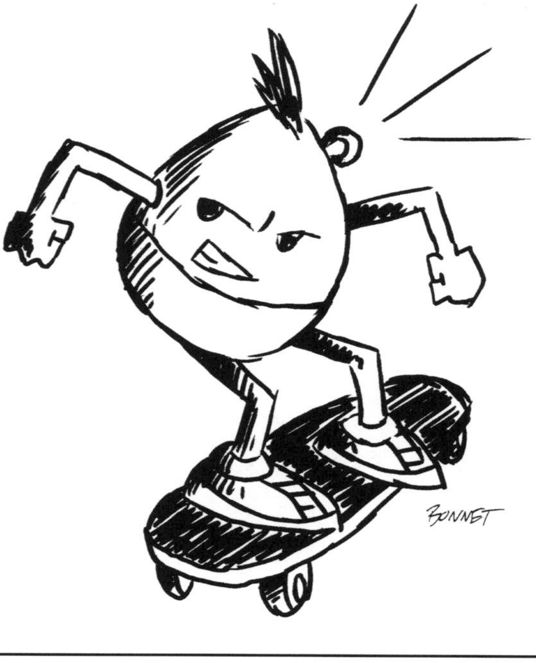
BONNET

6921408R0

Made in the USA
Charleston, SC
26 December 2010